Abuse of Power

Abuse of Power

*How Cold War Surveillance
and Secrecy Policy Shaped the Response to 9/11*

Athan G. Theoharis

TEMPLE UNIVERSITY PRESS / Philadelphia

TEMPLE UNIVERSITY PRESS
Philadelphia, Pennsylvania 19122
www.temple.edu/tempress

Library of Congress Cataloging-in-Publication Data

Theoharis, Athan G.
  Abuse of power : how Cold War surveillance and secrecy policy shaped the response to 9/11 / Athan G. Theoharis.
     p. cm.
  Includes bibliographical references and index.
  ISBN 978-1-4399-0664-4 (cloth : alk. paper) — ISBN 978-1-4399-0665-1 (pbk. : alk. paper) — ISBN 978-1-4399-0666-8 (e-book)
  1. Electronic surveillance. 2. Wiretapping. 3. Intelligence service.
4. Cold War. 5. September 11 Terrorist Attacks, 2001. I. Title.
  TK7882.E2T47 2011
  363.325′16—dc22

                                                    2010042416

Printed in the United States of America

2 4 6 8 9 7 5 3 1

To Jeanne, Ella, and Sophia,

two generations of achievement and promise

Contents

Acknowledgments

This book is the culmination of ongoing research of accessible FBI records dating from the mid-1970s. In the process of conducting this research, I have incurred a number of debts. First, I thank the Franklin and Eleanor Roosevelt Institute, the Harry S Truman Institute for International and National Affairs, and the Lyndon Baines Johnson Foundation for funding my research at presidential libraries. Second, and more important, my extensive use of the Freedom of Information Act to obtain hundreds of thousands of pages of FBI records was made possible through the support of the following institutions and individuals, whose funding helped defray the FBI's ten-cent-per-page processing fee: Marquette University, Field Foundation, Warsh-Mott Funds, C. S. Fund, Youth Project, Fund for Investigative Journalism, W. H. Ferry, Webster Woodmansee Fund, Scholarly Resources, University Publications, Albert Beveridge Award, and National Endowment for the Humanities. I also acknowledge the following people for their helpful insights and willingness to share FBI files: Kenneth O'Reilly, Christopher Gerard, Stephen Leahy, Douglas Charles, Robert Donnelly, Aaron Stockham, Linda Boss, Susan Dion, Patrick Jung, and Cathleen Thom (my former graduate students); Lew Paper, Ira Shapiro, John Elliff, Mark Gitenstein, Mike Epstein, Timothy Ingram, and Robert Gellman (congressional staff); Harrison Salisbury, Anthony Marro, Tony Mauro, Seth Rosenfeld, David Burnham, Steve Aftergood, James Rowen, and Scott Armstrong (reporters); and Victor Navasky, Bruce Craig, Percival Bailey, Kenneth Waltzer, Sigmund

Diamond, Alger Hiss, Boria Sax, Matthew Aid, James Dempsey, Jon Wiener, Alexander Charns, John Henry Faulk, Herbert Mitgang, John Stuart Cox, Gary May, Kai Bird, Douglas Cassel, Harold Weisberg, Morton Halperin, M. Wesley Swearingen, David Luce, Richard Criley, Steven Rosswurm, Dan Simoniski, Ellen Schrecker, Theodore Kornweibel, Sam Walker, Raymond Dall'Osto, Charles Martin, John Fuegi, Jessica Wang, Laura Kalman, David Kendall, and Kathryn Olmsted. Like the FBI, I am sorely deficient in the use of computers; I do not have an e-mail address, and I still use a manual typewriter. In my efforts to produce an electronic manuscript file, I have profited from the invaluable assistance of James Marten, the chair of Marquette's History Department, and the department's efficient administrative assistant, Jolene Kreisler. This study has also benefited from the perceptive criticisms and recommendations of Temple University Press's two readers, Richard Immerman and an anonymous reviewer. Last, I am particularly indebted to my daughter, Jeanne Theoharis, and the editor-in-chief at Temple University Press, Janet Francendese. Jeanne and Janet, at different times, urged me to abandon my original intent to edit a series of essays on the abuse of power theme in favor of writing a coherent, tightly focused, and comprehensive narrative, which became this book.

Introduction

Those who cannot remember the past are condemned to repeat it.

—GEORGE SANTAYANA, *The Life of Reason*

Blind-sided by the devastating terrorist attack of September 11, 2001, George W. Bush administration officials endorsed what they contended were unprecedented changes in federal surveillance policy. Such changes, they claimed, were essential to anticipating and preventing future terrorist attacks. First, administration officials drafted and successfully lobbied the Congress to enact the USA PATRIOT Act, a far-reaching law that legalized Federal Bureau of Investigation (FBI) interception of the communications and records of suspected terrorists without having to obtain a prior court warrant. Second, seven months later, in May 2002, at a joint press conference with FBI Director Robert Mueller III, Attorney General John Ashcroft issued new FBI investigative guidelines to change the "culture" of the FBI from that of a "reactive" law enforcement agency to one that was "proactive," put "prevention above all else," and would anticipate and prevent crime.

The administration's contentions, however, were misleading and, in fact, misrepresented the more complex history of long-term FBI operations and authority. For the FBI did not first abandon a law-enforcement approach in May 2002, having sixty-six years earlier (under a secret August 1936 oral directive of President Franklin Roosevelt) conducted investigations having as their objective to anticipate and prevent crime (in this case, espionage or sabotage orchestrated by Nazi Germany, the Soviet Union, and their American recruits). Thereafter, FBI intelligence operations exceeded those based on a criminal standard.[1] In Chapter 1,

I chronicle the evolution of the FBI's intelligence operations, the attendant changes in tactics and priorities instituted during the World War II and cold war eras, and the ways these changes transformed the FBI's culture, conduct, and approach.

Nor was it the case that FBI agents had been hamstrung in the months and years preceding the 9/11 attack because they were denied the authority essential to uncovering potential terrorist operations. In fact, FBI agents already commanded broad legal authority—under the 1968 Omnibus Crime Control and Safe Streets Act and the 1978 Foreign Intelligence Surveillance Act—to intercept domestic and international communications when conducting intelligence and counterintelligence operations. In addition, under a key provision of the 1996 Antiterrorism and Effective Death Penalty Act, investigations could be launched based on the nebulous standard that a suspected individual or organization provided "material support" to terrorism. Furthermore, dating from the 1980s and intensifying in the 1990s, counterterrorism became an FBI priority. Under new "domestic security/terrorism" guidelines that Attorney General William French Smith issued in March 1983, FBI agents were authorized to "anticipate or prevent crime" and "initiate investigations in advance of criminal conduct." Moreover, in the 1990s, FBI officials established special units to coordinate such investigations—a Radical Fundamentalist Unit in 1994 and an Usama[2] Bin Laden Unit in 1999.

Significantly, during the World War II and cold war years, even though the 1934 Communications Act banned wiretapping and the Supreme Court in 1937 and 1939 ruled that this ban applied to federal agents, FBI agents (under a secret presidential directive) employed wiretaps during national-defense investigations. FBI officials on their own authorized FBI agents to conduct break-ins, mail openings, and bugs when investigating suspected subversives. FBI officials privately conceded that such techniques were illegal or contravened the Fourth Amendment ban against unreasonable searches and seizures. In Chapter 2, I survey the history of FBI wiretapping authority; in Chapter 3, I identify the targets of such interceptions, some of which extended well beyond legitimate national-security threats.

Resisting public and congressional requests for access to records documenting FBI surveillance operations, Bush administration (and, subsequently, Barack Obama administration) officials claimed that disclosure would imperil the nation's security interests. Their claims reiterated the justifications of FBI and White House officials during the World War II and cold war years. In Chapter 4, I describe the various programs and procedures that were adopted during this earlier era to preclude discovery of the scope and targets of FBI surveillance operations.

Because of their ability to conduct policy in secret, FBI officials were able to preclude an independent assessment of the effectiveness of the FBI's counterintelligence operations, a history discussed in detail in Chapter 5. Chapter 6, in turn, discusses how FBI counterintelligence investigations moved far beyond legitimate security concerns to monitor the personal and political activities of prominent, as well as radical, Americans and then to act covertly to promote what has been inaptly described as "McCarthyism."

In contrast to other books and commentary on U.S. counterterrorist operations instituted in response to the 9/11 terrorist attacks, some of which criticized their violations of civil liberties, this book uses the lens of the World War II and cold war eras to examine current counterterrorism policy and does so for two reasons. First, a survey of World War II and cold war surveillance operations places those of the post-9/11 era in a needed historical context, highlighting the striking similarities of the response and the consequences of this expansion beyond the issue of the potential threat to civil liberties. This history moves the criticism of civil libertarians from the abstract and theoretical (potential for abuse) to the realm of predictable reality. Second, current stringent restrictions denying access to relevant records of 9/11 surveillance operations have inevitably precluded a fuller understanding of their scope and consequences and, in this respect, highlight the need to learn from the recently uncovered reality of the World War II and cold war eras.

There is a further dimension in light of the fact that the FBI's World War II and cold war surveillance programs became known only when the wall of secrecy that had theretofore shrouded FBI (but also National Security Agency [NSA] and Central Intelligence Agency [CIA]) operations was first breached by the so-called Church and Pike Committee hearings and reports of 1975–1976. The enactment of a series of amendments to the Freedom of Information Act (FOIA) in 1974 concurrently made possible an informed assessment of these operations for the first time. By exploiting the mandatory review and disclosure provisions of the amended FOIA, researchers were able to obtain some of the formerly secret FBI records.

Research in these released records documents that the FBI's intrusive investigations had not simply targeted suspected criminals and the nation's enemies (foreign spies and their recruits) but had extended, for example, to monitoring the political and personal activities of prominent Americans (First Lady Eleanor Roosevelt, Illinois governor and Democratic presidential nominee Adlai Stevenson, Ensign/President John F. Kennedy, the Reverend Martin Luther King, Jr.), an author of a critical history of the FBI (Max Lowenthal), and even an infamous influence-peddler (John Monroe) after senior FBI officials learned that he had privately bragged to being immune from prosecution because he could prove that J. Edgar Hoover was a homosexual. The released records further document that FBI officials, despite commanding broad powers, had in many instances neither anticipated nor apprehended those individuals who actually engaged in espionage. Having ensured their operations would remain secret through special records procedures to preclude the discovery of their abusive practices and the ineffectiveness of their counterintelligence programs, FBI officials purposefully used the acquired information (and misinformation). This acquired information did not molder in the FBI's massive records system, either because it was unusable for prosecution purposes (having been obtained illegally) or because an illegal activity was not confirmed. Instead, and on their own, FBI officials regularly and surreptitiously leaked this information to favored reporters and members of Congress with the objective either to discredit critics and/or to promote militantly anti-Communist politics.

Significantly, these revelations of widespread abuses and of the limitations of FBI counterintelligence capabilities had not been uncovered through the findings of the Church and Pike Committees or through the records released under the disclosure provisions of the amended FOIA. The FOIA might have provided the opportunity to obtain FBI records. Nonetheless, such access required, at minimum, that the requestor be able to identify the FBI's most-sensitive records and be willing to wait decades to obtain them. Diligence, creativity, and steadfastness have underpinned my most significant findings, detailed in the following chapters.

For, in contrast to other journalists, historians, and political activists, I have not simply requested FBI files on named individuals, cases, or organizations. Instead, I have sought to understand how FBI officials created and maintained sensitive records. Based on a careful reading of congressional hearings and reports; of court cases involving senior FBI officials; of released FBI files, some of which were declassified at presidential libraries; and of references in released CIA records, I have successfully identified and thereby obtained through the FOIA some of the FBI's most sensitive records: extant secret office files of senior FBI officials (Hoover, Clyde Tolson, Louis Nichols), code-named programs (COMRAP, CINRAD, COMPIC, American Legion Contact), and special policy files (SAC letters, FBI Manual of Rules and Regulations, June Mail, Surreptitious Entries, Symbol Number Sensitive Source Index [the last renamed the National Security Electronic Surveillance Index Card File]).

This successful identification strategy, however, did not ensure that the requested records were immediately released. I then encountered the reluctance of FBI officials to make public these records by adopting broad, at times capricious, interpretations of the FOIA's exemptive provisions (claiming "national security," "sources and methods," or "personal privacy" grounds and sometimes asserting two different grounds when withholding the same information on different occasions). My challenges to these withholding claims led to long delays in processing my ultimately successful appeals. For example, one of my requests, submitted in 1982, for former FBI Director Hoover's extant Official and Confidential File led to an appeal that continued for more than twenty years before the totality of this sensitive file was eventually released. When originally processing my request for this massive file (numbering 17,700 pages), the FBI released slightly more than 6,000 heavily redacted pages. Because of the publicity that my acquisition of this file triggered (which became the subject of *U.S. News and World Report*'s special "1984" edition of December 18, 1983), Justice Department officials granted me multiple appeals, eventually totaling five. I was able to successfully challenge the FBI's claimed withholdings. I could do so because of my acquired knowledge of the general contents of the withheld records, based on a review of the memoranda prepared for Attorney General Edward Levi in February 1975 that outlined the contents of each of the 164 folders composing the FBI director's secret office file and my evolving research in FBI records released in response to other FOIA requests or deposited in presidential libraries. The fact remains and bears emphasis: Bureau officials were committed to a stance of secrecy well after programs were no longer operational—and long after the end of the cold war.

This time-consuming and, at times, frustrating experience has direct relevance for an informed assessment of the post-9/11 history. It underscores the commitment of intelligence bureaucrats (and, as well, senior administration officials) to secrecy—highlighted by their resistance to releasing dated FBI records, some created eighty years ago. And although we currently know more about the FBI's World War II and cold war operations than contemporaries did during those eras, and also following the initial releases of FBI records during the 1970s and ensuing decades, the ability of intelligence bureaucrats to delay releasing these records does suggest that our evolving knowledge of dated policies and practices might not reflect the full reality. This experience has particular relevance for our understanding of current counterterrorist policy and practices.

Seemingly contradicting this latter contention, some of the surveillance programs and policies of the post-9/11 era became known within five years after the 9/11 attacks (not, as in the case of the World War II era, forty years later). These discoveries, it should be emphasized, were inadvertent. Furthermore, the basis for these discoveries indirectly confirms the limits of our current knowledge, for these discoveries were the results either of a series of isolated leaks of highly classified information to reporters of the *New York Times* and the *Washington Post* or the release by inspectors general (of the Justice Department and the intelligence agencies) of unclassified sections of reports on some of the post-9/11 surveillance operations. In the latter case, when enacting legislation rescinding the sunset provisions of the USA PATRIOT Act pertaining to the use of National Security Letters (NSL) or when legalizing the NSA's surveillance program and immunizing telecommunication companies from criminal prosecution, Congress had concurrently required that the inspectors general (of the Justice Department or the intelligence agencies) review and report on the FBI's uses of NSLs or the operation of the NSA surveillance program. Neither the leaked information nor the reports of the inspectors general constitute a comprehensive (let alone independently verifiable) account of post-9/11 surveillance operations. The releases do not, for example, describe the scope and the targets of these surveillance operations (and whether the interceptions as a whole advanced legitimate national-security interests) or how the acquired information was used and continues to be used (whether, as in the cold war era, to advance the policy and political interests of presidents and senior intelligence agency officials). There is no reason to believe that the politics of secrecy does not continue to undermine accountability and invite abuses of power.

Abuse of Power

1

A New Intelligence Paradigm

Surveillance and Preventive Detention

The crisis of the Great Depression transformed American politics. Capitalizing on the severe economic downturn and the seeming ineptitude of Herbert Hoover, the incumbent Republican president, Democratic presidential nominee Franklin Roosevelt easily captured the presidency in the 1932 election. Candidate Roosevelt, however, had offered no specific blueprint for the New Deal he pledged to enact if elected beyond promising bold new initiatives and a willingness to experiment. His commitment to change course and commanding personality, nonetheless, captured the public's mood, enabling the new president to steer through Congress in the ensuing years a far-reaching legislative agenda that radically expanded the federal government's regulatory and spending roles while at the same time focusing public attention on his leadership as president. In the process, Roosevelt undercut the checks on executive power that Congress and the media traditionally exercised.

Roosevelt's success in enacting the so-called New Deal for that very reason precipitated criticisms from many American conservatives and progressives. Roosevelt's conservative critics decried the undermining of limited government and the emergent more powerful presidency. For fundamentally different reasons, progressives also criticized Roosevelt's presidency, dismissing New Deal legislative reforms as half-hearted and as co-opting needed fundamental change. Conservatives and progressives, moreover, extended their divergent criticisms to the president's foreign-policy initiatives.

Their criticisms of Roosevelt's attempts to extend U.S. international commitments struck a responsive chord in the mid- to late 1930s, given the public's principal concerns, in the depths of the Great Depression, centering on the domestic economy and viewing with great skepticism an activist international role. Disillusioned over U.S. involvement in World War I, the public had come to perceive international involvement as unnecessary and counterproductive. This antipathy was greatly influenced by the highly publicized hearings conducted by the so-called Nye Committee during the years 1934–1937 that triggered enactment of the so-called Neutrality Acts of 1935, 1936, and 1937. Intended to avert U.S. involvement in foreign wars, these acts limited the nation's financial and commercial relations with belligerent powers and the president's discretion to counter Nazi Germany's expansionism. Moreover, by the mid-1930s, progressives and conservatives directly connected an interventionist foreign policy with the shaping of domestic reform. For many conservatives, President Roosevelt's justification for the expanded federal regulatory and spending policies under the New Deal as having precedence in the nation's emergency responses during World War I confirmed this connection, while for many progressives the consequences of President Woodrow Wilson's unneutral policies that resulted in U.S. intervention in World War I had created the repressive political climate that not only led to the Red Scare of 1920 but also underpinned the conservative politics of the 1920s.

These convictions shaped the political context that President Roosevelt felt compelled to address in the mid- to late 1930s through a series of tactical decisions to counter a perceived internal security threat that a resurgent Nazi Germany and Soviet Union posed. These governments, as "subversive" powers, Roosevelt feared, could influence the actions of the American Fascist and Communist movements. To contain this perceived subversive threat, Roosevelt concluded, required a fundamental shift in the role of the Federal Bureau of Investigation (FBI)—from a law enforcement agency that sought to develop evidence to prosecute violators of federal laws to an intelligence agency that would seek to acquire advance information about the plans and capabilities of suspected spies and saboteurs. Under this scenario, the FBI should anticipate and thereby frustrate potential acts of espionage and sabotage and furthermore contain "subversive" activists and movements from being able to influence the public debate about the president's interventionist initiatives. These goals, the president further concluded, could not be achieved through new legislation authorizing FBI intelligence investigations, given prevailing suspicions about executive and presidential powers. President Roosevelt, his attorneys general, and the FBI director instead opted for secret executive directives, a method that had as a central purpose the foreclosure of a potentially divisive and contentious debate. The FBI's new proactive approach meant that agents would seek to identify potential spies and saboteurs by adopting ideological and associational criteria.

Moreover, as in the case of the evolution of the domestic New Deal, this profound shift was effected not through a well-defined blueprint but through a series of ad hoc responses. President Roosevelt (abetted by the ambitious FBI director, J. Edgar Hoover) at first intended only to address a specific and immediate problem; the secrecy of his and Hoover's initiatives and the resultant undermining of accountability cumulatively and over time culminated in a vastly expanded and politicized FBI. With the onset of the cold war, Roosevelt's temporary, ad hoc initiatives gave rise to a permanent FBI intelligence role and, given the resultant obsession over the gravity of the Communist threat, a new conception of the nation's institutional relationships and priorities.

This new intelligence paradigm had its inception in a one-time initiative. Concerned over Nazi Germany's domestic propaganda activities, in May 1934, President Roosevelt convened a conference of representatives from the Secret Service, the Immigration Bureau, the FBI, and the Department of Justice. Following this meeting, Roosevelt ordered FBI Director Hoover to conduct "a very careful and searching investigation" into whether German embassy and consular officials "may have" a connection with American Fascist movements. Roosevelt's request had no law-enforcement purpose in that he sought to document the ideological orientation of American citizens and organizations. Indeed, Hoover's follow-up response reflected this reality, as FBI agents were ordered to investigate the "activities of the Nazi groups with particular reference to the anti-racial and any anti-American activities having any possible connection with official representatives of the German government in the United States." The resultant twenty-eight-month FBI investigation, not surprisingly then, uncovered no evidence of illegal conduct, as FBI agents monitored the political activities of various Fascist groups (notably, the German American Bund headed by Fritz Kuhn and the Silver Shirts headed by William Pelley) with Hoover submitting the resultant reports periodically to Attorney General Homer Cummings for transmittal to the president.[1]

Roosevelt's 1934 request had a limited one-time purpose. The reports that Hoover submitted, however, combined with an upsurge in Fascist and Communist activities heightened the president's concerns and led him in August 1936 to convene a meeting with Hoover at the White House. Roosevelt had a broader objective than in 1934, as he solicited the FBI director's input about "the question of subversive activities in the United States, particularly Fascism and Communism," the immediate catalyst being the various reports from Hoover, specifically one recounting that Catholic priest Charles Coughlin had asked retired general Smedley Butler to head a military expedition to Mexico.

At this meeting, however, Hoover focused not only on American Fascists but also on the Communist threat, citing Communist plans to "get control" of the International Longshoremen's and Warehousemen's Union, the United Mine Workers, and the Newspaper Guild. Should the Communists succeed in gaining control of these labor unions, Hoover explained, they could "paralyze the country in that they could stop all shipping in and out . . . stop the operation of industry . . . and stop publication of any newspaper in the country." Communists, he continued, had also infiltrated the National Labor Relations Board and had been instructed to vote for Roosevelt in the 1936 election.

Disturbed by this report, Roosevelt expressed an interest in "obtaining a broader picture of the general movement and its activities as may affect the economic and political life of the country as a whole" and asked how this could be achieved. No agency currently addressed that interest, Hoover reported, given the lack of authority to investigate such matters, but under a 1916 appropriation statute, the FBI was authorized to investigate "any matters referred to it by the Department of State." Roosevelt agreed to this proposed strategy but on the condition that it be accomplished without any leaks, and he proposed that the two of them meet with Secretary of State Cordell Hull.

The three men met the next day at the White House. Roosevelt began this meeting by citing the activities of Soviet consular official Constantine Oumansky, whom he described as "a leading figure in some of these activities in this country, so consequently, it was a matter which fell within the scope of foreign affairs over which the State Department would have a right to request an investigation to be made." When Hull then asked if such a request should be made in writing, Roosevelt demurred, preferring that this matter "be handled quite confidentially, and it will be sufficient that the President, the Secretary of State and [FBI director] should be the ones aware of this request." Only one written report about this decision remains extant, which Hoover had maintained in his secret office file.[2]

When meeting Hoover and then authorizing FBI noncriminal intelligence investigations, President Roosevelt had bypassed his attorney general, Cummings. Cummings first learned of Roosevelt's decision at a September 10 meeting with Hoover (with the FBI director misleadingly informing him that his meeting with the president had been held on September 1). Roosevelt's interest in secrecy had additional consequences beyond undermining the attorney general's supervisory authority, in that it enabled the ambitious and politically conservative FBI director to institute a broader surveillance initiative that extended beyond monitoring Nazi and Soviet agents and their American recruits. Hoover's August 25 order to his key aides outlining the "general classifications" that were to govern this new initiative captures this broader political surveillance purpose. The intended targets were "Maritime industry, Government affairs, steel industry, general strike activities, Armed Forces, educational institutions, general activities—Communist and affiliated

Organizations, Fascisti, anti-Fascisti movements, and adherents of organized Labor organizations." FBI agents were specifically directed to obtain information from "all possible sources" but not to initiate any investigation without "specific authorization" from FBI headquarters, a requirement intended to preclude the discovery of this broad-ranging intelligence operation.[3]

Expanding the FBI's authority to conduct intelligence investigations did not ensure that foreign-directed espionage or sabotage operations would be uncovered. This was particularly highlighted by the FBI's concurrent and inefficient handling of an investigation that had fortuitously uncovered a wide-ranging German espionage operation that the so-called Rumrich spy ring orchestrated.

Born in Chicago in 1911, Guenther Gustave Rumrich emigrated to Germany with his family in 1915, returning to the United States in 1929, whereupon he joined the U.S. Army in 1930 and then went AWOL in 1936. That year in May, Rumrich signed up as an agent of Abwehr, the German espionage service, in New York. Working closely the next two years with other recruited German agents (some of whom had begun spying for Abwehr as early as 1927), Rumrich helped steal and then transmit to Germany sensitive military data (including military technology and information about ship movements in the port of New York). His carelessness, however, led to his apprehension by State Department and New York City police investigators in February 1938. Rumrich's espionage activities were discovered as the result of an inquiry into his receipt of thirty-five blank passports. Rumrich eventually identified to State Department, New York police, and FBI investigators eighteen other participants in this spy operation. Only three of those whom he identified, however, were tried, as the other fourteen fled the country before they could be apprehended. The resultant adverse publicity about the long-term operation of this ring and the escape of the fourteen tarnished more than it enhanced the FBI's public reputation.[4]

Seeking to dispel public doubts and to address the seeming weakness of the federal government's counterespionage capabilities, President Roosevelt convened a cabinet meeting on October 14, 1938, at which he pointedly questioned Attorney General Cummings about the federal government's overall counterespionage operations. His department, Cummings responded, had a "well-defined system" in place, and no changes were needed. Roosevelt, however, was unconvinced and ordered his attorney general to chair a committee composed of representatives from the FBI, the Military Intelligence Division (MID), and the Office of Naval Intelligence (ONI) "to inquire into the so-called espionage situation" and to report back to him whatever additional appropriations would be needed to ensure an effective "domestic intelligence" program.

Cummings thereupon solicited Hoover's counsel. On October 20, 1938, the FBI director submitted a detailed plan that would require a significant increase in appropriations to "expand" the FBI's, the MID's, and the ONI's counterespionage operations. The FBI, Hoover reported, currently collected information "dealing with various forms of activities of either a subversive or so-called intelligence type" and had "a close and coordinated plan of cooperation" with the MID and the ONI. Hoover nonetheless emphasized that future operations should focus on "matters which do not themselves constitute a violation of a Federal Criminal Statute, such as subversive activities." This needed expansion, Hoover continued, could be best achieved "under present provisions" in the FBI's annual appropriations, much as Roosevelt himself had ordered at the earlier 1936 meeting with Hoover and Hull by honoring requests under the 1916 appropriations statute from the State Department. The language of the 1916 statute was "sufficiently broad to cover an expansion," which in turn would require an increase in FBI appropriations of $300,000. The proposed expanded FBI surveillance operations, the FBI director counseled Cummings, should be "proceeded with the utmost degree of secrecy in order to avoid criticism or objections which may be raised to such an expansion by either ill-informed persons or individuals having some ulterior motive." The "word 'espionage,'" Hoover pointedly observed, "has long been a word that has been repugnant to the American people and it is believed that the structure which is already in existence is much broader than espionage or counter-espionage but covers in a true sense real intelligence value" for the FBI, the MID, and the ONI. The FBI director explicitly advised against seeking "special legislation," as this "would draw attention to the fact that it was proposed to develop a special counter-espionage drive of any great magnitude." Immediately forwarded to President Roosevelt, Hoover's report was approved on November 1, although the president limited the proposed increase in FBI appropriations to $150,000.[5]

The onset of World War II, with the German invasion of Poland in September 1939 and U.S. military involvement in that ongoing conflict following the Japanese attack on Pearl Harbor in December 1941, emboldened the Roosevelt administration to seek further increases in FBI appropriations and personnel. Thus, during the years 1936–1945, and particularly in the years after 1939, FBI appropriations and personnel increased from $5,000,000 and 1,690 in 1936, to $6,578,076 and 1,912 in 1939, to $14,743,300 and 4,273 in 1941, to $44,197,146 and 11,792 in 1945. (The post-1940 figures, however, also included funding for the FBI's foreign-intelligence operations in Latin America, secretly authorized by President Roosevelt in June 1940. The FBI's foreign intelligence role, however, was terminated with the creation of the CIA in 1947.)[6]

Despite the 600 percent increase in personnel during the years 1936 through 1945 (and a 1,300 percent increase dating from 1932), FBI officials were not content to rely solely on an agent force to conduct secret intelligence operations. Paid informants (disgruntled former adherents and "patriotic" volunteers) were also recruited to infiltrate targeted organizations (such as the U.S. Communist Party). More ominously, dating from 1940, FBI officials also tapped into the ranks of conservative organizations, such as the American Legion, the post–World War I veterans' organization. Their institution of the formally code-named American Legion Contact Program in 1940 enabled FBI officials to monitor closely and intensively suspect "subversive" labor union and political activities.

Ironically, this program's inception contravened the original intention of senior Justice Department officials. In June 1940, American Legion officials had contacted Attorney General Robert Jackson and offered to monitor "subversive activities" and report their "findings to local law enforcement agencies." Rebuffing this offer, the attorney general urged the Legion to refrain from such investigations and instead act to reduce "mob violence and hysteria."[7]

Subsequently learning of Legion officials' adverse reaction to this rebuff (and the potential consequences for the FBI's intelligence activities), the head of the FBI's New York office, Special Agent in Charge (SAC) B. Edwin Sackett, contacted FBI Director Hoover and urged him to endorse a proposal to counter a Legion surveillance plan. Doing nothing, Sackett warned, could deny the FBI the Legion's support insofar as Legion officers intended to institute their own surveillance program, whether in cooperation with local and state police or with military intelligence. Sackett recommended that his FBI superiors allow him to attend a forthcoming conference of American Legion officials, having the purpose to "develop reliable [Legion] informants, outline the type of information the Bureau desires, and also tell the [Legion] Commanders when possible that we need them as confidential informants in . . . [defense] plants."[8]

Hoover endorsed Sackett's plan but demanded further refinement, adding that any plan would first have to be cleared with the attorney general. The FBI director promised to seek Jackson's approval by November 19, the date when Legion officers were scheduled to meet to approve their own surveillance program and which meeting Sackett would attend to brief Legion officers on the FBI's counterproposal.

The FBI director thereupon advised the attorney general of the Legionnaires' resentment over his earlier dismissal of their offer and their intention to approve a "broad program" to investigate "all information received concerning espionage, sabotage, subversive activities, un-American activities and other matters related in any manner to the national defense." The Legion intended to report the acquired information, Hoover added, to "local and state police agencies, ignoring the Federal Bureau of Investigation entirely." Because they would be conducted by "inexperienced men," he continued, the Legion's surveillance operations could adversely affect the FBI's carefully planned "national defense programs." But under an alternative FBI plan, the FBI could obtain the Legion's support and "keep the membership of that organization so occupied that there will be no attempt . . . to carry on actual investigative activity."[9]

Attorney General Jackson reluctantly approved Hoover's proposal but admitted that he "would much rather not do this but apparently something must be done." He did so on the understanding that Legionnaires would not conduct investigations but would only report to the FBI what they learned through everyday activities—that Legionnaires of German, Italian, French, and Russian nationality would keep the FBI apprised of the activities of their nationality groups and that Legionnaires employed in defense industries would become plant informants. Hoover did not disabuse Jackson of this belief or reveal his more ambitious intention to recruit Legionnaires as Confidential National Defense Informants.[10]

Briefed by Sackett on the FBI's counterproposal, American Legion officers wholeheartedly agreed to cooperate with the FBI. The arrangement finally agreed upon involved each SAC maintaining close contact with the Legion's regional officers, who would have been identified by the head of the Legion's National Americanism Commission, Homer Chaillaux. The SACs would then solicit from their region's state Legion officers the names of reliable Legion members in their area who could be "safely contacted" for recruitment. The net result would be the creation of a nationwide pool of informers who would be encouraged to provide information on a regular basis. Hoover, moreover, spelled out the criteria for selecting Legion recruits: "Good judgment, employment in important industrial or public utility plants and facilities or who have contacts with conditions in their communities relating to groups of foreign extraction or un-American sympathies." The program, the FBI director further emphasized, must "be kept strictly confidential and that no publicity whatsoever result."[11]

Hoover thereafter personally monitored the SACs' contacts with Legion officers and FBI agents' recruitment of Legion informers to ensure "intensive coverage." And, whenever learning that a field office had either delayed initiating this program or had not contacted members of the Legion's National Americanism Commission to serve as informers, he demanded that SACs immediately contact their state's Legion officers to ascertain which Legionnaires would be sufficiently reliable for recruitment as "confidential informants." Agents who were found to be derelict in making these contacts were either threatened with or given administrative sanctions. Hoover explicitly extolled the benefits of this recruitment program as enhancing the FBI's surveillance capabilities without having to seek additional appropriations from Congress to hire more agents. It might be "undesirable as a general rule to rely upon outside groups to render assistance to the FBI," he conceded but then added that Legion members were "substantial, patriotic citizens, whose assistance should be used to the utmost" and that SACs should thus "explore the possibility of utilizing the services of the American Legion to greater advantage."[12]

SACs and agents responded enthusiastically to Hoover's orders. By August 20, 1941, 813 American Legion department and division officers had been contacted and 46,864 potential informers identified, of whom 32,918 were contacted by FBI agents. The FBI supervisor responsible for administering the program at the time estimated that when the planning phase was completed, 43,000 informers would have been recruited from the Legion's 1,700 nation-wide posts.[13]

The FBI director, however, was not satisfied with these sizable numbers. When subsequently learning that many Legion post commanders had still not been identified as "reliable" Legionnaires and, further, that owing to their ignorance of the FBI's program some of them had offered to cooperate with the MID, Hoover ordered all SACs to secure immediately from their region's Legion department commanders a list of all posts that had already been contacted and then ask those who had not been whether they would cooperate with the FBI. His pressure brought about a further increase in the number of potential Legion informers to sixty thousand by October 1943.

The radical expansion in the FBI's ability to conduct intelligence investigations, because of the resultant focus on labor unions and political activities, did not lead to an increase in prosecutions during the World War II era, let alone the uncovering of planned espionage or sabotage operations. These paltry results did not dissuade FBI officials. Their concern in any event had never been simply to prosecute spies or saboteurs but to contain "subversive" influence. And thus, to achieve this preventative objective, FBI Director Hoover concurrently, in September 1939, instituted a formal emergency detention program code-named Custodial Detention.

Unilaterally instituted by the FBI director, this program was intended to identify "persons of German, Italian, and Communist sympathies" and those "whose interest may be directed primarily to the interest of some other nation than the United States" by having FBI agents review the subscription lists of German, Italian, and Communist newspapers; membership lists of Fascist and Communist organizations; agent and informer reports on meetings; and demonstrations of such organizations and, further, by developing confidential sources or conducting new investigations in "a discreet manner." The names of those so-identified aliens and citizens were then listed in a special Custodial Detention index, "on whom there is information available that their presence at liberty in this country in time of war or national emergency would be dangerous to the public peace and safety of the United States Government." Hoover recognized that the proposed investigations and listings lacked statutory authority and further focused on protected First Amendment speech and associations. Accordingly, he sought to limit the political fallout should the FBI's actions be discovered, admonishing SACs that "the purpose should be entirely confidential and it should be handled in the same manner as any investigation for the purpose of determining if the individual involved has violated the [Foreign Agent] Registration Act or is engaged in subversive activities. . . . [I]nquiries as to the reason for the investigation should be answered by reference to the Registration Act."[14]

This unilaterally instituted Custodial Detention program could not become operational, however, insofar as it lacked statutory authority. Belatedly, then, Hoover briefed Attorney General Jackson about this program nine months later, in June 1940. At this time, the FBI director solicited Jackson's guidance relative to the compilation of "a suspect list of individuals whose arrest might be considered necessary in the event the United States becomes involved in war" (masking the fact that he had already had agents compile such a list).[15]

Jackson concurred that such an index should be prepared and immediately directed the head of the Justice Department's newly created Neutrality Laws Unit to review the names of those whom the FBI listed. Hoover, however, had not anticipated that department officials would insist upon a supervisory role and objected to this requirement. The FBI's confidential sources could be compromised by such reviews, he protested, and the bureau's "counterespionage activities" could be adversely affected. He then demanded that the department personnel conducting such reviews should "be selected with a great deal of care" to preclude any leaks.

Department officials ultimately agreed to two modifications in Jackson's proposed review system. First, the department agreed not to indict a listed individual if this "might interfere with sound investigative techniques" (i.e., reveal the FBI's use of wiretaps, bugs, or break-ins). Second, no FBI recruited informer would be disclosed "without the prior approval of the Bureau." Assistant Attorney General M. F. McGuire then outlined for Hoover how the department planned to implement this program: Following a presidential proclamation, the attorney general would issue warrants for the arrest of alien enemies (based on the 1798 alien enemies statute), and a special department committee would decide whether listed American citizens "not subject to internment" should be prosecuted under the 1940 Smith Act (which made it a crime to advocate or belong to an organization that advocated the violent overthrow of the government) "or some other appropriate statute."[16]

Hoover also concurrently briefed President Roosevelt in October 1940 about this FBI program of "preparing and maintaining" a list of "several thousand individuals" whose activities "are considered potentially inimical to the welfare of the United States." Those listed, Hoover explained, would be detained in "the event of a declared emergency or the enactment of additional legislation." He identified those whom the FBI planned to list as "German groups and sympathizers, Communist groups and sympathizers, Fascist groups and sympathizers, Japanese and others."

Neither President Roosevelt nor Attorney General Francis Biddle (Jackson's successor) subsequently decided to implement a detention program based on the FBI's Custodial Detention listings. Instead, following the Japanese attack on Pearl Harbor, Biddle, on December 12, 1941, authorized the detention under the 1798 Alien Enemies Act of those German, Italian, and Japanese alien residents who were listed in this special index (totaling 2,541). Citizens listed in this index (as well as suspected Communists) were not subject to this order. In addition, President Roosevelt in February 1942 authorized the now-infamous Japanese internment program, the vast majority of whom had not been identified under the FBI's relatively circumscribed listing of "dangerous" Japanese aliens and citizens.[17]

FBI officials nonetheless continued to compile and maintain a Custodial Detention index that included the names of citizens and aliens who were not identified with the Axis powers but were listed because of their suspect Communist Party membership or sympathies. Attorney General Biddle soon questioned the value of maintaining such an index, having concluded that "these dangerous classifications . . . serve no useful purpose." The Justice Department's Alien Control Unit, the attorney general informed FBI Director Hoover in July 1943, had found the FBI's Custodial Detention classifications to be useless.[18] "There is no statutory authorization or other present justification," Biddle continued, "for keeping a 'custodial detention' list of citizens. The Department fulfills its proper functions by investigating the activities of persons who may have violated the law. It is not aided in this work by classifying persons as to dangerousness." Accordingly, the attorney general barred the future use of this classification and demanded the insertion of a card in the files of those persons who were listed in the Custodial Detention index stipulating that "this classification is unreliable, it is hereby cancelled, and [it] should not be used as a determination of dangerousness or of any other fact."[19]

The FBI director, however, did not comply with the intent of the attorney general's order. Instead, all SACs were ordered in August 1943 that henceforth the "character of investigations of individuals (other than alien enemies) who may be dangerous or potentially dangerous to the public safety or internal security of the United States shall be 'Security Matter' and not 'Custodial Detention.' The phraseology, 'Custodial Detention,' shall no longer be used to designate the character of the investigation, nor shall it be used for any purpose in reports or other communications." Almost in passing, the FBI director alluded to the attorney general's order that "the dangerousness classification previously made by the Special Defense Unit and its successor, the Special War Policies Unit, be not used in the future for any purpose whatsoever."

Hoover had technically complied with Biddle's requirement in that the attorney general had not specifically banned the compilation of listings of "dangerous" individuals under a different name. "Henceforth," the FBI director thus stipulated, "the cards known as Custodial Detention Cards will be known and referred to as Security Index Cards, and the list composed of such cards will be known as the Security Index." And, to foreclose the possibility that his insubordination could be discovered, SACs were directed that "the fact that the Security Index and Security Index Cards are prepared and maintained should be considered as strictly confidential, and should at no time be mentioned and alluded to in investigative reports, or discussed with agencies or individuals outside the Bureau other than duly qualified field representatives of the Office of Naval Intelligence and the Military Intelligence Service, and then only on a strictly confidential basis."[20]

The principal catalyst to President Roosevelt's secret authorization of FBI intelligence investigations might have stemmed primarily from his concerns about German espionage and sabotage activities and secondarily the "subversive" threat that the Soviet Union and American Communists posed. Nonetheless, FBI intelligence investigations during World War II had focused intensively on what the FBI director and his senior aides perceived to be the Communist threat. FBI officials could not at the time act on the information contained in the FBI's burgeoning files. Their concern, however, soon led them to continue and, after 1945, to intensify surveillance of Communists and those whom they believed to be Communist sympathizers. They were emboldened to do so owing to the radically altered political climate of the cold war years. The deterioration in U.S.-Soviet relations after 1945 combined with the discovery in late 1945 of wartime Soviet espionage operations (in the United States and Canada) led to White House endorsement of continued FBI intelligence investigations. As one result, with the exception of the formal termination in 1947 of the FBI's foreign intelligence role in South America (thereby temporarily reducing FBI appropriations and personnel), FBI appropriations and personnel never returned to their pre-1936 levels and instead increased steadily thereafter from $43,900,000 and 9,300 in 1948 to $256,857,000 and 18,028 by 1970.[21]

Nonetheless, in their efforts to contain the Communist "subversive" threat, FBI officials once again sought to enhance their monitoring capabilities by continuing the wartime liaison relationship with the American Legion. Legion recruits, FBI Director Hoover advised his key aides, were a "valuable pool of information which should be used to the fullest extent by the Bureau, both in security matters and other matters coming within the jurisdiction of the Bureau."[22] SACs were accordingly ordered in February 1945 to review their

American Legion files "with the thought of having as much coverage as possible in the postwar period . . . in general investigative as well as in National Defense matters."[23]

Under this revised program, however, SACs were directed to discontinue "developing" new Legion contacts and to instead retain already recruited Legionnaires as potentially valuable informers who were to be "appropriately indexed as Confidential Informants, Sources of Information, or Contacts." "A close relationship with the American Legion" must be maintained, Hoover emphasized, as "it is more vital than ever at this time to retain the continued support and active cooperation of this ever-increasingly important organization."[24]

Thus, FBI agents continued to solicit information from their established Legion informers. The outbreak of the Korean War in June 1950, however, led to a reassessment, as Hoover decided to reactivate the wartime American Legion Contact Program in light of the FBI's "most cordial" relationship with the Legion (a "powerful, numerically large group of citizens in active participation in the affairs of this country"). But rather than recruiting Legionnaire informers solely on the basis of their usefulness, SACs were to contact "all reliable Post Commanders and Adjutants" to "prevent their offering their services to other agencies" and were to focus on selective-service matters. While imposing a heavy burden on the FBI's resources, senior FBI officials conceded, this reactivated program would nonetheless provide FBI agents "entree to persons and organizations in all walks of life" and at the same time dissuade Legionnaires from instituting their own internal security program.[25]

FBI officials, however, decided that "it was not necessary to contact the [Justice] Department prior to starting this program." The FBI Executives Conference, composed of senior FBI officials at FBI headquarters, instead "felt that the initial step should be personal contact by [FBI Inspector and liaison to the American Legion] Lee Pennington with the National Commander of the American Legion."[26] This reactivated program greatly expanded the FBI's surveillance capabilities. By June 20, 1953, 100,880 informers were recruited from the Legion's active posts. Nonetheless, by then FBI agents in the field had come to question the value of the program, given the amount of time required to contact and recontact Legion officers and the limited quality of the acquired information. Their complaints, however, were summarily dismissed by senior FBI officials, who extolled the program's "good public relations."[27]

Then, in 1954, FBI Inspector C. W. Stein, the official having administrative responsibility over the program, recommended its discontinuance. Based on his survey of all FBI personnel who supervised the program, Stein concluded that the program "contributed no information of value" and constituted a costly use of limited FBI manpower. He proposed instead to limit FBI contacts to the Legion's national officers, with agents only honoring any and all speaking requests from Legion posts. Stein's recommendation was summarily rebuffed, although Hoover agreed to limit the required SAC contacts on the condition that agents would not overlook "the possibility that some of these Legion contacts may be developed as security and criminal informants or sources of information."[28]

The Legion program as such limped along mindlessly until the 1960s, when FBI Supervisor Fred Baumgardner, citing the upsurge of racial unrest, proposed to senior FBI officials in 1964 and again in 1965 the reactivation of the FBI's liaison relationship with the Legion to "increase the quality and quantity of coverage of racial matters." Such reactivation, Baumgardner argued, could provide "a limited and selective means of obtaining resources at the community level." Legion informers, Baumgardner continued, "should be made aware of the Bureau's interest in racial activities," as the FBI must "consider every possible step toward a position in which we will be aware of all racial activities." Baumgardner cited as the proposal's added benefit "the public relations gained and education of such [Legion] officials and workers" regarding the FBI's "responsibilities and jurisdiction."[29]

The FBI Executives Conference, however, never formally considered Baumgardner's recommendation. To the contrary, on March 7, 1966, FBI Director Hoover approved Baumgardner's quite different recommendation to terminate the American Legion Contact Program on the grounds that "the expenditure of time and money in making yearly contacts" with Legion commanders and adjutants was no longer warranted.[30]

Despite its long tenure, the FBI's American Legion Contact Program furthered no legitimate security interest. Its sole value was to increase the accumulation of information about liberal and radical political activities and to enhance the FBI's reputation with this conservative veterans' organization. Indeed, senior FBI officials, when endorsing its continuance, cited only that it cemented a favorable relationship with this powerful veterans' organization and at the same time enhanced the monitoring of suspect radical activities. Indeed, this had been the program's underlying objective all along, with Hoover, in 1940 with the inception of the program, explicitly affirming its value in addressing "the vital need of the Bureau to know conditions in various localities throughout the country." He particularly specified the political intelligence value of the Bureau's recruitment of Legion contacts:

In communities where groups or settlements of persons of foreign extraction or possible un-American sympathies are located, it is important that the Bureau know the identity of leaders of these groups, the location of their meeting places, the identity and scope of operation of their social clubs, societies, language schools, etc.; whether persons are sent into the communities to spread propaganda; to raise funds for various purposes or for the purpose of agitating such foreign extraction groups.[31]

FBI Supervisor Baumgardner's 1965 review of the program's history confirmed Hoover's original assessment that this program helped promote FBI officials' ideological and bureaucratic interests. Citing the "considerable value [to the FBI] in the public relations field and . . . in deterring the American Legion from embarking on security-type investigations," Baumgardner emphasized that "it is extremely desirable" that the FBI maintain "our excellent relations" with the Legion, "a numerically strong and powerful militant group." The Legion's vast membership, he continued, "has in the past given the Bureau entree to organizations and persons in all walks of life. The limited program now in effect permits the Bureau to maintain its relations with the leading officials in the Legion without undue burden on investigative personnel."[32]

FBI officials, at the same time, remained committed after 1945 to a preventive-detention program, even though the Custodial Detention program had never become operational and Attorney General Biddle had, in 1943, ordered that such listings were to be terminated. Hoover's secret renaming of this list as a Security Index might have ensured the continued collection of information about suspect individuals. Nonetheless, given Biddle's order, those listed could not be detained. The opportunity to resolve this dilemma presented itself with Tom Clark's replacement of Biddle as attorney general in September 1945. Clark held a more expansive conception of internal security threats than had Biddle and was less concerned that listing individuals because of their beliefs or associations could threaten civil liberties and amount to a repudiation of congressional authority.

Seeking to exploit the opportunity, given the changed political climate with the deterioration of U.S.-Soviet relations, FBI Assistant Director D. Milton Ladd in February 1946 urged Hoover to secure Clark's support for a "study as to the action which could be taken in the event of an emergency." As justification, Ladd cited the serious domestic threat that American Communists posed owing to their allegiance to the Soviet Union and control of key labor unions. Only a preventive-detention program could address this threat, a program that would not "only" apprehend Communist Party leaders or "more important figures" but would also investigate and identify "all known members of the Communist Party." Such a Security Index program could be instituted, Ladd continued, only by "finding legal authority," since under current law enemy aliens alone could be interned.[33]

Hoover briefed the attorney general the next month but did not at the time inform Clark that the FBI had already instituted a Security Index program in technical violation of Biddle's 1943 order. He misleadingly urged Clark to approve a new program to address an imminent espionage and sabotage threat. FBI officials, Hoover advised Clark, had "found it necessary to intensify [the FBI's] investigation of Communist Party activities and Soviet espionage cases" and had also taken steps to "list all members of the Communist Party and others who would be dangerous in the event of war" or of a break in U.S. diplomatic relations with the Soviet Union. American citizens might also have to be detained in a future crisis, Hoover emphasized and accordingly urged Clark to conduct a study to "determine what legislation is available or should be sought to authorize effective action . . . in the event of a serious emergency."[34]

Clark agreed to the proposed study. Department officials, however, eventually concluded that, rather than seeking legislation authorizing a detention program, the government should during an emergency either declare martial law or suspend the writ of habeas corpus. FBI officials dissented from this plan of action, emphasizing that "statutory backing for detention" was needed and that the detention standards should be broadened to include persons "holding important positions who have shown sympathy for Communist objectives and policy." Investigations for such listings should extend to fields where Communists were "promoting Communist Party objectives and principles," citing as examples organized labor; civil-rights, nationality, and youth groups; elementary and secondary schools and colleges and universities; and "informers in the major political parties or in other political bodies."[35]

Justice Department officials agreed to the bureau's broad standards but not the recommendation to seek legislative authorization. "The present is no time to seek legislation," they contended: "To ask for it would only bring on a loud and acrimonious discussion." They instead opted for a strategy whereby the president would proclaim an emergency, at which time legislation would be introduced to authorize a detention program. In addition, they proposed launching a campaign that year to educate the public to the seriousness of the Communist threat, to be achieved by seeking the indictment and prosecution under the 1940 Smith Act of the national leadership of the U.S. Communist Party. Department officials nonetheless feared that this prosecution strategy would fail, as the courts might reject the indictments, which would then require "sufficient courage to withstand the courts . . . if they should act."[36]

Hoover again dissented from this assessment of the congressional mood, arguing that needed legislation would "be adopted readily by Congress." On August 3, 1948, ignoring Hoover's advice, Clark secretly instituted the proposed detention program (formally named the Department's Portfolio). Under this program, FBI officials were empowered to compile a Security Index listing dangerous individuals who would be apprehended at a time of "threatened invasion" under a master warrant issued by the attorney general and by suspending the writ of habeas corpus. FBI agents could conduct searches at the time of an arrest and confiscate contraband, while specially established courts would review within forty-five days the appeals of those apprehended. These hearings, however, would not be bound by rules of evidence, and their adverse rulings could be appealed only to the president. Finally, to address the statutory problem, Clark proposed a strategy based on ex post facto congressional approval. Under this plan, the Department's Portfolio contained two drafts: the first of a presidential proclamation to be issued during the anticipated crisis and the second of a joint resolution to be submitted for congressional approval following the issuance of the president's proclamation.[37]

Attorney General Clark briefed the National Security Council (NSC) in late 1948 about his decision to establish the Security Index program and also "cleared" the plan "on Cabinet level." Thereafter, FBI Director Hoover regularly reported to the NSC on the program's "progress," citing the numbers of individuals listed for possible detention. By October 1952, the numbers totaled 19,436 and reached 26,174 by December 1954.[38]

The intensification of the cold war and the resultant obsession over the Communist internal security threat, however, had by 1950 led the conservative congressional leadership, in the midst of the Korean War, to introduce legislation to strengthen internal security safeguards, including authorization of a preventive-detention program. Congressional proponents, however, were unaware that the Harry Truman administration had already secretly instituted a preventive-detention program. Their proposed standards as a result differed substantially from those of the secret Department's Portfolio. Congress eventually approved such legislation, the Internal Security (or McCarran) Act in September 1950, overriding President Truman's veto.

The disparity between the congressionally mandated standards and those of the Security Index, as a result, posed serious problems for the FBI and the Justice Department. The Internal Security Act did not authorize the suspension of the writ of habeas corpus; limited detentions only to those individuals who were active members of subversive organizations since January 1, 1949; and permitted apprehensions only in the event of an actual invasion, insurrection, or declaration of war. Federal officials were further required under the act to obtain individual warrants before apprehending an individual and had to convene detention hearings within forty-eight hours after the apprehension, which hearings had to be conducted on the basis of rules of evidence with an adverse rulings appealable to any U.S. Court of Appeals.[39]

Given these vastly different standards, FBI Director Hoover immediately asked Attorney General McGrath whether the act's emergency detention requirements superseded those currently in force under the Department's Portfolio.[40] McGrath responded by directing Hoover to disregard the act and to "proceed with the program as previously outlined."[41]

McGrath's order had been conveyed orally during a meeting with the FBI director but was subsequently reaffirmed in writing by Assistant Attorney

General James McInerney. Addressing the evident conflict between Title II of the Internal Security Act and the Department's Portfolio, McInerney wrote that in the event a detention program would have to be implemented, the department would introduce legislation to amend the 1950 act. Department officials, McInerney added, considered many of the act's provisions "unworkable."[42]

McGrath and McInerney, however, had counseled Hoover only about the department's future legislative strategy. The FBI director, accordingly, asked the attorney general to specify which standards the department proposed to follow in the interim when conducting reviews of the FBI's detention listings. The department, Deputy Attorney General Peyton Ford replied, currently lacked the personnel to review all the FBI's listings. In the "event of an emergency" requiring that a detention program be instituted, Ford continued, "all of the persons now or hereafter included by the Bureau on the Security Index should be considered subjects for immediate apprehension thus resolving any possible doubtful cases in favor of the Government."[43]

Ford, however, had not offered a legal rationale for a decision to essentially not comply with the legislated standards, a failure that was clearly important, since many of the 19,577 individuals listed in the FBI's Security Index did not meet the act's more restrictive standard (active involvement in subversive activities after January 1, 1949, in contrast to the Portfolio standard of individuals "who had at any time been actively engaged in subversive activity"). The act also limited detentions to situations of "actual" invasion (whereas the department's standard was of "threatened" invasion), required the issuance of individual warrants based on probable cause, did not suspend the writ of habeas corpus, and did not authorize FBI agents to search and confiscate contraband when apprehending suspect detainees. Accordingly, FBI officials once again requested a departmental review of their Security Index listings to ensure that "the Bureau would not be open to an allegation of using Police State tactics." How would the detention program be handled, they inquired, pointing out that "prominent persons" were listed in the Security Index whose apprehension "might cause the Bureau some embarrassment." Responding for the department, Assistant Attorney General Raymond Whearty, the head of the Criminal Division, assured FBI officials that the department considered the provisions of the 1950 act unworkable and that the FBI should operate under the 1948 standards. Apprised further of Justice Department attorneys' intention to review the FBI's Security Index listings, the FBI director demanded that his aides search FBI files for any background information about the department attorneys who would conduct the proposed reviews—in the process highlighting FBI officials' expansive conception of security risks.[44]

The FBI director's underlying concern in any event was that the department would not remain committed to the 1948 standards, a concern that proved to be well founded. In June 1951, Deputy Attorney General Ford instructed

Hoover that the Security Index standards should be revised "to conform more closely" with the provisions of the 1950 act. Interested less in clarification than in ensuring that department officials remained committed to the 1948 program, Hoover immediately contacted Ford to emphasize the "wide disparity" between these standards, pointing out that individuals could not be listed under the 1950 act if they were not proven members of a revolutionary group, were no longer involved in "current activity of a subversive nature," or were not people "whose association and activities are closely affiliated with individuals or organizations having a definite foreign interest or connection contrary and detrimental to the interests of the United States." The FBI director demanded "a prompt resolution" of this disparity in standards.[45]

When departmental officials did not respond promptly, FBI Assistant Director Alan Belmont and FBI Supervisor Baumgardner raised the standards issue directly during a meeting with Whearty, protesting that the department was apparently "interpreting" the 1950 act and "hedging" its previous stand of adherence to the 1948 standards. There should be no doubt, they insisted, that the FBI was operating under standards "specifically authorized" by the attorney general. Furthermore, they observed, in the event a preventive-detention program was implemented, the department's "broad interpretation" of the 1950 act might not stand up. Reiterating that the department intended to proceed under the 1948 plan and not the unworkable 1950 act, Whearty advised that the already drafted presidential proclamation would be issued in an emergency and that the department would seek the repeal of Title II by bringing to Congress's attention the "unworkability" of the act.[46]

Justice Department officials might have consistently dismissed the 1950 act as unworkable; they never explicitly ordered FBI officials to ignore its provisions. This ambivalence haunted FBI officials, as at times it appeared that department officials had decided to ignore the act and, at other times, had seemingly concluded that the act could not be ignored. This question was seemingly resolved in October 1952, when Attorney General James McGranery informed FBI Director Hoover that the department intended to seek new preventive-detention legislation. Until then, McGranery wrote, when reviewing the files of individuals subject to apprehension and detention, department officials would be guided by Title II of the 1950 act.[47]

Hoover, however, refused to accept this decision as final. He immediately informed McGranery that this decision posed serious problems for the bureau, FBI planning having always been based on the 1948 standards. The FBI director then specifically queried: Did McGranery agree with the FBI's conceptions of this program and the Security Index standards as outlined in his June 1951 memorandum to Deputy Attorney General Ford?

Senior FBI and Justice Department officials met to address the FBI director's demands. No definitive solution was reached, as the participants agreed only to study the matter further. Hoover thereupon ordered FBI Assistant Director Ladd to draft specific recommendations for appropriate action. When reporting back later that month, Ladd emphasized that the FBI could operate "more effectively" under the 1948 plan than the 1950 act. "Many" of the 19,577 individuals listed in the FBI's Security Index "do not fall within the provisions" of the 1950 act, he observed, and thus should the department proceed under this act, "many people who are now included in our Security Index" would be excluded. The FBI, Ladd continued, could not wait until an emergency to discover which standards would apply. Accordingly, he recommended:

> While ... I firmly believe that the internal security of the country could best be protected in the time of an emergency if we proceed under the plans set forth in the Department's Portfolio, I do not believe that it is desirable that the Bureau go on record with recommendations to the Department concerning this matter. The Department's Portfolio contains a plan for the suspension of the Writ of Habeas Corpus which without question will be a highly controversial subject and will undoubtedly cause considerable debate in the event it is ever openly proposed. Other questions will be raised as to why it is necessary to proceed under a plan devised by the Department of Justice when there is a law on the statute books which ostensibly covers the purpose for which the Department's plan was set up to handle. . . . Obviously the Department does not want to be placed in a position of having stated that it is not going to pay attention to the Internal Security Act of 1950. They have hedged in this matter in the past and it is to our interest that we receive from them a positive expression of approval for our concepts of the Emergency Detention Program and our concepts of the standards for including individuals in the Security Index which is tantamount to scheduling these persons for apprehension. I believe that we should continue to call for a positive statement from the Department and that we should under no circumstances make any commitments regarding the desirability of proceeding under the Emergency Detention Program or under the Internal Security Act of 1950.

Ladd urged Hoover to send the enclosed draft memorandum to McGranery detailing the FBI's position and requesting "a definite and clear cut answer." The FBI director agreed to send the memorandum, adding, however, that "I do think we are hedging in not at least being on record as to what is best for the internal security of the country + then leaving it to Dept to decide whether to adopt it."[48]

FBI officials had never been willing to defer to the attorney general and to senior departmental officials. Their consistent objective had always been to force their ostensible superiors to direct the FBI to ignore the will of Congress. This strategy failed as, when finally replying, McGranery did not explicitly direct the FBI to flaunt Congress's legislated standards. The attorney general, however, was unwilling to defy Hoover's demand that he explicitly endorse the standards of the 1948 Department's Portfolio. In his "Top Secret" response to "the questions" raised in Hoover's October 15, 1952, memorandum, McGranery merely affirmed "the Department's intention in the event of an emergency to proceed under the program as outlined in the Department's Portfolio." In effect representing this as the FBI's position, McGranery simply wrote that his "approval, of course, indicates agreement with your Bureau's concepts of the Detention Program and the Security Index standards as outlined in your memorandum of June 28, 1951."[49]

In this attempt to avoid having to direct the FBI explicitly to ignore an act of Congress, McGranery had purposefully responded not to Hoover's November 14 memorandum; instead, he only acknowledged the FBI director's earlier memorandum of October 1952. The attorney general thereby avoided going on record directing the FBI not to comply with the legislatively mandated standards. He had decided to resolve an administrative problem alone—advising FBI officials which criteria should govern the FBI's listing of individuals. McGranery at the same time purposefully sidestepped the broader issues that Hoover had raised in his November memorandum—whether to suspend the writ of habeas corpus, base apprehensions on individual or general warrants showing probable cause, base detention hearings on rules of evidence, grant detainees the right of appeal to the courts, and allow agents to conduct searches and confiscate contraband when apprehending individuals. Having simply affirmed the department's "intention," the attorney general represented this decision as concurrence with the "Bureau's concepts" of the emergency detention program and Security Index standards.

McGranery's willingness to ignore the legislatively mandated detention standards was not binding on his successors. Thus, following Dwight Eisenhower's election to the presidency, FBI Director Hoover solicited the views of the new attorney general, Herbert Brownell, about the detention program's standards and apprehension procedures. Brownell thereupon authorized Hoover to "implement the apprehension and search and seizure provisions of the program immediately upon ascertaining that a major surprise attack upon Washington, D.C., has occurred," specifying that all those listed in the FBI's Security Index were to be apprehended.[50]

Although never formally implemented,[51] the FBI's Security Index program continued through the John Kennedy, Lyndon Johnson, and Richard Nixon administrations. During the 1960s, however, the listing standards were broadened to include individuals involved in civil-rights, youth, and anti–Vietnam

War activities. After reviewing the program in 1968, however, Justice Department officials amended the listing standards to ensure that they conformed to the 1950 act's authorization requirements, modified to include individuals who were members of violent revolutionary organizations that were first established during the 1960s, such as the New Left and black nationalist organizations.[52]

Although never implemented, the revised detention program became the subject of quite different interest in the wake of the charged political atmosphere provoked by U.S. involvement in the Vietnam War. In contrast to the Korean War era, this military conflict provoked widespread public dissent and gave rise to public skepticism about the actions of presidents and intelligence bureaucrats. This skepticism extended to the preventive-detention program following the disclosure that the Justice Department had established facilities to detain individuals scheduled for detention at Avon Park, Florida; Allenwood, Pennsylvania; El Reno, Oklahoma; Wickenburg, Arizona; Florence, Arizona; and Tule Lake, California. Already suspicious about FBI surveillance, many activists and influential liberals depicted these as concentration camps and pressured Congress in September 1971 to rescind the detention section of the 1950 act.

Rather than complying with this legislative rescission, however, FBI officials instead urged Attorney General John Mitchell to continue a preventive-detention program as a necessary component of the FBI's "basic responsibility for protecting the Nation's internal security." Such a program should be maintained, FBI Supervisor Richard Cotter argued, given that "the potential dangerousness of subversives is probably even greater now than before the repeal of the Act, since they no doubt feel safer now to conspire in the destruction of this country." Congress's rescission of Title II, Hoover further advised Mitchell, "does not limit the FBI's authority and responsibility to keep and maintain administrative records, including various indices, which may be necessary to" fulfilling the FBI's "responsibility and authority" to investigate subversive activities. Hoover asked whether Mitchell concurred with his "opinion that the repeal of the Emergency Detention Act does not prohibit or limit the FBI's authority to keep and maintain . . . an administrative index." Mitchell concurred, authorizing the FBI to compile and maintain an Administrative Index to make "readily retrievable and available the results of its investigations into subversive activities and related matters."[53]

Attorney General Mitchell's authorization of an Administrative Index might have violated the spirit and intent of Congress's action when rescinding Title II of the Internal Security Act in 1971 (and, in effect, repeated Hoover's 1943 renaming of the Custodial Detention Index as the Security Index). Mitchell's secret decision soon proved to be vulnerable in the changed political climate that emerged in response to President Nixon's controversial "national security" and "executive privilege" claims when seeking to contain the impact of the so-called Ervin Committee's investigation of the Watergate break-in and cover-up. Thereupon, FBI Director Clarence Kelley, recognizing the political risk inherent in Hoover's 1971 decision to flaunt Congress's intent, on June 7, 1973, decided that the Administrative Index should be considered "strictly an administrative device" that henceforth would play no part "in investigative decisions or policies."[54] Termination of the FBI's detention program, however, did not mean that FBI agents ceased monitoring suspected "subversive" activists and organizations. The establishment of the so-called Church and Pike Committees in 1975, however, led to a new assessment of FBI policies and procedures and, as a byproduct, the cost of unquestioned deference to the national-security claims of presidents and national-security bureaucrats.

2
A History of FBI
Wiretapping Authority

President Franklin Roosevelt's unprecedented authorization of Federal Bureau of Intelligence (FBI) "intelligence" investigations, combined with the similarly secret authorization (whether by presidents, attorneys general, or the FBI director) of other preventive detention and informer programs, had shifted the focus of FBI investigations from law enforcement to monitoring the political and personal activities of suspected "subversives." And yet, despite commanding this increased authority, appropriations, and their successful recruitment of paid and volunteer informers (as, for example, under the American Legion Contact Program), FBI officials could not achieve their objective of learning in advance about the plans and capabilities of suspect individuals and organizations through legal means. Physical surveillance (whether by FBI agents or recruited informers) produced only limited and not always reliable information. FBI officials accordingly sought alternative means to acquire such information. And, because their objective was not to obtain evidence to prosecute but to advance intelligence, they were willing to employ intrusive, if illegal, investigative techniques—break-ins, mail opening, bugs, and wiretaps. The most controversial of them, because it was the subject of public debate, involved wiretapping.

Coincidentally, at the very time when FBI officials obtained presidential authorization to conduct intelligence investigations, Congress had recently banned wiretapping. In 1934, when enacting the Communications Act to regulate the communications industry (radio, telephone, telegraph), Congress adopted Section 605, which barred any "person not authorized by the sender [to] intercept any [wire or radio] communication or divulge or publish the existence, contents, substance, purport, effect or meaning of such intercepted communication to any person."[1]

Claiming privately that this legislative ban applied only to private individuals and corporations and not to federal agents, Justice Department officials continued to authorize the FBI to employ wiretaps during criminal investigations.[2] The Supreme Court, however, struck down this interpretation of the statute in 1937 in *Nardone v. U.S.* In his majority opinion, Justice Owen Roberts held that, "taken at face value," the 1934 act's ban applied to federal agents. Roberts rejected the government's argument that the "construction" of the statute did not apply to federal agents and thus that Congress had not intended to "hamper and impede" investigations to detect and prosecute federal crimes. As a matter of "policy," Roberts countered, Congress "may have thought it less important that some offender should go unwhipped than that officers should resort to methods deemed inconsistent with ethical standards and destructive of personal liberty."[3]

In light of this ruling, FBI Director J. Edgar Hoover solicited Assistant Attorney General Alexander Holtzoff's guidance over "the significance to the Bureau of the Supreme Court decision," fearing that bureau agents could be "prosecuted for violating the [1934 act's] penal provisions." Holtzoff, however, opined that the Court's decision had been "misinterpreted" by the press, as wiretaps per se had not been prohibited but rather the "intercepting and divulging" of communications. The Justice Department, Holtzoff assured Hoover, would "not authorize any prosecution against its own employees in those cases where the employees were proceeding in a course of official conduct authorized" by the FBI director. The prohibition, he further pointed out, applied to interstate and not "local calls" and that although any information obtained through the interception of an interstate call could not be introduced in evidence, FBI officials could act "in an investigative capacity" upon information developed through the tap. Based on Holtzoff's assurance, Hoover instructed FBI personnel to continue installing wiretaps. He nonetheless conditioned his approval, emphasizing "as previously we will not authorize any except in extraordinary cases & then not to obtain evidence but only for collateral leads."

Concurrently, Holtzoff urged Attorney General Homer Cummings not to make a public statement about the department's intention to continue authorizing wiretaps, as this could "evoke hostile comments from the papers and periodicals" and could "lead some Members of Congress who believe in sedulously conserving individual rights to introduce a bill that would expand the scope of the *Nardone* decision, which would be an undesirable consummation." Instead, Cummings instructed his key aides to consider "the question

[of] whether an amendment to the [1934] law should be suggested." No consensus on a preferred bill was reached, however, with Hoover objecting to one proposal that would have required that the FBI secure the advance approval of an assistant attorney general. Justice Department officials ultimately recommended that the attorney general consider banning wiretapping "at least until Congress or the courts carve out an exception."[4]

In a follow-up ruling of 1939, again *Nardone v. U.S.*, the Supreme Court explicitly repudiated Holtzoff's private assessment. The Court at this time extended its earlier ruling holding that the divulgence of "the exact words" had not simply been banned but the "derivative use" of such illegally intercepted communications, and thus any indictment or conviction based on information obtained through a wiretap would require the dismissal of the case. Writing for the majority, Justice Felix Frankfurter held that the ban intended that "not merely evidence so acquired shall not be used before the court, but that it shall not be used at all."[5]

Hoover once again sought Assistant Attorney General Holtzoff's guidance. The assistant attorney general reaffirmed the department's earlier position that only "intercepting and divulging" wiretap information had been banned and that "consequently the Bureau was under no legal or implied prohibition from utilizing telephone taps for investigative purposes only in cases of major importance." The FBI director, however, had serious reservations about continued usage of wiretaps and urged department officials to seek legislation to amend the 1934 act. Unwilling personally to publicly endorse such a legislative change, Hoover proposed that should the department "see fit to indorse [*sic*] some type of wiretapping it should only be done after some outstanding lawyers, with liberal reputations [citing, for example, ACLU Counsel Morris Ernst], were consulted as to the type of legislation to be drafted." In the wake of the Court's *Nardone* ruling, Attorney General Robert Jackson was unwilling at this time to press for such legislation and, instead, in March 1940 issued an executive order barring "wire tapping, entrapment, or the use of any other improper, illegal, or unethical tactics."[6]

Jackson's prohibition, however, was secretly repudiated six weeks later. FBI Director Hoover had in the interim privately advised the attorney general that the wiretapping ban could render "impossible" FBI investigations of kidnapping and espionage. Such disasters as a 1915 bombing incident, the FBI director then argued, "must be anticipated," but the FBI "cannot cope without wiretaps." A future national catastrophe, Hoover warned, could "focus the spotlight of public indignation upon the Department because of the failure to prevent some serious occurrence." Hoover on his own broached this matter with Secretary of the Treasury Henry Morgenthau, who endorsed the FBI director's dire assessment of such threats and the government's responsibility to anticipate and prevent them; accordingly, he urged White House aide

Edwin Watson to have President Roosevelt authorize FBI wiretapping of Axis embassies and suspected Nazi agents. When Watson observed that such an action would be "illegal," Morgenthau blithely replied, "What if it is illegal?"[7]

President Roosevelt, already concerned about German and Soviet involvement in "the organization of so-called 'fifth columns' and in the preparation for sabotage, as well as actual sabotage" in Spain, France, and the Western Hemisphere, on May 21, 1940, secretly authorized FBI wiretapping during "national defense" investigations. In its recent rulings, Roosevelt contended, the Supreme Court "never intended any dictum . . . to apply to grave matters involving the defense of the nation." FBI agents should employ wiretaps in such situations, Roosevelt ordered, but conditioned such uses on the prior review and approval, on a case-by-case basis, of the attorney general. Such uses, the president stipulated, were to be confined to investigations "of persons suspected of subversive activities against the United States, including suspected spies" and were to be "conducted to a minimum and to limit them insofar as possible to aliens."[8]

Roosevelt's secret directive did not legalize FBI wiretapping. The president's circumvention of the Court's ruling was based on the premise that the objective was not to prosecute suspected spies or saboteurs but rather to enable FBI agents to anticipate and thereby prevent the commission of acts of espionage or sabotage. This decision nonetheless was risky politically and created a serious dilemma for the attorney general. Committed to averting the discovery of FBI wiretapping practices and his own required authorization, Jackson instructed Hoover on May 28 of his intention not to maintain a "detailed record" of approved wiretaps. The only record of FBI requests and his approval, the attorney general continued, would be maintained in "a memorandum book" in the FBI director's office that would list "the times, places, and cases in which this procedure is utilized."[9]

Jackson's decision to minimize the discovery of this secret wiretapping policy had far-reaching consequences and in effect subverted Roosevelt's complementary requirement that the Justice Department exercise tight oversight over such FBI uses. Succeeding attorneys general could learn of an ongoing wiretap only if briefed by the FBI director. Jackson's further failure to limit the duration of approved wiretaps and to require that continuance demand his reauthorization ensured that FBI wiretaps could be extended indefinitely and without FBI officials having to prove that the originally stated claim of a security threat existed and had been addressed.

A genius at bureaucratic politics, Hoover readily exploited this wide latitude. Thus, an FBI wiretap of a branch of the National Association for the Advancement of Colored People installed in the 1940s extended for decades until Attorney General Edward Levi inadvertently discovered it in the 1970s. Attorneys general until the mid-1960s, furthermore, rarely evaluated whether the originally stated purpose for an FBI wiretap request had been met. Last, FBI officials did not in all cases honor the requirement that they obtain the attorney general's advance review and approval and in some cases authorized particularly sensitive wiretaps on their own—a practice confirmed by the happenstance preservation of seventeen wiretap authorization cards relating to wiretaps installed during World War II that FBI Assistant Director D. Milton Ladd had originally maintained in his secret office file.

These seventeen cases do not necessarily constitute the totality of all unilaterally instituted FBI wiretaps. In this instance, when Ladd retired from the FBI in 1954, these authorization cards were transferred to FBI Assistant Director Louis Nichols, where they were maintained in his secret office file until his retirement. Alone among the secret office files of FBI assistant directors, which pursuant to Hoover's March 1953 directive were to be regularly purged every six months, Nichols's office file remains extant. The cards confirm that some of the taps had been authorized by Hoover alone and others by FBI Assistant Directors Ladd, Edward Tamm, or Clyde Tolson. Of these taps, six had been installed during criminal investigations (involving bribery, extortion, stolen property, or treason) and seven (in the FBI's terminology) involved "special inquiry" or "SPECIAL sur[veillance]." investigations. The authorization cards list the dates when these taps were installed and discontinued and bear the notation "not included in running memo"—that is, they were not included in the "memorandum book" of approved FBI wiretaps that Hoover maintained in his office.[10]

One of Hoover's top aides and the FBI director's liaison to Congress and the media, Nichols began to maintain (on Hoover's explicit order) his own secret Official and Confidential File in October 1941. FBI Director Hoover had specifically authorized the creation of this secret office file to supplement his own "confidential" office file "in which are kept various and sundry items believed inadvisable to be included in the general files of the Bureau."[11]

Ladd had originally been instructed that "no one can look" at these wiretap records without the FBI director's approval. Furthermore, a memo recording Nichols's receipt of these cards from Ladd confirms that Ladd had also maintained five other categories of wiretap records: a wiretap of a [name withheld] individual; wiretaps installed on the authority of the FBI director for which the attorney general's subsequent approval was obtained and "if approved put in active drawer"; "active" wiretaps identified by FBI field office; "Disapproved requests + 20 or so never used"; and one "Top Secret" wiretap installed by the Washington field office. Nichols's memo, however, does not describe the disposition of these other wiretap records.

Jackson's recognition of the political risks attendant to Roosevelt's secret directive led him to seek to redress this problem by coordinating with liberal Democratic Congressman Emanuel Celler, who on May 27, 1940, introduced a joint resolution to amend Section 605 of the 1934 Communications Act. The proposed bill would permit FBI wiretapping "during security investigations, subject to the direction of the Attorney General, to ascertain, prevent, and frustrate any interference with the national defense by sabotage, treason, seditious conspiracy, espionage, violations of neutrality laws, or any other matter." This bill, Celler contended, would promote the prosecution of so-called "fifth column activities" that threatened the nation's security, stressing that "spies are in great numbers in the United States at this very moment" and that the FBI could not "apprehend them and cannot get the proper evidence to convict them without wire tapping." Attorney General Jackson publicly endorsed Celler's bill as essential to permit wiretapping "under some appropriate safeguard" in "a limited number of cases, such as kidnapping, extortion, and racketeering." This "cannot be done," Jackson emphasized, under the "existing state of the law and [Court] decisions" unless Congress "sees fit to modify the existing statute." The attorney general further claimed that the 1934 act only prohibited the interception *and* divulgence of "any communication" and that any person "with no risk of penalty may tap . . . and act upon what he hears or make any use of it that does not involve divulging or publication." In February 1941, moreover, President Roosevelt endorsed the proposed bill, writing Congressman Hatton Summers that wiretapping "should be used against those persons, not citizens of the United States, and those few citizens who are traitors to their country, who today are engaged in espionage or sabotage."[12]

Congress, however, ignored Jackson's endorsement and did not approve Celler's bill. (Celler's resolution passed the House but was never considered by the Senate.) Conservatives, on the one hand, feared that passage of Celler's resolution would lead to a "New Deal wiretapping Gestapo or Ogpu [the Soviet spy agency and predecessor to the KGB]," creating a dictatorship in the United States. Liberals, in contrast, doubted that wiretapping uses would be confined to legitimate security threats and instead would adversely affect civil liberties, the organized labor movement, and political activists. Federal, state, or local authorities, they contended, would wiretap to further either partisan or antiunion objectives. Indeed, Senators cited these concerns as their reason for conducting radically different hearings to investigate wiretapping practices.[13]

In articulating their reason for convening hearings to investigate past wiretapping practices, which hearings extended from May 21, 1940, through February 15, 1941, members of a Subcommittee of the Senate Committee on Interstate Commerce stressed that such hearings could help determine whether further legislative safeguards were needed to deter the use of wiretaps. Senators expressed a quite different concern from that articulated by Roosevelt, Jackson, and Celler—that government agencies had used and would continue to use wiretaps to investigate the political activities and beliefs of public employees and private citizens despite the ban of Section 605. The abuses that had been publicized through these hearings, the Senate report on this investigation warned, would be repeated; police agencies would not likely abide by antiwiretapping prohibitions.[14]

U.S. military involvement in World War II following the Japanese attack on Pearl Harbor in December 1941 only slightly altered this hostile political climate. In a renewed attempt to exploit this new political setting, on April 23, 1942, Congressman Celler introduced another bill to legalize wiretapping. His proposal, however, differed from that of 1940 in that it would waive Section 605 only in the "interest of prosecution of the war." The report accompanying his proposed bill extolled the importance of wiretaps as a counterespionage tool and dismissed as unwarranted criticisms that individual rights would be affected. Wiretapping would be permitted only for the duration of the war and then only for counterespionage cases.[15] Celler's 1942 initiative once again failed. Despite this rejection, the FBI continued to wiretap for the duration of the war, based solely on President Roosevelt's secret directive and with the realization that any information so obtained could not be used as evidence.

The Roosevelt administration might have failed to convince Congress to legalize FBI "national-defense" wiretapping. FBI officials' actions were not that risky, given the crisis atmosphere of World War II and the broad consensus over the need to defeat the Axis Powers. The end of the war, however, removed this potential cover, all the more so since the FBI's actual wiretapping practices had exceeded the president's "national-defense" rationale and had extended to monitoring a host of political activists involved in radical labor-union and civil-rights activities (including the National Maritime Union, the National Union of Marine Cooks and Stewards, the March on Washington Movement, and the Communist Party's headquarters and branch offices, prominent Communist Party members, and radical German émigrés Bertolt Brecht and Thomas Mann). Tom Clark's appointment as President Harry Truman's attorney general in 1945, given his broader conceptions of national security threats combined with the sharp deterioration in U.S.-Soviet relations after 1945, encouraged FBI Director Hoover to devise a crafty strategy to resolve this FBI dilemma, in this case by seeking Clark's (and Truman's) authorization for the FBI's broader wiretapping operations. Hoover did not do so directly and instead, in July 1946, drafted a letter that he urged Clark to send to the president, purportedly to seek Truman's "reaffirmation" of FBI wiretapping as had been authorized under President Roosevelt's secret May 1940 directive. Clark signed and sent this letter to President Truman—requesting that he indicate his approval by signing the bottom of the letter and not by issuing his own directive.

Hoover's letter, however, distorted the scope and intent of Roosevelt's secret directive. It began by quoting from the final authorization paragraph of

Roosevelt's May 21, 1940, directive but purposefully dropped the last qualifying sentence "to limit [the use of wiretaps in] these investigations so conducted to a minimum and to limit them insofar as possible to aliens." Approving this request, Hoover's drafted letter continued, President Truman would simply reaffirm existing policy (further claiming that this policy had been approved by Clark's predecessors as attorneys general, Jackson and Francis Biddle) given "the present troubled period in international affairs, accompanied as it is by an increase in subversive activity here at home." Citing further the recent "very substantial increase in crime," the letter acknowledged the attorney general's reluctance to employ "these special investigative measures in domestic cases" but added that "it seems to me imperative to use them in cases *vitally affecting the domestic security*, or where human life is in jeopardy" (emphasis added).[16]

In reality, by approving the Hoover-drafted letter, President Truman extended FBI wiretapping authority to a broad range of undefined "subversive" activists and in the process formally abandoned Roosevelt's "national-defense" rationale. The unqualified phrase "vitally affecting the domestic security, or when human life is in jeopardy" would encompass such uses during kidnapping investigations and the targeting of radical and left-liberal political activists. In effect, by signing this letter, Truman had inadvertently unleashed the FBI and had done so without the White House staff's conducting an independent review of this proposal (as would have been the case had he issued his own directive rather than simply sign the Hoover-drafted letter). Indeed, the subjects of FBI wiretaps after 1946 included not only Communist leaders and Communist Party offices but also a host of radical and liberal activists, organizations, and even reporters, including Muhammad Ali; Martin Luther King, Jr.; Stokely Carmichael; Elijah Muhammad; Malcolm X; H. Rap Brown; Roy Cohn; Benjamin Spock; the National Lawyers Guild; the Southern Christian Leadership Conference; the Student Non-Violent Coordinating Committee; the Socialist Workers Party; the Black Panthers; the Nation of Islam; Thomas Corcoran; Bartley Crum; William Beecher; Lloyd Norman; Hanson Baldwin; Marvin Kalb; Hedrick Smith; I. F. Stone; Edward Prichard; William Safire; Morton Halperin; and Anthony Lake.

Because Truman's wiretapping directive, much like that of Roosevelt, did not legalize FBI wiretapping, Justice Department officials concurrently lobbied Congress to legalize this practice. They originally included a section in a comprehensive internal security bill introduced in 1949. Two and a half months later, however, department officials abandoned this legislative initiative, in this case owing to the controversy that the Judith Coplon case precipitated.[17]

An employee of the Justice Department's alien registration section, Coplon was arrested by FBI agents on March 4, 1949, as she was about to deliver twenty-eight FBI reports to Valentin Gubitchev, a Soviet agent employed by the

United Nations. Coplon was eventually indicted and tried in Washington, D.C., and New York City—the Washington indictment for unauthorized possession of classified documents and the New York indictment for the further crime of attempting to deliver the FBI reports to an agent of a foreign government.

At the onset of her Washington trial, Coplon's attorney convinced the presiding judge, Albert Reeves, to order the submission as evidence of the twenty-eight FBI documents so the defense could evaluate the legitimacy of the national-security classified claim. FBI officials pressured the Justice Department to oppose this request, on claimed "national-security" grounds, and then preferred that the case be dropped rather than honor Judge Reeves's subsequent disclosure order. Attorney General Clark, however, overruled their objection. The FBI reports, when released, did not reveal any national secrets but did prove to be deeply embarrassing for FBI officials, as they documented first that the subjects of FBI investigations included political activists and further that some of the information reported in fifteen of the twenty-eight reports had been obtained from wiretaps. Seeking to quell the resultant furor over the seeming confirmation of extensive FBI wiretapping, Justice Department officials claimed in a March 31, 1949, press release that the FBI had wiretapped "in limited cases with the express approval in each instance of the Attorney General. There has been no new policy or procedure since the initial policy was stated by President Roosevelt and this has continued to be the Department's policy when the security of the nation is involved."

Coplon's attorneys at the time sought to exploit this confirmation of extensive FBI wiretapping and requested that the judge approve a pretrial hearing to ascertain whether Coplon had been wiretapped. Objecting to this motion as a "fishing expedition," U.S. Attorney John Kelley, Jr., succeeded in averting discovery. This, however, proved to be a temporary victory. In Coplon's New York trial, the presiding judge honored a similar request. The result of these discovery proceedings proved to be further embarrassment for FBI officials. For one, the released records confirmed that FBI agents had wiretapped Coplon before and after her arrest (raising the further question of the interception of her privileged conversations with her attorney) and, more embarrassingly, that the FBI agent who originally testified to not knowing whether Coplon had been wiretapped had been the recipient of Coplon's wiretap logs and that FBI officials had ordered the destruction of the wiretap logs in view of the "imminence of her trial." Seeking once again to quell this heightened furor, Justice Department officials issued another press release on January 8, 1950, that reiterated, "There has been no new policy or procedure since . . . President Roosevelt." Attorney General J. Howard McGrath alarmingly added that "in view of the emergency which still prevails and the necessity of protecting the national security, I see no reason at the present time for any change."

McGrath, however, was not content to rely simply on the department's claim that there had been "no new policy or procedure" since Roosevelt's presidency and accordingly urged President Truman to release the text of Roosevelt's May 21, 1940, directive to establish that the FBI had been acting under proper authorization. President Truman need not, McGrath added, release his 1946 order, claiming that the president would "protect" himself by doing so. Rather than blindly acquiesce as he had when signing the Hoover-drafted letter in July 1946, Truman had the White House staff review his own 1946 and President Roosevelt's 1940 directives. White House aide George Elsey subsequently informed Truman that Clark's (Hoover-drafted) letter had dropped the final qualifying sentence of Roosevelt's directive. Truman immediately responded by endorsing Elsey's further recommendation to rescind his 1946 directive and issue a more restrictive wiretapping authorization limiting such uses to "cases where the national security requires it" and further requiring the attorney general to "establish appropriate means of control to assure this result."[18]

President Truman, however, never issued this revised directive. Given the heightened anti-Communist climate of the time, captured in the meteoric rise to national prominence that spring of the junior Senator from Wisconsin, Joseph McCarthy, the White House eventually decided that it would be too costly politically to in effect restrict the FBI's wiretapping authority. Instead, in 1951, the Truman administration urged Congress to legalize FBI wiretapping subject only to the review and approval of the attorney general. Republican Congressman Kenneth Keating, however, introduced an alternative bill that would legalize wiretapping but only if based on a prior court order.

FBI officials closely monitored the ensuing congressional debate, preferring the administration's proposed bill. Congress ultimately declined to enact either bill—a development privately welcomed by the FBI director, who preferred "no legislation at all" rather than have FBI wiretapping requests subject to court approval.[19]

The Coplon case, moreover, precipitated a further internal review of FBI wiretapping practices, triggered by the reversal of Coplon's conviction by the court of appeals, in part on grounds of illegal FBI wiretapping. The court's ruling placed FBI officials in a difficult position, raising as it did the possibility of further exposés of FBI wiretapping practices. Accordingly, in October 1951, FBI Director Hoover solicited Attorney General McGrath's guidance about the FBI's current wiretapping practices. Citing the 1934 act's prohibition and the Supreme Court's rulings in the *Nardone* cases, Hoover observed that "allegations will be made that this Bureau is engaging in illegal practices" and that FBI agents "may incur citations for contempt of court by declining to produce wire tap information and prosecutions may be dismissed if such information is not produced." Wiretaps, Hoover emphasized, enabled the FBI to protect the national security, and "the use of wire tapping is a valuable and highly productive technique in intelligence coverage of matters relating to espionage, sabotage and related security fields." He then asked McGrath to "consider" whether the FBI "should continue to employ this technique as at present, or discontinue it entirely." The FBI director furthermore, in a seemingly unrelated matter, blindsided the attorney general by soliciting his guidance about the FBI's current uses of bugs, including bugs installed by means of trespass. Conceding the illegality of this practice, Hoover defended such uses as "of an intelligence nature only" and thereby "highly pertinent to the defense and welfare of this nation." The FBI director inquired whether the bureau should "continue to utilize this technique on the present highly restrictive basis, or whether we should cease the use of microphone coverage entirely in view of the issues currently being raised."

Responding on February 26, 1952, McGrath did not "alter the [department's] existing" wiretap policy "under the present highly restricted basis and when specifically authorized by me." The attorney general then addressed Hoover's bugging request, asserting that installing microphones without trespass "would seem to be permissible under the present state of the law." Installations involving trespass, he continued, would violate the Fourth Amendment, "and evidence so obtained and from leads so obtained is inadmissible." Observing that the issue of FBI microphone surveillance had not been "presented before," McGrath concluded that "I cannot authorize the installation of a microphone *involving a trespass* under existing law."[20]

McGrath might have been unwilling to authorize such bugging installations. Nonetheless, he had not explicitly banned this practice. As a result, FBI officials continued to authorize bugs, but on a more restricted basis owing to their "importance and value." FBI Director Hoover, nonetheless, imposed strict conditions on such uses and explicitly required his own "specific authorization in each and every instance."

Then, with McGrath's forced resignation as attorney general in early 1952, FBI officials lobbied his successor, James McGranery, to permit such installations, which the FBI director claimed had been installed "on a very limited basis" and "only in cases which directly affect the internal security of the United States." Unwilling to issue a formal directive authorizing this practice, McGranery agreed to "leave it to" FBI Director Hoover's judgment "as to the steps to take." Hoover assured McGranery that this "authority would only be used in extreme cases and only in cases involving the internal security of the United States."[21]

The election of Dwight Eisenhower in 1952 potentially could have led to major changes in FBI wiretapping and bugging policy insofar as the authority for the use of these techniques had derived from secret executive directives (whether issued by the president or the FBI director) and not law. No change in policy ensued, however. To the contrary, the Eisenhower administration (which had won office on a militant anti-Communist platform of decrying the Truman administration's "softness toward communism") unsuccessfully lobbied Congress—in 1953, 1954, 1955, 1958, and 1959—to legalize FBI wiretapping practices during national-security investigations subject only to the prior approval of the attorney general. Fearful that "any legislation on this subject would open up discussion which might lead to requiring court permission," Attorney General Herbert Brownell asserted that "the Justice Department would prefer no legislation at all rather than such a change." As in 1951, however, alternative bills were introduced conditioning FBI wiretapping on court-ordered warrants. Once again, FBI officials privately lobbied against these measures. Indeed, in 1953, FBI officials prepared a memo containing "derogatory data" on eight federal judges for possible off-the-record use "in connection with proposed wire-tapping legislation." The memo questioned whether certain judges could be trusted to handle "confidential information from our files in security matters."[22]

Either when proposing or testifying before Congress on bills to legalize wiretapping, Eisenhower administration officials extolled the necessity of wiretapping, reiterated Attorney General Jackson's 1941 claim that the 1934 act had only prohibited the divulgence of information secured through wiretaps, and warned that vesting oversight in the courts would ensure delay and "leaks."[23] Attorney General Brownell, however, in effect rejected his predecessors' apologetic stance about FBI wiretapping when forthrightly admitting that the number of FBI wiretaps in operation reached as high as two hundred at any one time. He cited these figures as evidence of the department's vigilance.[24]

The proposed bills and the resultant hearings, moreover, highlighted how the congressional debate had shifted from the earlier questioning of the effect of FBI wiretapping on privacy rights. The central issues that members of Congress raised instead became: What procedures or guidelines should be established to govern such uses; what specific uses should be legalized; and should the final authority for approving the use of wiretaps be vested in the attorney general or in federal judges? Indeed, in 1953, Congressman Celler described the purpose of the congressional hearings as not to investigate incidents of wiretapping but to spell out the appropriate provisions that should govern the legal use of evidence obtained through wiretaps. The resultant congressional report, reflecting this new stance, criticized the ban of Section 605 of the 1934 Communications Act as harming "national security" and endorsed the legalization of wiretapping in those cases where the attorney general determined that "national security" would be adversely affected.[25]

No member of the Judiciary Committee, moreover, even attempted during the 1953 hearings to define precisely the meaning of the term "national security." Congressman Celler's bill, for example, delineated national security as encompassing "treason, sabotage, espionage, sedition, sedition conspiracy, violation of the neutrality laws, violation of the Act requiring the registration of agents of foreign principals . . . violation of the Act requiring the registration of organizations carrying on certain activities within the United States . . . [and] violation of the Atomic Energy Act of 1946."[26] Furthermore, none of the bills that the administration endorsed defined what constituted subversive or "certain" activities but simply granted Justice Department officials broad authority to employ wiretaps during investigations of those who affected "national security."

One such bill introduced in 1953 repeated this deference to the attorney general. "National security" was defined as "treason, sabotage, espionage, sedition, conspiracy, violation of Chapter 115 of Title 18 of the United States Code, violation of the Internal Security Act of 1950, violation of the Atomic Energy Act of 1946 . . . and conspiracies involving any of the foregoing." This same language was repeated in the other bills to legalize wiretapping that were introduced throughout the 1950s, with the exception of one introduced by Congressman Keating in 1958.[27] Congress enacted none of the proposed bills, however, remaining unwilling to grant to the attorney general the sole authority to determine whether a tap should be installed, although the momentum for passage had increased and members of Congress were no longer reluctant to legalize wiretapping during claimed "national-security" investigations.

A significant change in emphasis, nonetheless, surfaced in the 1960s, captured in a clause in a bill that had been introduced by Congressman Celler in 1959 that would have authorized wiretapping during kidnapping cases.[28] The Kefauver and McClellan Committees' disclosures of 1950 and 1957 of the insidious influence of organized crime introduced a new rationale beyond "national security"—the value of wiretaps in combating organized crime. The "national-security" rationale nonetheless was repeated in proposed bills of 1961 and 1962 to legalize wiretapping—defined as "any offense punishable by death or imprisonment for more than one year under Chapter 37, 105, or 115 of Title 18 of United States Code, Sections 224–227 inclusive of the Atomic Energy Act of 1954 . . . , as amended, or conspiracy to commit any such offense." But now proponents offered an additional rationale for legalizing wiretapping to counter "any offense involving murder, kidnapping or extortion under Title 18 of the United States Code, any offense under Sections 201, 202, 1084, or 1952 of the United States Code, any offense under any law of the United States involving the manufacture of, importation, receiving, concealment, buying, selling or otherwise dealing in narcotic drugs, marihuana or any conspiracy to commit any of the foregoing offenses."[29] The continued antipathy toward what was still perceived to be a Big Brother tactic, however, once again led Congress to stymie the proponents of legalization.

Throughout the 1950s and 1960s, despite the failure of these legislative initiatives, FBI agents continued to employ wiretaps, and, when their uses were publicized in isolated cases, Justice Department officials defended the practice. For example, in 1959, Attorney General William Rogers informed a Senate committee investigating the use of wiretaps that the FBI currently employed seventy-four wiretaps, all of which were used in "national-security" investigations, while in 1961 Assistant Attorney General Jack Miller during Senate testimony similarly admitted that the FBI had eighty-five wiretaps at that time, all authorized on "national-security" grounds.[30] Justice Department officials even admitted in 1968 that some of the evidence in more than thirty cases was possibly tainted, because it was obtained from illegal wiretaps or bugs.[31]

FBI bugging operations, in any event, posed quite a different political problem for FBI officials, all the more so because of Attorney General McGrath's written conclusion that he could not approve bugs installed through trespass, as this practice was illegal. McGranery's willingness to grant FBI officials a green light to continue to employ bugs during "national-security" investigations did not resolve this dilemma insofar as the attorney general had simply deferred to the FBI director. The opportunity to resolve this problem first surfaced with the election of the Eisenhower administration in 1952, given the militant anti-Communist stance it had adopted during the presidential campaign. Accordingly, FBI Director Hoover solicited the endorsement of the new attorney general, Brownell, of a "less restrictive interpretation of the law pertaining to microphone surveillances." Brownell concurred, advising Hoover that he agreed "upon a new legal approach under which microphones installed through trespass would not be seen as the result of an illegal entry because the entry was not for the purpose of a search and seizure and thus not within the proscription of the Fourth Amendment."

Unwilling to rely on this tortuous interpretation, FBI officials pressed the department again, proposing that the same process be applied for bugs as wiretaps—the prior approval in each case by the attorney general. FBI Assistant Director Nichols pointed out that the FBI required the department's "backing" in the event that an FBI microphone installation was discovered, as this "would precipitate considerable adverse publicity in the press and result in embarrassment" for the FBI and the Justice Department. Brownell again demurred, claiming that the department would be "in a much better position to defend the Bureau in the event there should be technical trespass if he had not heretofore approved it."

FBI officials were not dissuaded and soon exploited a subsequent Supreme Court ruling in *Irvine v. California*[32] to propose again the adoption of the prior-review-and-approval procedure. Instead, on May 20, 1954, Attorney General Brownell issued a broadly worded secret directive authorizing FBI microphone installations, including by means of trespass, "in connection with matters relating to internal security" (a broader standard than "national defense" or "national security"). Stressing the need for and value of such uses in "uncovering the activities of espionage agents, possible saboteurs, and subversive persons," Brownell stipulated that "the Department approves" FBI microphone installations, including by "means of trespass to fulfill its intelligence function in connection with internal security matters." "In resolving the problems which may arise in connection with the use of microphone surveillances," Brownell added, the department "will review the circumstances in each case in the light of the practical necessities of investigation and of the national interest which must be protected . . . [and would thus] adopt that interpretation which will permit microphone coverage by the FBI in a manner most conducive to our national interest." Brownell concluded by commenting that for the FBI to "fulfill its intelligence function, considerations of internal security and the national safety are paramount and, therefore, may compel the unrestricted use of this technique in the national interest."[33]

Brownell's unwillingness to exercise strict oversight over FBI bugging operations (by creating records of his authorization, thereby repeating Attorney General Jackson's similar unwillingness of 1940) once again invited senior FBI officials to expand their uses of microphones even beyond the broader "internal security" standard. Embarrassed by the highly publicized so-called Apalachin incident of 1958[34] that contradicted his public denial that an organized nationwide crime syndicate, or Mafia, existed and to counter this adverse publicity and criticisms of the FBI, Hoover that year instituted a code-named Top Hoodlum program to enhance FBI investigations of organized crime bosses. As part of this intensified monitoring effort, FBI officials on their own in July 1959 decided to employ microphones "against top hoodlums on the basis of the threat to society from organized crime." They did so without consulting the attorney general and by interpreting the "terminology 'national safety'" of Brownell's 1954 directive as authority for their decision to install bugs during FBI criminal investigations. FBI officials explicitly decided not even to brief attorney general William Rogers about their interpretation of Brownell's directive.[35]

Attorneys General Brownell's and Rogers's deference continued during Robert Kennedy's attorney generalship. The new attorney general, moreover, personally was convinced about the value of wiretaps to advance an effective anticrime agenda, the central plank of his administration. Frustrated by the restrictions on the use of evidence obtained from wiretaps, in 1961 and 1962, he pressured Congress to legalize wiretapping and privately reaffirmed what he understood Brownell's policy to be concerning FBI microphone installations—that Brownell had permitted the FBI to install bugs without having to obtain the advance approval of the attorney general. Kennedy's successors, Nicholas Katzenbach and Ramsey Clark, however, rejected this policy of abject deference and instead instituted stricter rules to enhance their ability to monitor FBI wiretapping and bugging practices.[36] Thus, on March 30, 1965, Attorney General Katzenbach issued a new order requiring the attorney general's advance approval for wiretaps and bugs and limiting the duration of approved wiretaps and bugs to six months, after which FBI officials would have to secure the attorney general's reauthorization. Each request to install a tap or bug, moreover, had to be justified in writing. In September 1966, Katzenbach furthermore ordered FBI officials to create a special ELSUR (Electronic Surveillance) Index that listed all individuals whose conversations had been intercepted, whether directly targeted or intercepted through a tap or bug of a specified target. Clark, who succeeded Katzenbach as attorney general in 1966, tightened these reporting procedures in June 1967. All FBI wiretaps and bugs would be subject to "tight administrative control" to ensure that they "will not be used in a manner in which it is illegal and that even legal use will be strictly controlled." Clark required his advance approval for wiretaps and bugs, adding that "special problems with respect to the use of [bugs and wiretaps] in national security investigations shall continue to be taken up directly with the Attorney General in light of existing stringent restrictions."[37] As one direct consequence of Katzenbach's and Clark's administrative rules, the number of FBI wiretaps and bugs declined substantially between 1965 and 1968: from 233 wiretaps in 1965, to 174 in 1966, to 113 in 1967, and to 82 in 1968; and from 67 bugs in 1965, to 10 in 1966, to 0 in 1967, and 9 in 1968.[38]

Reflecting the changed political climate shaped by the waning of the cold war and the resurgence of a renewed concern about the threat such intrusive techniques posed to civil liberties, in 1967, a Senate subcommittee conducted hearings on a proposed bill, S. 928, to prohibit the interception or divulgence of any wire communication or use of electronic eavesdropping devices sold in interstate commerce. This bill nonetheless contained a new "national-security" exception: "Nothing contained in this chapter or in section 605 of the Communications Act of 1954 . . . shall limit the constitutional power of the President to take such measures as he deems necessary to protect the Nation against actual or potential attack or other hostile acts of a foreign power or any serious threat to the security of the United States or to protect national security information against foreign intelligence activity."[39]

During the resultant hearings, Attorney General Clark admitted that the FBI had presently installed thirty-eight wiretaps "in cases directly affecting the national security." Clark added that the FBI engaged in "no [other] wiretapping or other electronic surveillance." Questioned by Senator Edward Long regarding whether the language "any serious threat to the security of the United States" included organized crime or other criminal cases, Clark replied,

"We are speaking only of matters that directly affect the national security and are a threat to the Nation. This bill would, therefore, prohibit use of wiretapping for investigation of gambling, numbers, prostitution and such things as that."[40] This proposed bill was again not enacted in 1967.

In 1968, however, proponents of legalization encountered a more receptive political climate, triggered by that decade's sharp increase in urban crime and the frequency of militant anti–Vietnam War and civil-rights demonstrations. A new politics of "law and order" had emerged that served as an additional rationale for proposed initiatives to legalize wiretapping and bugging. The appeal of "law and order" culminated with the enactment of the Omnibus Crime Control and Safe Streets Act of 1968.

When debating this bill, a majority of the members of Congress rejected what heretofore had been the guiding premise that law enforcement was primarily a local and state responsibility. They were now willing to expand the federal government's role. As originally drafted and enacted by the House, the proposed law, however, did not legalize wiretapping. Such a section was added during Senate deliberations. Ironically, in this case (in contrast to legalization initiatives dating from 1940), representatives from the Lyndon Johnson administration did not actively lobby in support of the legalization of wiretapping. Instead, two constituencies that had traditionally opposed it, whether on states-rights grounds or opposition to centralized executive powers, provided the crucial support to expand federal law-enforcement authority—Southern Democrats and conservative Republicans. As drafted during deliberations by the Senate Judiciary Committee, the proposed bill legalized wiretapping and bugging during criminal investigations subject to a court-ordered warrant requirement. Proponents of this section, however, endorsed a broad exception to the court-review requirement, stipulating:

> Nothing contained in this statute or in Section 605 of the Communications Act of 1934 . . . shall limit the constitutional powers of the President to take such measures as he deems necessary to protect the Nation against actual or potential attack or other hostile acts of a foreign power, to obtain foreign intelligence deemed essential to the security of the United States, or to protect the United States against the overthrow of the Government by force or other unlawful means, or against any other clear and present danger to the structure or existence of the Government. The contents of any wire or oral communication intercepted by the authority of the President in the exercise of the foregoing powers may be received in evidence . . . only where such interception was reasonable, and shall not be otherwise used or disclosed except as is necessary to implement that power.[41]

The majority report of the Senate Judiciary Committee wholeheartedly endorsed this exception. Never defining the limits to executive "national-security" wiretapping, although professing their commitment to prohibit abuses of unauthorized wiretaps, proponents argued that "whatever means are necessary should and must be taken to protect the national security interest." Describing wiretaps and bugs as "proper means" to acquire "counterintel-ligence against hostile actions of foreign powers," the writers of the report denied that the proposed legislation would "disturb the power of the president in this area," adding that limitations that "might be deemed proper in the field of domestic affairs become artificial when international relations and internal security are at stake." Proponents elaborated:

> Nothing in the proposed chapter or other act amended by the pro-posed legislation is intended to limit the power of the President to obtain information by whatever means to protect the United States from the acts of foreign powers including actual or potential attack, of foreign intelligence activities, or any other danger to the structure or existence of the Government. When foreign affairs and internal security are involved, the proposed system of court ordered electronic surveillance envisioned for the administration of domestic criminal legislation is not intended to be applicable. . . . The only limitation recognized in this use is that the interception be deemed reasonable based on an ad hoc judgment taking into consideration all of the facts and circumstances of the individual case.[42]

This broad language, proponents of this section maintained, would not lead presidents to authorize FBI wiretapping of political activists or to vio-late constitutional rights.[43] In fact, Senator John McClellan, the bill's floor manager, during floor debate contended that the "first major purpose" of the bill's wiretapping section "is to protect privacy of communication." The bill, McClellan continued, "has been carefully drafted to meet both the letter and spirit" of the Supreme Court's rulings in the recent *Berger* and *Katz* cases. He emphasized that "electronic surveillance is authorized but only under strict controls. Broadly, Title III creates a court order system of electronic surveillance," limits approval to "certain carefully detailed conditions," and "narrowly assures that electronic surveillance is intended to be the exception, rather than the rule." The act, McClellan continued, "envisaged that these techniques will be employed in only limited numbers and kinds of criminal investigations. On the federal level, the two chief areas are national security matters and organized crime."

Senators Edward Long and Philip Hart pointedly challenged McClellan's benign characterization. In their minority report, Long and Hart contended that the proposed Title III was "unconstitutional, as it provides for unreasonable searches and seizures." Hart specifically condemned the bill's reference "against any clear and present danger to the structure or existence of the Government." "On his own motion," Hart argued, a president "could declare a militant right-wing group (i.e., the minutemen) or left-wing group (i.e., black nationalists), a national labor dispute, a concerted tax avoidance campaign, draft protesters, the Mafia, civil rights demonstrators, a 'clear and present danger to the structure of the Government.' Such a declaration would allow unlimited unsupervised bugging and tapping . . . [and give] the President a blank check to tap or bug without judicial supervision when he finds, on his own motion, that an activity poses a 'clear and present danger to the Government.'"

Hart repeated these objections during the ensuing floor debate, specifically pinpointing the bill's failure to define the limits to executive authority or a national-security exception. Future presidents, Hart presciently warned, could interpret the vague language of the section as authorizing wiretapping radical groups, such as the Black Muslims, the Ku Klux Klan, draft dodgers, and civil-rights advocates. Were his reading correct, Hart averred, this section "grants unlimited tapping and bugging authority to the President. And that means there will be bugging in areas that do not come within our traditional notion of national security." Hart then inquired whether McClellan agreed that this was a fair reading of the wiretapping section.

Replying evasively, McClellan defended this language as having been "drafted by the Administration, the Justice Department. I was perfectly willing to recognize the power of the President in this area. If he felt there was an organization that was plotting to overthrow the government, I would think we would want him to have the right." The president's powers, McClellan continued, need not be defined; the language merely reflected the "spirit of permitting the President to take such action as he deems necessary when the government is threatened."

McClellan implied that only groups or individuals planning overt revolutionary acts but not those involved in radical politics could be monitored. Yet, because this distinction had not been made explicit in the majority report or in the language of the bill, Hart demanded that McClellan clarify what he understood to be a president's constitutional powers and the limits to a president's actions in the national-security area. If we are saying, Hart said, that "so long as the President thinks it is an activity that constitutes a clear and present danger to the structure and existence of the government, he can put a bug on without restraint, then clearly I think we are going too far." Responding, Senator Spessard Holland claimed that Hart was "unduly concerned about this matter." This section, he contended, did not "affirmatively" give any power to a president but simply stated that presidential power was not restricted. McClellan concurred that "there is nothing affirmative in the statement."

Agreeing that Congress could not expand presidential powers, Hart nonetheless maintained that the section's language did not define the limits to a president's national-security powers. "As a result of this exchange," he added, "I am now sure no President thinking that just because some political movement in this country is giving him fits, he could read this as an agreement from us that, by his own motion, he could put a tap on." There was not "a single indication that anything affirmative is being done," Holland reiterated and then added that Congress was not foolishly seeking to "negate" a president's constitutional powers.

The question of the scope of presidential powers permitted by this loophole was not clarified during the following House debate over this legislative initiative. Because the bill that the House had approved earlier did not include a wiretapping section, Congressman Celler, the chair of the House Judiciary Committee, requested House approval to refer the bill to conference. House conservatives submarined this initiative and instead demanded that the House approve the Senate bill, an action that captured the current fearful "law and order" mood, heightened by the recent assassinations of civil-rights leader King and Democratic presidential candidate Kennedy. Under stringent time restrictions governing floor debate, opponents had great difficulty in rallying opposition to or raising probing questions about the meaning of the bill's wiretapping provisions.

At best, the analysis of the bill's provisions by members of the House during floor debate was perfunctory and ill-informed. No member singled out for criticism the section granting the president broad authority in national-security cases or seemingly permitting the targeting of political activists. Indeed, the sole direct comments on the wiretapping section by two of the bill's proponents, Congressmen William Randall and Howard Pollock, conveyed their own misunderstanding of what exactly was being approved. For example, Randall claimed that Title II limited any possibility of abuses by requiring court approval. "Only in the case of national security," the Missouri Congressman argued, "can wire taps be made without a court order. And even these are invalid if application for such order is not made within forty-eight hours after such surveillance is undertaken." Pollock repeated this error when affirming that law-enforcement officers had to secure court approval except in certain "limited" cases where wiretapping would be permitted for forty-eight hours "if it concerns national security or organized crime" that were of an "emergency" nature.[44]

Randall's and Pollock's comments indicate how far the public and Congress had departed from what had been a traditional antipathy toward secret, centralized executive power. The dramatic revelations of presidential and intelligence agency abuses, publicized first during the highly publicized Senate Watergate hearings of 1973 and then the Church and Pike Committees hearings of 1975, rekindled these concerns. Nonetheless, these concerns proved to be temporary, as members of Congress were unwilling to abandon the belief that presidents and intelligence agency bureaucrats should be accorded limited latitude in their efforts to safeguard the nation's internal security from suspected threats.

3

The Politics of Wiretapping

The rationale for President Franklin Roosevelt's secret wiretapping directive was that this technique would enable the FBI to anticipate threats to the "national defense"—that is, planned acts of espionage or sabotage. President Harry Truman's unknowing broader authorization of Federal Bureau of Investigation (FBI) wiretapping of "subversive activities" and Attorney General Herbert Brownell's authorization of FBI bugging during "internal security" investigations were also intended to anticipate foreign-directed operations that could threaten the nation's security. Indeed, some FBI wiretapping and bugging operations did address legitimate security threats. Beginning in 1940, for example, the FBI wiretapped the German, Japanese, Italian, and Soviet embassies. Thereafter, and in succeeding years, the FBI wiretapped and/or bugged the offices of the Soviet Government Purchasing Commission (stationed in the United States during World War II to expedite the Lend-Lease program), the residence of Soviet consular official Peter Ivanov, the headquarters of the U.S. Communist Party and various Communist Party branch offices, prominent Communist Party members (Earl Browder, Steve Nelson, Alexander Bittelman, William Dieterle, James Miller, John Lawson, Waldo Scott, Herbert Biberman), six pro-Fascist and pro-Nazi organizations (including the pro-German Peace Now Movement), and suspected Soviet spies (including Alger Hiss, Judith Coplon, Victor Kravchenko, Boris Morros, Jean Tatlock, Haakon Chevalier, J. Robert Oppenheimer, Emmanuel Larsen, Andrew Roth, Bernard Redmont, William Remington, Felix Inslerman,

George Silverman, Harry Dexter White, Nathan Gregory Silvermaster, Alfred Stein, Elizabeth Sasuly, Irving Kaplan, Victor Perlo, Donald Wheeler, Michael Greenberg, Joseph Gregg, Maurice Halperin, Peter Rhodes, James Harper, Ronald Humphrey, Ronald Pelton, John Walker, Aldrich Ames, Brian Kelley, and Robert Hannsen).

FBI wiretapping and bugging operations, moreover, extended beyond legitimate security threats to encompass a disparate group of radical and left-liberal activists and organizations whose political activities senior FBI officials believed were potentially treasonous. Those tapped and/or bugged included radical activists (David Dallin, Charles Malamuth, C. B. Baldwin, Frank Oppenheimer, Bertolt Brecht, Thomas Mann, Heinrich Mann, Helene Weigel, Berthold Viertel, Anna Seghers, Bodo Uhse, Richard Criley, Frank Wilkinson), prominent liberal and radical attorneys (Bartley Crum, Martin Popper, Thomas Corcoran, David Wahl, Benjamin Margolis, Carol King, Robert Silberstein, National Lawyers Guild, Fred Black), radical labor leaders and unions (Harry Bridges; United Auto Workers; National Maritime Union; National Union of Marine Cooks and Stewards; United Public Workers; United Electrical Radio and Machine Workers; Food, Tobacco, Agricultural and Allied Workers; International Longshoremen's and Warehousemen's Union; CIO Maritime Committee; Congress of Industrial Organizations Council), journalists (I. F. Stone, Philip Jaffe, Kate Mitchell, Mark Gayn, Leonard Lyons, William Beecher, Marvin Kalb, Henry Brandon, Hedrick Smith, Lloyd Norman, Hanson Baldwin, Inga Arvad), civil-rights activists and organizations (Martin Luther King, Jr.; Malcolm X; Southern Christian Leadership Conference; National Association for the Advancement of Colored People; March on Washington Movement; Gandhi Society for Human Rights; Elijah Muhammad; Nation of Islam; Stokely Carmichael; H. Rap Brown; Student Non-Violent Coordinating Committee; Alabama Peoples Education Association; Committee to Aid the Monroe Defendants; Southern Conference for Human Welfare; Black Panther Party; Universal Negro Improvement Association; African Liberation Day Committee), the Students for a Democratic Society, Ku Klux Klan, National Committee to Abolish HUAC, Socialist Workers Party, Washington Bookstore Association, Northern California Association of Scientists, Federation of American Scientists, American Association of Scientific Workers, pre–World War II isolationists (Henry Grunewald, Ethel Brigham, John O'Brien, Lillian Moorehead, Laura Ingalls, America First, Jehovah's Witnesses, Los Angeles Chamber of Commerce), and even prominent personalities (Joe Namath, Harlow Shapley, Edward Condon, Edward Prichard, Muhammad Ali, Benjamin Spock).[1]

The shift in FBI wiretapping from national defense to political surveillance began within a year after President Roosevelt issued his secret wiretapping directive in May 1940. In June 1940, FBI officials, at the request of the White

House, initiated an investigation of Henry Grunewald based on uncorroborated allegations that Grunewald headed a German espionage ring. Resuming this investigation of Grunewald in May 1941, FBI agents this time tapped him, the resumption having been triggered by a report from military intelligence (the military's source, however, was the same individual who had triggered the FBI's 1940 investigation). Installed on June 4, 1941, this tap continued until September 13, 1941. The resultant investigation uncovered no information that Grunewald was a spy but did record his political and shady business contacts. FBI agents, moreover, tapped Grunewald again on June 22, 1945, owing to his close relationship (as a private detective) with prominent Washington attorney Thomas Corcoran. FBI officials discontinued this tap a year later on September 10, 1946.[2]

These two separate taps of Grunewald reflected different political considerations and were determined by the political interests of the two incumbent Democratic presidents, Roosevelt and Truman. A self-employed private detective, Grunewald had moved to Washington, D.C., in the mid-1930s and thereafter maintained close ties with conservative businessman Henry Marsh (to whom he reported regularly on developments in New Deal Washington), isolationist Republicans (notably Senators Gerald Nye and Styles Bridges) and former Roosevelt White House aide and Washington attorney Corcoran (for whom he served as an investigator). Given these associations, the 1941 Grunewald tap and other FBI surveillance inevitably uncovered, among other matters, crucial information about the plans and political tactics of President Roosevelt's isolationist critics in Congress. FBI Director J. Edgar Hoover shared the acquired information about the president's isolationist critics with the Roosevelt White House, although without disclosing how it had been obtained. The FBI's 1945 tap, in contrast, was installed for a quite different purpose and was intended to complement the FBI's investigation of Corcoran, whom Grunewald assisted as an investigator. This tap was installed at the specific request of the Truman White House, eager to learn about Corcoran's contacts (and influence)[3] with the president's liberal critics in Congress, the media, and throughout the federal bureaucracy.[4]

The Roosevelt White House's interest in obtaining advance intelligence about the plans of the president's isolationist critics also underpinned its approval of two other FBI wiretaps on John G. O'Brien and Lillian Moorehead. An officer in the army reserve, O'Brien was activated in 1942 and assigned to the provost marshal's office in Washington. His principal associates were prominent anti–New Deal conservatives in the business, military, and social or societal communities (notably, Provost Marshal General Allen W. Guillon and wealthy socialite Moorehead).

Prior to entering military service, O'Brien had, since 1923, served as an aide to Hearst columnist Cornelius Vanderbilt. Although he was the heir to a sizable fortune, Vanderbilt was politically liberal and, in his gossipy column for the Hearst newspaper chain, commented on the foibles of the wealthy from a New Deal perspective. His contacts in the military (where he served in the army reserve and during World War II held a wartime assignment in New York) and in high society made him a valued recruit for the White House and the FBI, as he willingly alerted them to the plans and activities of conservative activists. Indeed, dating from at least 1941, Vanderbilt "served in a confidential capacity in the Federal Bureau of Investigation by order of the President." "From time to time," Vanderbilt briefed FBI Director Hoover about "matters which he believed should be brought to the attention of the President and which he is reluctant for personal or official reasons to forward through official channels in the War Department."[5]

One of Vanderbilt's reports cited O'Brien's relationships with General Guillon, Moorehead, and a number of other individuals whose names the FBI has redacted but which included a wealthy businessman whom Vanderbilt claimed was "willing to finance" a conspiracy "centered around" Guillon to overthrow the Roosevelt administration. Vanderbilt's reports described Guillon as heading a "constantly growing group who contemplate a military dictatorship in the United States and whose objective is 'to put Jews in their place' and to remove the 'left-wing friends of Mrs. Roosevelt' from public affairs." These "anti-administration" conspirators had allegedly boasted that "the Army will be in complete control of the Government prior to the next elections, which move is contemplated to save the Government 'from the revolutionary group of Mrs. Roosevelt's friends.'" Briefing Attorney General Francis Biddle on these unsupported allegations, Hoover secured his "oral" approval to wiretap O'Brien. Based on information obtained through this tap and from FBI agents' surveillance of O'Brien, Hoover the next month solicited and obtained Biddle's approval to wiretap Moorehead.[6]

Stressing the "extremely delicate" nature of this matter in view of O'Brien's and Moorehead's prominence, Hoover directed FBI agents to install these wiretaps "without the assistance of the telephone company and without the knowledge of any person in a way that it could not under any circumstance be traced back to the Bureau." The taps and FBI agents' physical monitoring of O'Brien and Moorehead, however, uncovered no evidence of a "conspiracy to overthrow" the government. Agents learned only that both commented critically about the Roosevelt administration and the FBI.[7]

The FBI's wiretaps and surveillance might have failed to uncover information of a military conspiracy. They did provide advance intelligence about the political activities of the president's conservative critics and enhanced FBI Director Hoover's standing with the White House. This, however, was not the sole FBI wiretapping operation installed for the purpose of abetting President Roosevelt's political interest in obtaining advance intelligence about the plans and associations of his administration's conservative critics. An even more sensitive operation involved Inga Arvad, a gossip columnist whom the bitterly anti–New Deal *Washington Times-Herald* employed.

FBI officials' interest in Arvad was first kindled in November 1940 with the receipt of an unsolicited report from one of Arvad's classmates in a Columbia University journalism class. Arvad's classmate claimed only that Arvad was pro-German and anti-Semitic. Her report did not at this time trigger an intensive FBI investigation. The repetition of this rumor in December 1941 and a further uncorroborated allegation that Arvad, by then employed by the *Times-Herald*, had been a publicity agent for Nazi leader Adolf Hitler during the mid-1930s and was possibly a German spy elicited intense interest among senior FBI officials, all the more so because the allegation was made in the immediate aftermath of the Japanese attack on Pearl Harbor and the German declaration of war against the United States. This source had offered no hard evidence to support these sweeping allegations; nonetheless Arvad's employment with the isolationist, anti–New Deal *Times-Herald* led FBI Director Hoover to order the FBI's Washington field office to launch a "discreet" investigation of Arvad, with the results to be submitted "in the near future."[8]

As a columnist who wrote about the social activities of prominent Washingtonians, Arvad regularly contacted private citizens and federal employees. These frequent contacts were uncovered during the ensuing investigation and the Washington Special Agent in Charge (SAC) S. K. McKee immediately alerted Hoover to the possibility that Arvad and her associates "may be engaged in any subversive or un-American activity." Sharing this suspicion, the FBI director promptly sought Attorney General Biddle's approval to wiretap Arvad. As justification, Hoover claimed that the FBI's "current investigation of this woman as an espionage subject" had "determined that in the short period she has been in Washington she has established close personal and professional contacts with persons holding important positions in the Government departments and bureaus vitally concerned with the national defense." These "facts," Hoover emphasized, "indicate a definite possibility that she may be engaged in a most subtle type of espionage activity against the United States." Uncritically accepting this contention at face value, in part because of his own suspicions about the motivations of the Roosevelt administration's conservative media critics, Biddle approved the Arvad wiretap.[9]

Almost from its inception, the Arvad investigation acquired a further dimension, triggered by the FBI's discovery of Arvad's association with an unnamed naval ensign (soon to be confirmed as John F. Kennedy) and a report from the Office of Naval Intelligence (ONI) concerning this relationship. Briefing the FBI director about this development, McKee portrayed the Arvad case as having "more possibilities than anything I have seen in a long time." He specifically cited Arvad's sexual affairs (with another ensign as well as Kennedy), particularly with naval ensign Kennedy. In response, Hoover ordered the FBI's Washington field office to give the Arvad investigation "close supervision" and to "be fully cognizant of the potentialities." The FBI director concurrently ordered all other FBI field offices to forward their own investigative findings relative to Arvad and her associations to the Washington field office "not less frequently than weekly."[10]

From their ONI counterparts, FBI agents soon learned that Kennedy, during his temporary assignment in Washington, D.C., and prior to being transferred to Charleston, South Carolina, had "spent the night with [Arvad] on several occasions." FBI officials briefed Hoover about this discovery and their further discovery, through the tap on Arvad, that she planned to visit Kennedy in Charleston during the weekends of February 6–9 and then February 20–23, 1942. Hoover thereupon ordered the Savannah, Georgia, SAC to bug Arvad's hotel room during these weekends but—pointing out that should the FBI's monitoring of Arvad become known to the *Times-Herald*, that newspaper "would be quick to expose any investigation by the FBI"—he demanded that the SAC exercise great caution. The SAC did, the bug was installed, and the SAC duly reported that Arvad and Kennedy had "engaged in sexual intercourse on numerous occasions" during these two weekend visits.[11]

In addition to tapping Arvad and physically monitoring her activities and contacts in Washington, FBI agents broke into her Washington apartment to photocopy her papers and closely reviewed her published columns. No evidence of her "most subtle type of espionage activity" was uncovered then or in the ensuing months, however. Furthermore, when Kennedy learned from contacts in naval intelligence that his activities were under surveillance and relayed this discovery to Arvad, the FBI wiretap intercepted this briefing and Arvad's intention to confront the FBI director. Alerted to this potential problem, Hoover ordered agents to discontinue the wiretap and the Arvad investigation. The FBI director's termination order, however, was countermanded within the month when President Roosevelt, on May 4, demanded that Arvad be "specially watched," having found suspicious Hoover's reports about her associations. FBI officials thereupon resumed the wiretap and investigation for another two months.[12]

Neither Biddle nor Roosevelt ever inquired whether FBI agents had uncovered any evidence of espionage activities from the wiretap or agent investigations—and never learned that the FBI had only discovered Arvad's affair with Kennedy. Their indifference, particularly that of the attorney general, allowed Hoover to retain the discretion to exploit as he saw fit this sensitive personal information about the Kennedy-Arvad affair.

From its inception, FBI officials handled this investigation of Arvad differently from other FBI investigations, even those purportedly seeking information about subversive activities. The distinctiveness of the Arvad investigation in 1942 stemmed from the fact that its subject was an employee of the arch-conservative *Washington Times-Herald*. Fully aware of the possible adverse ramifications should their targeting of a media critic of the president be discovered, FBI officials adopted a series of safeguards. First, the reports on the Kennedy-Arvad affair were submitted under one of the FBI director's special procedures: "Personal and Confidential Letters." Upon receipt at FBI headquarters, these communications were routed to FBI Assistant Director Louis Nichols's office rather than being filed in the FBI's central records system. This handling would enable FBI officials to truthfully deny that FBI agents were investigating a *Times-Herald* employee. Maintaining such records in Nichols's office file would allow them to affirm that the FBI's central records system contained no records that FBI agents had investigated Arvad (including her sexual affair with Kennedy), nor did it retain any records of an Arvad investigation.

This system proved to be of crucial importance in the long run in that it provided FBI director Hoover with potential leverage vis-à-vis the liberal Democratic politician. Indeed, on July 13, 1960, the date Kennedy won the Democratic presidential nomination, Hoover's aides compiled a memorandum summarizing whatever derogatory information the FBI had accumulated about Kennedy's personal and political activities over the years—a seemingly normal practice, as senior FBI officials had also, in 1952 and again in 1956, compiled similar memoranda summarizing whatever derogatory information the FBI had accumulated about another liberal Democratic presidential nominee, Adlai Stevenson.

The summary memorandum on Kennedy reminded Hoover, among other matters, about Kennedy's 1942 affair with Arvad. Thereupon, on July 14, the massive file on the Kennedy-Arvad affair that since 1942 had been maintained by Nichols's secret office file was immediately transferred to the FBI director's secret office file.[13]

In the Arvad case (but as well when wiretapping Grunewald, O'Brien, and Moorehead), Hoover had been more than willing to advance the political interest of the Roosevelt White House and in the process confirm the FBI's value as the political intelligence arm of the president. This questionable practice contravened the FBI's legal responsibilities and would not necessarily continue. To forestall a possible loss of influence, FBI Director Hoover sought to sustain this support in April 1945, following Truman's unanticipated elevation to the presidency with Roosevelt's death that month. In this case, the FBI director willingly exploited the new president's insecurity and doubts about the personal loyalty of those holdovers from Roosevelt's presidency he had inherited and who remained on the staffs of the White House and executive agencies. In no position to clean house and at first dependent on these appointees for background information about Roosevelt's decisions, Truman nonetheless was committed to firing those who secretly plotted to undermine his major domestic- and foreign-policy initiatives.

Having served in the Senate since 1934, Truman had joined the Roosevelt administration belatedly with his inauguration as vice president in January 1945—three months before Roosevelt's sudden death. In the interim between his selection as Roosevelt's running mate at the Democratic National Convention in the summer of 1944 and Roosevelt's death in April 1945, Truman had not been fully briefed about Roosevelt's major domestic- and foreign-policy plans and past decisions and furthermore did not command the unquestioned loyalty of his predecessor's aides—many of whom had at the past summer's Democratic National Convention supported the retention of Henry Wallace as Roosevelt's running mate. Committed to continuing Roosevelt's policies, the new president nonetheless intended to exercise power in his own right and almost immediately replaced many of the current high-level White House and Cabinet appointees. His replacements, because they were more conservative than their predecessors, troubled many of the remaining Roosevelt holdovers as well as liberal activists in Congress and on the staff of the Democratic National Committee, as well as liberal columnists. To prevent what these loyal New Dealers feared amounted to a betrayal of the Roosevelt agenda, some of these holdovers sought to undercut the new president by leaking inside information about Truman's plans and decisions to their allies in the media and Congress. Their most troubling action for Truman involved a leak to syndicated columnist Drew Pearson about the recent discussions of White House emissary Harry Hopkins with Soviet Premier Joseph Stalin. An already insecure Truman became infuriated by this insubordination and its effect on his exercise of power.

President Truman acted quickly to curb future leaks, an objective that required the identification of the disloyal advisers. With this objective in mind, he purposely solicited Hoover's assistance.[14] Contacting the FBI director on behalf of the president, White House aides Edward McKim and James Vardaman specifically requested that the FBI "investigate suspected White House aides, wiretap Edward Prichard [an aide to the director of the Office of War Mobilization and Reconversion and Truman's appointee as Treasury Secretary Fred Vinson] and study the operations of the White House with the objective of offering recommendations to improve its efficiency." (The troublesome leak to syndicated columnist Pearson had triggered the latter request.) Vardaman asked that the FBI director "secure all information possible on White House employees and . . . intercepts of their phone conversations would be of extreme value." He imposed one condition, however: Should these investigations become known, "it would be incumbent upon both the President and him [Vardaman] to deny any such investigation had been ordered." More than willing to further the president's political objectives, Hoover authorized the

Prichard wiretap and concurrently launched a top-secret code-named White House Security Survey program to identify the source of the leak to Pearson and "secure all information possible on White House employees."[15]

Independent of this initiative, President Truman soon learned about another current FBI investigation, in this case involving the leak of classified documents to the radical journal of Far Eastern affairs, *Amerasia*. Truman urged the FBI to conduct a vigorous investigation of this leak, perceiving this as setting "an example to other persons in the Government who may be divulging confidential information."

The *Amerasia* case had its origins in the discovery by agents of the Office of Strategic Services (OSS), through a March 11, 1945, break-in of the office of *Amerasia*, of thousands of pages of classified OSS, State Department, and Navy Department documents. OSS officials had thereupon reported this discovery to the FBI, and FBI officials launched an intensive investigation to identify the federal employees who had leaked these documents. During the ensuing investigation, FBI agents monitored and wiretapped the *Amerasia* office and in addition broke into the journal's office and the residence of *Amerasia* editor Philip Jaffe. Agents also broke into the residences of a suspected State Department source (Emmanuel Larsen) and of a freelance reporter (Mark Gayn) affiliated with the journal. Their investigation led to the discovery of the suspected involvement of another *Amerasia* editor, Kate Mitchell; ONI employee Andrew Roth; and another State Department employee, John Stewart Service. This investigation culminated with the arrest of the six suspects, only three of whom were indicted (Jaffe, Larsen, and Roth) for either having possessed or having transmitted without authorization classified records. The timing of the arrests, however, provoked senior Navy and State Department officials to oppose prosecuting these suspects, fearing the adverse effect of any trial on the already-deteriorating U.S.-Soviet relations. President Truman rejected this counsel, obsessed as he was to stop leaks, and indeed instructed the FBI's liaison to the White House, Myron Gurnea, to notify him directly should any federal-agency official refuse to cooperate with the FBI investigation.[16]

The *Amerasia* and White House Security Survey investigations inadvertently became intertwined as the indirect by-product of the FBI wiretap of Prichard (the only known White House employee tapped under the White House Security Survey program). Prior to tapping Prichard, FBI agents had uncovered his derogatory comments about Truman's abilities and the quality of the president's major administrative appointments. Hoover immediately reported this information to the White House. White House aide Harry Vaughan subsequently personally informed the FBI director that the president had read the FBI's report about Prichard's comments "with great interest." The president, Vaughan advised Hoover, believed that "future communications along that line would be of considerable interest whenever, in your opinion, they are necessary."[17] Hoover accordingly on May 8, without seeking the attorney general's approval, authorized the Prichard wiretap. This tap in time precipitated two additional Truman White House wiretap requests.

On May 29, Hoover forwarded to White House aide McKim the transcripts of Prichard's intercepted conversations with Supreme Court Justice Felix Frankfurter and subsequently forwarded transcripts of Prichard's conversations with syndicated columnist Pearson and former Roosevelt aide and prominent Washington attorney Corcoran. Prichard had earlier clerked for Frankfurter and continued a close friendship with the justice and, as a New Deal liberal, remained close to Corcoran. The intercepted conversations recorded Frankfurter's and Prichard's critical comments about the abilities of Truman's appointees, Prichard's agreement with Frankfurter's suggestion to leak information about the president's policy decisions to Pearson, and also confirmation that Prichard had shared inside information directly with Pearson and Corcoran. McKim subsequently thanked Gurnea for the FBI's "hell-of-a-swell job," asked him to relay the president's "personal gratitude" to the FBI director, and reported that "we are taking corrective action." McKim then asked to be "currently" advised of "any" similar conversations, adding that we "want to keep that tap on." The White House aide conveyed the White House's particular interest in learning about Pearson's and Corcoran's contacts within the administration, their apparent influence, and, further, whether the FBI could identify "any other" of Pearson's sources in the administration. The president had been particularly incensed over a June 12, 1945, Pearson column that was based on a leak concerning White House emissary Hopkins's conversations with Soviet Premier Stalin in Moscow.[18] The White House aide thereupon asked on behalf of the president that the FBI wiretap Pearson and Corcoran.

Hoover agreed to tap Corcoran but not Pearson (given the syndicated columnist's prominence and disturbing ability to learn about closely held secrets from his extensive contacts in the federal bureaucracy and in Congress). The FBI director fully understood the political risks that the Corcoran wiretap posed (given the Washington attorney's prominence as a New Deal Democrat and extensive contacts in the Washington political and journalist communities). Gurnea did create a written record of this discussion with McKim. Truman, however, could claim deniability, not having been a direct party to this request. Hoover's decision to tap Corcoran and Prichard, moreover, made him particularly vulnerable, since these taps had been instituted on his own, without even seeking the approval of Attorney General Tom Clark, thereby contravening the requirement of Roosevelt's May 1940 directive. Furthermore, the FBI director had done so, as recorded in Gurnea's memo on this meeting, despite McKim's having explicitly told Gurnea that "nothing was said in any way, shape or form as to the consequences should this [wiretap on Corcoran] ever become known. It was highly confidential." White House aide Vaughan more fully spelled out the meaning of this conversation—if the Corcoran tap "should ever become known it would be our [the FBI's] baby," as he "would deny any knowledge."[19]

The FBI's taps of Corcoran and Prichard and intensive investigation under the White House Security Survey program failed to uncover the source of the troublesome Hopkins leak.[20] The Corcoran tap, nonetheless, proved to be extremely valuable as a source of political intelligence, given the Washington attorney's extensive contacts throughout the federal bureaucracy, Congress, the Supreme Court, and the Democratic Party. Through this wiretap, the White House was soon alerted to the plans of the president's critics, whether in Congress, the Democratic Party, and on the Supreme Court, as well as the prospective commentary of liberal columnists Pearson, Irving Brant, and Ernest Cuneo.[21]

The Corcoran tap consolidated Hoover's position as FBI director, beyond winning favor with the Truman White House. The tap, in addition, also unexpectedly provided a further benefit for Hoover, which the politically astute FBI director later exploited as political leverage in 1950 and 1953, ironically against the Truman White House.

The FBI director's first-known exploitation of this leverage occurred in July 1950. The specific occasion involved hearings conducted by the so-called Tydings Committee into Senator Joseph McCarthy's claim to have evidence that 81 "known" Communists were employed in the State Department. In the course of these hearings, the committee examined the Justice Department's actions in the disposition of the *Amerasia* case in 1945 and specifically focused on the department's failure to have indicted two of those who had been originally arrested (Mitchell and Service) and agreement to a lenient plea bargain with the three indictees (Jaffe, Larsen, and Roth).

Subpoenaed by the Tydings Committee, senior Justice Department officials planned to testify that the FBI's illegal conduct during its investigation in this case had forced the department to abort prosecution of the defendants. Apprised of this planned testimony, an angry FBI Assistant Director Nichols warned Deputy Attorney General Peyton Ford that, unless the department defended the FBI's conduct before the committee, FBI officials would be forced to release information obtained from the Corcoran wiretap that recorded Corcoran's behind-the-scenes intercession with senior Justice Department officials (Attorney General Clark and Assistant Attorney General James McGranery) in the summer of 1945. The intercepted conversations recorded Corcoran's purposeful effort to avert the indictment of State Department officer John Stewart Service and his intercession at the request of State Department Counsel Benjamin Cohen. When Ford admitted to knowing about the Corcoran tap, adding that "of course, we would never admit this," Nichols responded, "We wouldn't want to admit it, but if we were ever forced into a position the only thing we could do would be to tell the truth and point out we were ordered to do this."[22] The threat succeeded, in the process undercutting the administration's efforts to subvert Republican efforts to exploit how the *Amerasia* case had been handled as a further indication of the administration's "softness toward communism."

FBI officials upped the ante in 1953, on this occasion in a crassly partisan action to promote the political objectives of the recently elected Dwight Eisenhower administration. Having orchestrated a successful strategy, as Eisenhower's campaign manager during the 1952 presidential election, that criticized the Roosevelt and Truman administrations for failing to address the Communist threat, Attorney General Brownell, speaking to a Chicago businessmen's group in early November 1953, charged that in 1946 President Truman had ignored FBI reports that questioned the loyalty of his proposed appointee to head the International Monetary Fund, Harry Dexter White. The White case, Brownell contended, captured the contrasting relationships of Truman and Eisenhower with the FBI and underpinned the Republican administration's successful purge of suspected subversive employees. Infuriated by this aspersion on his loyalty, Truman responded by accusing Brownell of McCarthyism. To rebut the former president, Brownell arranged a joint appearance of FBI director Hoover and himself before the Senate Internal Security Subcommittee later that month. Then, when preparing for his public testimony about this matter, with the central question being how Truman had handled FBI reports, the FBI director considered publicizing Corcoran's intercepted initiatives in the *Amerasia* case, fully cognizant that the attorney general and the Republican leadership of the Internal Security Subcommittee would welcome any additional information that might tarnish the Truman administration and the Democrats. Hoover, however, was reluctant to publicize this discovery of Corcoran's actions, which had been obtained through a wiretap, unless he could document that President Truman had known of and had authorized this tap. Releasing the reports of the meetings of FBI Assistant Director Gordon Nease and FBI Inspector Gurnea with McKim, Vardaman, and Vaughan in 1945 could backfire on the FBI. For one, these reports documented that Hoover had been willing to act as the political agent of the White House. The reports, moreover, did not confirm that President Truman had personally requested the Corcoran tap or had read the transcripts of the Corcoran wiretap sent to the White House. Seeking such confirmation, Hoover ordered FBI Assistant Director Nichols to search FBI files for any records that would at a minimum confirm President Truman's receipt of the Corcoran wiretap transcripts and thus his knowledge of Corcoran's actions involving Service. After reviewing the wiretap summaries and the cover letters that had been submitted with these transcripts, Nichols reported back, "There are no such letters which I can recall or find" covering the 1945 period. Owing to Nichols's failure to produce the desired documentation, Hoover decided to abandon a strategy of disclosing the Corcoran wiretap information during his testimony before the subcommittee.[23]

This was not the sole instance where senior FBI officials exploited the fruits of FBI wiretaps to further their own personal agendas. Another instance involved a Washington-based businessman and influence peddler, John Monroe. FBI officials were first alerted to Monroe's illicit activities in 1943, triggered by disclosures in the news media of a seemingly major scandal. These press reports described Monroe as the host of the "big red house on R Street" (reviving images of Warren Harding–era scandals) who had, through his contacts with federal officials and members of Congress, secured the favorable disposition of wartime contracts.[24]

A congressional hearing was convened to corroborate the sensational press reports, but no evidence of Monroe's involvement in criminal conduct was uncovered beyond his entertaining prominent Washingtonians. Monroe, however, remained a subject of FBI interest and the next year became the target of an FBI bribery investigation into whether he had arranged to secure the dismissal of an Office of Price Administration (OPA) suit against a Brooklyn cake company through his "connections in government circles" and his "alleged friend, Congressman [name withheld]."[25]

This investigation, however, produced another discovery, one that was of particular interest to senior FBI officials—the claim of an FBI informer that Monroe had bragged that "he had no fear of the FBI inasmuch as he 'was the only one who had positive proof that J. Edgar Hoover is a fairy.'" This informer further charged that Monroe was confident of being immune from any criminal inquiry, attributing this to having "slept with" Gladys Drexel, reportedly the niece of Attorney General Biddle.[26] Briefed on these allegations, Hoover's interest in this relatively unimportant case changed dramatically.

When briefing the FBI director about the homosexual allegation, New York SAC E. E. Conroy sought to explain why he had delayed reporting this information. Conroy's dilemma stemmed from the fact that an FBI agent had learned of the homosexual allegation on December 17, 1943, but that the SAC did not report it to Hoover until January 18, 1944. Rightly anticipating the FBI director's ire, Conroy assured Hoover that "the series of situations of this type are being called to the attention of the [FBI] Supervisors [in the New York office] at the meeting today and to the Agents at the next Agents' conference, with the warning that information of this nature should be conveyed to the Special Agent in Charge of the office immediately upon its receipt."[27]

Conroy was nonetheless chastised for having "grossly mishandled" this matter, as Hoover demanded to know "why the matter was not reported from Dec 17 to Jan 18." "Vigorous action" must be made to address this "failure to promptly or properly report this," and Monroe should "'put up or shut up' both as to this statements re A. G. [Attorney General] & myself."[28] The FBI director also instructed FBI Assistant Director Nichols to meet Monroe to "dress down" the businessman on both alleged defamatory statements and to threaten him with "crim[inal] slander unless [he] can prove [them]." During this meeting, Monroe denied having made either allegation and agreed to sign a statement to that effect.[29]

The FBI's investigations, whether in 1943 or 1944, uncovered no evidence justifying an indictment of Monroe. FBI officials, nonetheless, continued to monitor Monroe's activities and initiated another investigation in March 1945 of his possible involvement in a conspiracy to violate OPA price ceilings. This investigation led to Monroe's arrest, indictment, and eventual conviction. Monroe received a sentence of two years imprisonment and a fine of $100,000.[30]

Yet, even though Monroe was the subject of an FBI criminal investigation, the FBI wiretapped him, although the precise date when this tap was installed cannot be pinpointed. Incomplete FBI records document that the tap began at least in August 1945 (the month before Monroe's arrest), was resumed on September 5 (two weeks before his arrest), and continued until December 22, 1945 (two months after his indictment). An October 17, 1946, routing slip, accompanying an attached October 16, 1946, wiretap summary, suggests that the FBI wiretap was installed in August 1945, three months after the FBI's investigation of the OPA violation had been concluded (in May), was terminated in December (three months before the start of his trial), and resumed for a day in October 1946. At minimum, then, Monroe's conversations with his attorneys, business associates, members of Congress, and federal bureaucrats were intercepted and provided FBI officials with valuable intelligence about his pretrial and trial strategy.

The undeniably incomplete wiretap summaries raise an additional question beyond whether FBI officials had exploited this tap to ensure Monroe's conviction. For one, these summaries suggest that one purpose of the FBI's investigation had been to harass Monroe because of his alleged homosexual remark. A secondary benefit of the tap was that it accorded FBI officials advance intelligence about a bureaucratic nemesis, Harry Cooper.

An investigator who had been assigned to the Commerce Department's Surplus Property section during World War II, Cooper had developed excellent contacts with high-level Commerce and Treasury Department and OSS officials as well as a close personal relationship with Monroe. Upon leaving government service, Cooper roomed with Monroe and later became his business partner. If not the direct target, the Monroe wiretap's interception of his and Cooper's conversations with a variety of federal agency officials provided FBI officials with invaluable intelligence that advanced their own bureaucratic interests.[31] At minimum, Hoover learned that Bernard Gladieux (Secretary of Commerce Wallace's executive assistant) intended to recruit army and navy investigators to improve the Commerce Department's investigative capabilities and thereby forestall FBI investigations of Commerce Department cases; newly appointed Treasury Secretary Vinson intended to ensure that the FBI would not displace other departmental investigative units to "find work" for the FBI's wartime expanded agent force (which had increased from 7,441 in 1940 to 11,792 in 1945), because "if they can they're going to take every damned job any other investigative agency's got in the government service"; Commerce Department officials did not intend "to turn anything which has a relation to the Department of Commerce over to the FBI to investigate at any step of the game"; other government officials distrusted Hoover's megalomania and manipulation of Attorney General Clark; Monroe and Cooper planned to counteract Hoover's attempt to sustain the FBI's postwar status by bringing together key leaders of Congress (Senator Francis Myer and Congressman Kenneth Keating) and prominent officials (ONI Director Ernest King and James King, an assistant to OSS Director William Donovan); the Surplus Property agency intended to phase out its investigative division by transferring civil service personnel to the Reconstruction Finance Corporation.[32]

This same interest in furthering their own personal agendas underpinned a November 1945 debate among senior FBI officials over how to handle wiretaps of three Congress of Industrial Organizations (CIO) unions. These taps, FBI Assistant Director Edward Tamm informed Hoover on November 5, 1945, "from time to time" had uncovered significant information that "has constituted an 'item of interest' in connection with memoranda which we have prepared, either upon our own initiative or upon the request of an outside agency, for transmittal to the White House, the Attorney General, the Secretary of the Navy, and others." Unfortunately, Tamm continued, "in spite of our information about these Communist activities in these units, in strikes, and in various every-day occurrences, nothing whatsoever is done by the policy-making agencies of the Government about this Communist activity." Lamenting this failure to take "affirmative" action "upon the information which we furnish," Tamm recommended that "we might as well face the fact that our effort is practically wasted." Hoover rejected Tamm's recommendation to terminate these three taps, contending that "I do think there have been too many unproductive technicals [wiretaps] installed but in these 3 cases they are highly informative on an aspect of Communist activities of considerable importance."[33]

FBI wiretapping and bugging activities captured the changed political reality that the political crisis of the cold war triggered. Potential security threats had become a major priority, and, as a result, FBI officials commanded greater latitude to exploit public concerns, in the process undermining meaningful congressional and media oversight over FBI operations. And, much as in 1945 President Truman had become obsessed over leaks to the media, emboldening him to solicit the FBI's monitoring of administration personnel whom he suspected had leaked classified information to the media, so, too, did President Kennedy respond to what he concluded were leaks in 1961 and 1962. Indeed, Kennedy's dissatisfaction over the FBI's inability to identify the source(s) of these leaks ironically led him to turn to the Central Intelligence Agency (CIA) under a code-named Project Mockingbird program.

In June 1961, President Kennedy concluded that a recent *Newsweek* article about U.S. plans concerning Germany had been based on classified information and thereupon requested an FBI investigation to identify the source of this leak. After first ascertaining that Lloyd Norman had written the offending article, FBI agents wiretapped the reporter's residence (the tap was installed on June 28 and discontinued on July 3). FBI agents were unable, however, to identify the source of this leak and indeed concluded that an intelligent reporter could have written the offending article without access to classified records.

This same scenario was repeated in 1962, triggered this time by a July 1962 article by the eminent *New York Times* military correspondent Hansen Baldwin about Soviet missile systems. An FBI investigation was once again requested to uncover the source of this leak. And the FBI wiretapped reporter Baldwin, but also his secretary, beginning on June 27 and continuing until mid-August. Once again, FBI agents could not positively identify the source of the suspected leak. A suspected individual, however, was identified whom President Kennedy concurred might have been the source.[34]

Kennedy's concern over leaks stemmed from his conviction, expressed in an April 1961 address to the American Newspaper Publishers Association, that press stories had alerted Cuban Premier Fidel Castro to the CIA's orchestration of the Bay of Pigs invasion earlier that month. Denying that he intended to impose any form of press censorship, the president claimed that his sole purpose was to encourage the publishers in attendance to consider not only whether to publish an article but also whether doing so would be "in the interest of national security." In a companion initiative, in October 1962, Kennedy barred State and Defense Department personnel from holding one-on-one meetings with reporters. Should they do so, they had to report such contacts "promptly and in writing."

Kennedy's interest in safeguarding classified information underpinned his frustration over the FBI's failure to identify Baldwin's source. The president in fact raised this matter during an August 1, 1962, meeting with members of the Foreign Intelligence Advisory Board. Board member and MIT president James Killian, after characterizing the Baldwin leak as "one of the most dangerous in recent history and a tragically serious breach of security," contended that the "F.B.I. may not be the best agency to follow up on security leaks." Another board member, prominent Washington attorney and former Truman White House aide Clark Clifford, concurred and recommended the creation of a "full time small group devoting themselves to this all the time" but then added that the FBI "has never been effective" in uncovering the source of leaks. "Nobody knows now. The FBI doesn't know," Clark continued; presumably, an expert group would be better able to "follow the press to identify a troublesome reporter's" contacts and thereby secure evidence of "trends." The president endorsed this proposal and concluded the meeting by asking CIA Director John McCone to "develop an expert [CIA] group that would be available at all times to follow up on security leaks . . . a team available to [McCone] operating under his direction."

At a follow-up meeting with the CIA director on August 22, Kennedy inquired about the "set up in the Baldwin leak." Assuring the president that the CIA had developed a "plan" to address the leak problem, McCone confided that he had established a "task force" that would be "a continuing group reporting to me."

Eventually, in 1963, this task force wiretapped, at a minimum, two syndicated columnists, Robert Allen and Paul Scott. The columnists had been targeted, because administration officials suspected that one of their recent columns had been based on classified "national-security information." The installed wiretaps lasted from March 12 through June 15, 1963; at the same time, task-force members set up an observation post across the street from the columnists' offices to track their movements and their contacts. As their FBI counterparts, however, CIA operatives could not identify the source of the suspected leak. Their monitoring activities nonetheless were considered to have been "very productive," as the wiretaps intercepted the columnists' telephone conversations with twelve Senators and six Congressmen. Continuing in operation for two years, the task force was abandoned in 1965.[35]

President Kennedy might have been dissatisfied by the FBI's failure to uncover the source of the Baldwin leak. Nonetheless, he had not abandoned reliance on the FBI's resources and secret wiretapping capabilities to advance his administration's policy objectives. One such occasion involved his response to the CIA's discovery in February 1961 that officials of the Dominican Republic "intensely desired passage of a sugar bill" pending before Congress and were lobbying key members of Congress to secure a quota "favorable" to their country. As the Kennedy administration was at the time exerting economic pressure on the Dominican government to institute economic and political reforms, congressional approval of the quota would undermine this initiative. Attorney General Robert Kennedy accordingly requested an FBI investigation to "develop intelligence data" that would provide President Kennedy "a picture of what was behind pressures exerted on behalf of the Dominican Republic regarding sugar quota deliberations in Congress." FBI officials in response briefed administration officials that representatives of the Dominican government may have bribed (either monetarily or through other gifts) influential Congressmen and Agriculture Department officials to sustain their nation's sugar quota. Attorney General Kennedy thereupon authorized FBI wiretaps of the residences of three suspected Agriculture Department officials, the residence of the secretary to the chairman of the House Agriculture Committee (Harold Cooley), and the residence and office of a Washington lobbyist registered as a foreign agent of the Dominican government. On his own authority, FBI Director Hoover authorized FBI agents to bug Congressman Cooley's New York hotel room to intercept his conversations during a scheduled meeting in New York with representatives of the Dominican government in mid-February 1961.

No evidence of payoffs was uncovered, but the taps did obtain valuable political intelligence—that the lobbyist for the Dominican government was "working on the Senate and has the Republicans all lined up"; that he had seen two "additional" members of the House Agriculture Committee and had concluded that one was opposed and the other was neutral and possibly supportive; and that Congressman Cooley had been unable to exercise his influence on this matter, as he "had been fighting over the Rules Committee and this had interfered with his attempt to 'organize.'"

The acquired intelligence abetted the administration's successful congressional lobbying effort regarding the sugar-quota legislation. The resultant bill, in fact, granted the president discretionary authority to deny quotas to countries for foreign-policy reasons. Attorney General Kennedy thereupon alerted Courtney Evans, the FBI's liaison to the administration, that "now that the law was passed he did not feel there was justification for continuing this extensive investigation." (Interestingly, an internal FBI report concluded that the FBI's wiretaps had "undoubtedly . . . contributed heavily to the Administration's success" in securing passage of desired legislation. White House officials concurred in this assessment, with CIA analyst William Brubeck writing National Security Council aide McGeorge Bundy that "the action taken by the House of Representatives" in passing the sugar-quota bill "has created a furor in the Dominican Republic," with that country's officials complaining that Congress's action "would be disastrous" to the Republic's "economy.") Then, when alerted by the FBI in 1962 that officials of the Dominican Republic might again seek to influence congressional deliberations over sugar-quota legislation, Attorney General Kennedy once again authorized FBI wiretaps of five foreign establishments, the office phone of the Washington attorney representing the republic, and the residence of the clerk of the House Agriculture Committee.[36]

The Kennedy (and Truman) administrations were not alone in soliciting FBI investigations to identify the source of leaks, requests shaped less by legitimate "national-security" concerns than by their desires to control the public debate over their secret foreign-policy initiatives. This objective also led President Richard Nixon to solicit an FBI investigation in 1969 to identify the source(s) of an apparent leak to *New York Times* Pentagon correspondent William Beecher. In a May 9, 1969, article, Beecher had reported that U.S. bombing operations in Vietnam had extended to North Vietnamese supply dumps in Cambodia. As this was a highly secret bombing operation—with administration officials purposefully misleading Congress and the press about the targets of U.S. bombing raids—President Nixon and NSC aide Henry Kissinger immediately demanded that the FBI identify the source of this leak. In response, FBI Director Hoover (based on a list of possible suspects that Kissinger provided) authorized FBI wiretaps of Beecher (and three other Washington-based reporters); NSC staff members Morton Halperin, Anthony Lake, Winston Lord, Helmut Sonnenfeld, Daniel Davidson, Richard Moose, and Richard Sneider; White House aides William Safire, John Sears, and James McLane; and three low-level State and Defense Department employees. The political sensitivity of this wiretap operation—targeting prominent reporters as well as members of the president's own White House and NSC staffs—led FBI officials to adopt special procedures to minimize discovery of this operation.

The wiretapping program lasted for almost two years. Once again, FBI agents could not identify the source(s) of the leak. Furthermore, Halperin and Lake continued to be tapped after they left the NSC and joined the campaign staff of Senator Edmund Muskie, at the time the acknowledged front-runner for the 1972 Democratic presidential nomination. By then, the wiretaps had acquired a far different purpose: providing valuable advance intelligence to the Nixon White House about the plans of the president's partisan adversaries. Indeed, one such FBI report elicited White House aide John Ehrlichman's enthusiastic assessment: "This is the kind of early warning we need more of—your [White House aide H. R. Haldeman] game planners are now in an excellent position to map anticipatory action."

This FBI wiretapping operation, for this reason, posed potentially serious problems for the Nixon administration. FBI Assistant Director William Sullivan recognized these consequences when alerting the White House to his possession of copies of the intercepted conversations following a falling out in October 1971 with FBI Director Hoover that led to his forced dismissal. Before leaving office, he alerted Assistant Attorney General Robert Mardian about these transcripts' "blackmail potential," adding that he currently maintained the copies in his office separately from other FBI wiretap records. Mardian thereupon briefed the White House about Sullivan's warning and shortly thereafter ordered Sullivan to deliver the logs to the White House for safekeeping in what was a purposeful attempt to stymie any possibility that the FBI director might attempt to exploit them as leverage against the president.[37]

The Nixon administration might have contained this potential threat to expose its exploitation of FBI wiretapping capabilities to further its political agenda. The same interest in foreclosing discovery of his administration's secret abuses of power underpinned a quite different response to the possible disclosure of the National Security Agency's (NSA's) sensitive wiretapping operation, an operation that had been initiated in 1967 two years before Nixon assumed office.

Because he was convinced that the demonstrations and protest activities of militant civil-rights and anti–Vietnam War activists were conducted under the direction of international Communism, President Lyndon Johnson sought confirmation of such a link and accordingly first pressured the FBI and the CIA to conduct investigations with the hope that they could document it. As their agencies were unable to develop the desired hard information, FBI and CIA officials turned to the NSA in 1967, intending to exploit that agency's capability to intercept international communications.[38] NSA officials agreed, and CIA and FBI officials submitted lists of specific individuals whose international communications should be intercepted. Cognizant that this cooperation violated domestic law and transcended the NSA's authorized counterintelligence responsibilities, NSA officials instituted special records procedures to preclude discovery of their participation in an illegal program. This "watch list" program was subsequently refined and expanded following Nixon's accession to the presidency in 1969 and was formally code-named Operation MINARET.

The special procedures that had been instituted to avert the discovery of this highly sensitive program, however, proved to be inadequate, as Operation MINARET's existence could have been compromised in June 1973 owing to the inadvertent and simultaneous timing of two separate developments that month. The first involved the disclosures by the special Senate Committee investigating the so-called Watergate Affair (chaired by Senator Sam Ervin) of the Nixon administration's authorization of a series of "clearly illegal" programs (specifically, the so-called Huston Plan). The second occurred in the course of a trial held in a federal district court in Detroit that was presided over by Judge Damon Keith and involved fifteen members of the radical Weatherman faction of the Students for a Democratic Society. Keith's role as the presiding judge proved to be especially important, since his earlier ruling rejecting President Nixon's claimed absolute right to authorize warrantless wiretaps in another case had been upheld by the Supreme Court in June 1972 in *U.S. v. U.S. District Court*.

During pretrial proceedings in the 1973 trial of members of this radical group, Judge Keith on June 5 honored a request from the defendants' attorneys and ordered government attorneys to inform the court and defense counsel by June 18 of any illegal activity (specifically, wiretaps, bugs, mail opening, break-ins, sabotage, espionage, provocateurism) that had been employed against the defendants or their counsel by representatives of the White House staff, the FBI, the CIA, the NSA, or the Defense Intelligence Agency (DIA). The defense attorneys had based their broad discovery motion on the Ervin Committee's revelation earlier that summer of the so-called Huston Plan that the Nixon White House instituted in June 1970. Under this highly secret plan, the Nixon White House had lifted restrictions on FBI, CIA, and NSA operations to permit the employment of recognizably illegal techniques (wiretaps, bugs, mail opening, break-ins, and the interception of international communications) during investigations of radical activists.

Assistant U.S. Attorney Will Ibershof immediately questioned Judge Keith's order, specifically whether the government had to comply fully with the required disclosures involving the various intelligence agencies. Ibershof instead submitted an affidavit on June 25 stipulating only that the FBI had not engaged in illegal wiretapping, break-ins, sabotage, provocateurism, or any other "unauthorized" activities during the bureau's investigation of the Weatherman defendants. No FBI records relating to the case had been lost or destroyed, he added. His submission was confined to the FBI and purposely avoided having to disclose the NSA's highly secret Operation MINARET interception program. Unknown at the time, his denial of illegality was solely based on the premise that the FBI's actual receipt of the NSA's intercept records under Operation MINARET was not unauthorized. Since the FBI was the chief investigative agency in the Weatherman case, Ibershof contended, it was sufficient to inquire only into the bureau's activities. The assistant U.S. attorney added tersely: "The government doesn't believe this is a proper forum for a trial of government misconduct."[39]

Judge Keith, however, rejected the prosecution's response as "perfunctory" and stipulated in detail the information that the prosecution had to provide by September 4—"by filing sworn statements from a person or persons with full knowledge of each specified group or agency" (the FBI, the CIA, the NSA, the DIA, the White House Plumbers, the Treasury Department's investigative division). Evidentiary hearings on this matter were to be held on September 24, at which time "the defense and prosecution shall be permitted to call all witnesses deemed appropriate by them to further this inquiry into governmental illegality."

Unable to comply with Judge Keith's order by the September 4 deadline, the prosecution sought a thirty-day extension. As justification, government attorneys emphasized that, for the first time, they had been required to seek affidavits from sensitive intelligence agencies that were not subject to Justice Department jurisdiction. At the hearing on this motion on September 12, U.S. Attorney Ralph B. Guy, Jr., advised the court that he would present, as an in camera submission to Judge Keith alone, an affidavit from an unspecified federal agency (actually, the NSA). The interception cited therein, Guy maintained, did not affect the prosecution of this case but did involve a sensitive national-security matter. Should Keith rule that this affidavit must be turned over to the defense, Guy added, "the government requests that the exhibit be returned to them and that they be given the liberty of exercising their option to dismiss the proceedings."

Defense attorney William Goodman immediately attempted to learn the specific nature of the material to be submitted for in camera examination. Guy replied elliptically that "the in camera exhibit contains information involving the interception of communications of individuals, none of whom are defendants presently before the court, by an agency of the federal government to obtain foreign intelligence information deemed essential to the security of the United States." Goodman thereupon posed a series of pointed questions: Was this interception a break-in, mail cover, wiretap, or bug? Which agency was involved? When did this occur? Guy refused to provide any additional information at the time except that the interception involved an individual in fugitive status.

Judge Keith granted Goodman a week to prepare for arguments on the in camera submission issue and agreed to the thirty-day extension. "This will be the last continuance of this matter," the judge asserted. "If there is a further request for continuance someone from Washington would have to come [before his court] to explain why this extension was requested and to submit to questioning from defense counsel." (Goodman had previously demanded the appearance of Guy Goodwin, the head of the Justice Department's Internal Security Section, arguing that Goodwin, unlike Guy or Ibershof, had first-hand knowledge regarding why the affidavits had not been produced. Keith's warning meant that, in the event of further delays, defense attorneys would be allowed to inquire whether the delays were the result of political pressure from the White House or from senior officials in the U.S. intelligence community.)

On October 4, government attorneys informed the court that all the required affidavits had been received. They requested that none of the affidavits be turned over to the defense until the in camera ruling was made. Otherwise, they argued, by process of elimination, the identity of the federal agency under question would have been revealed. Keith agreed to this request and set October 15 for oral arguments on the in camera submission matter. Then, in a surprise action and without waiting for Judge Keith's ruling on the in camera matter, the government on October 15 moved to dismiss the case.[40]

Unknown to Judge Keith or to defense attorneys at the time, Keith's orders had posed a serious risk for the Nixon administration and the NSA—the exposure of the Operation MINARET program. At first, NSA Director Lewis Allen was undaunted by the problems posed by Judge Keith's disclosure order and assured FBI Director Clarence Kelley that the NSA would continue to inter-cept the communications of targeted individuals. He nonetheless conditioned this continued assistance on assurances that such intercepts would be "prop-erly handled" in light of the "ever increasing pressures for disclosure of sources by Congress, the courts, and the press." Allen, however, soon abandoned his willingness to continue this assistance, a decision that the actions of Attorney General Elliott Richardson triggered.

Richardson first became aware of the FBI's participation in the Opera-tion MINARET program when briefed about the problems the prosecuting attorneys confronted in responding to Judge Keith's disclosure orders. The attorney general had thereupon concluded that this program was illegal in light of the Supreme Court's ruling in *U.S. v. U.S. District Court* and ordered the FBI to "cease and desist" submitting names to the NSA. He then advised NSA Director Allen to "immediately curtail the further dissemination" of intercepted communications to the FBI. Operation MINARET, Richardson wrote Allen, "raises a number of serious legal questions," and he specifically cited the *U.S. v. U.S. District Court* ruling concerning "domestic-security" investigations. He nonetheless added that the NSA could continue to forward to "appropriate" agencies (i.e., not the FBI) "relevant information acquired by [the NSA] in the routine pursuit of foreign intelligence information." Richard-son's holding put Allen in a bind. Unwilling to continue this secret program in this altered setting, Allen informed the attorney general that he had "directed [that] no further information" be disseminated to the FBI. The NSA director in addition formally terminated Operation MINARET and issued a directive to "preclude the resumption of such activity."[41]

Operation MINARET was terminated not because of its illegality but because of the risk of public disclosure in the more skeptical political climate of the early 1970s. Senior FBI, CIA, and NSA officials had long been aware that their interception activities were illegal; they nonetheless had conducted them because of their confidence that their actions would be immune from public scrutiny. Congressional deference, combined with the prevailing con-sensus that secrecy was essential for national-security reasons, had until the mid-1970s encouraged intelligence agency officials to risk the possibility that their illegal actions could not be discovered—a possibility that they had sought to avert by their decisions over the years to devise special record and record-destruction procedures.

4

A Commitment to Secrecy

Senior Federal Bureau of Investigation (FBI) officials' authorization of illegal investigative techniques (wiretaps, bugs, break-ins, mail openings), willingness to service the political and policy interests of the White House, and, conversely, willingness to subvert the political interests of liberal presidents by covertly assisting their conservative critics in Congress and the media posed serious political risks. The discovery of their actions could provoke demands for the dismissal of FBI Director J. Edgar Hoover, a thorough housecleaning of the senior ranks of the FBI, the institution of more-stringent congressional oversight, and the enactment (at a minimum) of an FBI legislative charter to define by statute the parameters of FBI investigative authority. The exposure of the wide-ranging abuses of power that were characteristic of FBI surveillance operations throughout the cold war years would inevitably raise serious questions about the commitment of presidents, their attorneys general, and the FBI director to meeting their supervisory responsibility while further confirming that Congress, the media, and the general public should abandon their uncritical acceptance of "national-security" claims.

When addressing these potentially disabling exposes, FBI officials confronted a seemingly insurmountable institutional reality. As the investigative division of the Department of Justice, the FBI was theoretically subject to the close supervision of senior Justice Department officials and would have to comply with their record requests. And, given their role as the appointee of the president (with attorneys general from J. Howard

McGrath in 1949 through John Mitchell in 1972 having served as the presidents' campaign managers and close political advisers), theoretically FBI officials could not risk the attorney general's discovery of their covert assistance to the president's congressional and media adversaries. As a federal agency whose appropriations were set by Congress and whose operations were subject to congressional inquiry, FBI officials would have to comply with congressional subpoenas and be subject to critical examination during scheduled congressional hearings. As a federal law-enforcement agency whose investigations and personnel provided the evidence for criminal indictments, FBI actions were potentially vulnerable to court-ordered discovery motions and questioning by defense attorneys that could establish whether evidence leading to an indictment or supporting a conviction had been illegally obtained. Last, as a federal agency subject to the record-retention requirements of the Federal Records Act of 1950, FBI officials' record-disposition decisions should have been reviewed and approved by the National Archives to ensure the preservation of records of "historical value" that would adequately and properly document the FBI's "organization, functions, policies, decisions, procedures and essential transactions" or would be essential to protect the "legal" rights of "persons affected by the Government's actions." In sum, on a government organizational chart, FBI actions as recorded in created records would theoretically be subject to a number of different reviews. In theory, at least, the threat of such discoveries should have deterred FBI officials from resorting either to illegal or to politically motivated (even partisan) abusive practices.

Yet what in theory should have been major constraints in practice proved not to be. FBI officials instead successfully shrouded their operations from and ensured that their most problematic decisions could not become subject to critical outside scrutiny. Their commitment to secrecy, indeed, underlay the various decisions adopted over time by senior FBI officials regarding the maintenance and accessibility of especially sensitive records.

Dating from his appointment as director of the Bureau of Investigation[1] in May 1924 and refined in succeeding decades, Hoover proactively and, on occasion, retroactively instituted a series of special records and record-destruction procedures to preclude the discovery of his own and senior FBI officials' authorization of sensitive or illegal operations.

Almost immediately upon assuming the directorship of the bureau in 1924, Hoover maintained a secret office file (soon expanded to two such files—an Official and Confidential File and a Personal and Confidential File)[2] to which were assigned "various and sundry items believed inadvisable to be included in the general files of the Bureau." In a 1941 memorandum, Hoover explicitly described the kind of information maintained in this file as including "confidential information on [phrase redacted]," information relating to "Communist infiltration of the Department of Justice," and "confidential items of a more or less personal nature of the Director's and items which I might have occasion to call from time to time, such as memoranda to the Department on the Dies Committee, etc." Creating a secret office file was not a simple administrative action; the underlying purpose was to enable the FBI director to deny, truthfully, that the FBI's central records system contained any records documenting that prominent Americans were investigated or illegal investigative techniques authorized. Then, in October 1941, in a decision to advance his recent designation of FBI Assistant Director Louis Nichols as FBI liaison to Congress and the media, Hoover authorized Nichols to maintain a similar "confidential" office file.[3]

Concurrently, Hoover circumvented an order that Attorney General Harlan Fiske Stone instituted in 1924 to confine bureau investigations to violations of federal statutes and to cease bureau monitoring of political activities, He did so first by encouraging interested conservative activists to continue submitting reports on "subversive" activities, then by having agents monitor press reports about the activities of radical activists and organizations, and finally by having agents disguise their sources in their reports on political activities as not from their own investigations but from "confidential informants," a "very reliable source," a "delicate and confidential source," or a "very confidential source."[4]

Hoover further refined the FBI's unauthorized political-surveillance practices of the 1930s, directing the heads of FBI field offices (Special Agent in Charge [SAC]) to employ "personal and confidential letters" whenever reporting "some matter that you wish be brought to my personal attention before correspondence is opened and indexed in the file room" at FBI headquarters— a procedure that ensured that these communications would not be serialized and indexed in the FBI's central records system. He specified that SACs should employ this procedure particularly when reporting about "subversive activities." This reporting system should also be used, Hoover continued, "if the communication pertains to official matters of a highly confidential nature which are deemed of sufficient importance to be brought to the Director's personal attention."[5]

Hoover's willingness in essence to flaunt Stone's prohibition and then to have agents continue to monitor political activities on its face would seem to have been risky, if not suicidal. His decision, after all, had been made in the immediate aftermath of the highly publicized series of scandals involving FBI abuses of the civil rights of American citizens and alien residents during World War I and the immediate postwar years. The publicity surrounding the revelations of 1917–1920 culminated with the discoveries of 1923–1924 of FBI monitoring of labor-union activities and of members of Congress demanding an inquiry into the Teapot Dome affair,[6] leading Attorney General Stone to dismiss Bureau Director William Burns and to appoint Hoover as his temporary replacement in May 1924. Hoover's creation of a secret office file and special record–submission procedures minimized the risk that his insubordi-nation could be uncovered at the very time of his preliminary appointment as bureau director in May (made permanent in December 1924). And although his decision to create a secret office file to house particularly sensitive records was not known, his authorization of continued monitoring of radical activities was not unduly risky, at least in the conservative political climate of the 1920s, given the prevailing nativist hostility toward recent immigrants and antipathy toward the conventional trade unionism of the American Federation of Labor. A cautious bureaucrat, Hoover nonetheless recognized that the prevailing strong commitment of conservative activists to states' rights combined with their antipathy toward a strong federal government and liberal fears that the FBI might again monitor labor-union and political activists required admin-istrative procedures that would minimize the discovery of his authorization of recognizably illegal activities and agents' monitoring of personal and political conduct.

The FBI director's companion strategy to achieve his ambitious agenda by creating a highly centralized and disciplined agency with rules set at the top, however, required, at a minimum, that records would be created to define permissible methods and would subject the actions of agents and SACs to the oversight review of officials from FBI headquarters. The inevitable creation of written records to achieve this administrative purpose could have been counterproductive—particularly in the decades after the early 1940s, when the FBI director purposefully authorized FBI personnel to employ "clearly illegal" techniques or "sources illegal in nature" or to report "facts and information which are considered of a nature not expedient to disseminate, or which would cause embarrassment to the Bureau, if distributed" outside the FBI.

Hoover presciently addressed this administrative problem in the early 1940s, necessitated by the FBI's secret evolution into a political-surveillance agency. Committed to enhancing the FBI's monitoring capabilities, the FBI director as such recognized the value of break-ins as an essential tool for installing bugs and photocopying the records of targeted individuals or orga-nizations. Privately conceding that such actions were "clearly illegal," the FBI director also recognized that, for that reason, he could not seek authoriza-tion from the attorney general. To minimize the discovery of this practice, he instituted a special Do Not File procedure in 1942, which SACs were to employ whenever seeking his advance authorization to conduct a break-in. Break-ins, he had then emphasized, were an "invaluable technique in combat-ing subversive activities of a clandestine nature aimed at undermining and destroying our nation." Yet to ensure that this illegal practice was neither done mindlessly nor without adopting safeguards to avert discovery, SACs were required to seek Hoover's approval before break-ins were conducted. Written requests for approval would have to "completely justify the need for the use of this technique and at the same time assure that it can be safely used without any danger of embarrassment to the Bureau." Normally, communications seeking approval of (or reporting results to) FBI headquarters would have been serialized and indexed in the FBI's central records system, thereby creating a retrievable record of this communication. As such, the serialization of all field office (and headquarters) communications would have made it impossible for FBI officials to withhold a specific record (whether responsive to a court-ordered discovery motion or congressional subpoena) without its absence becoming known (as the records in FBI files relating to a specific organization would have been numbered consecutively). The Do Not File procedure finessed this problem, as this caption ensured that all communications requesting his authorization of a proposed break-in would not be serialized or indexed in the FBI's central records system but immediately routed either to Hoover's office or the office of a designated FBI assistant director. In addition, SACs were required to file "an informal memorandum" relating to this request in their office "safe" and to retain these memoranda "until the next inspection by Bureau Inspectors, at which time [they are] destroyed." Hoover's ingenious order accordingly ensured that he and his key aides could tightly monitor break-in practices in the field (to ensure that appropriate safeguards were adopted and that the value of the to-be-acquired information justified the risk) and yet prevent the created written record from being discovered. In the event of an independent inquiry about a target of a break-in, FBI officials could truthfully respond that a search of the FBI's central records system uncovered no record of illegal conduct.[7]

The Do Not File and "informal memorandum" procedures were spin-offs of an earlier 1940 order of Hoover's (refined in 1941–1943) governing the creation and maintenance of especially sensitive communications among senior FBI officials at FBI headquarters. Memoranda "written merely for information purposes, which need not be retained for permanent filing," Hoover stipulated in April 1940, should be "prepared without abstracts and without carbon copies" on special blue paper bearing the notation on the bottom "Informative Memorandum—Not to Be Sent to Files Section." He added that should such memoranda "reach the Files section," they would be returned "to the Director's Office for appropriate disposition." However, in 1942, when Justice Department officials unknowingly required that all intradepartmental correspondence be prepared on blue paper, Hoover changed the color of paper to pink, bearing the notation on the bottom "This Memorandum Is for Administrative Purposes—To Be Destroyed After Action Is Taken and Not Sent to Files." Pink paper, he emphasized, should be used when preparing memoranda "solely for the benefit of the Director which will possibly be seen by the Director and other officials and eventually be returned to the dictator [of the memorandum] to be destroyed or retained in the Director's office." Then, when the pink-memorandum procedure was unexpectedly compromised in December 1949, with the public release of one such memorandum during pretrial discovery proceedings in the Judith Coplon case, Hoover terminated this procedure and, instead, orally directed senior FBI officials that henceforth such communications should be submitted as "informal memoranda." In contrast to blue and pink memoranda, informal memoranda were prepared on plain white, nonletterhead stationery that carried no printed notation but nonetheless were not indexed or filed in the FBI's central records system; instead, they were maintained in either the office files of the writers of the memoranda or sent to the FBI director's office.[8]

Do Not File and blue/pink/informal memoranda were intended to foreclose serialization and indexing and were routed to and maintained in the office files of senior FBI officials. And although they could be (and, indeed, were to be) safely destroyed, these records were not always destroyed once they had outlived their usefulness. Accordingly, in March 1953, Hoover issued new rules to limit the time period for retention of such records. FBI assistant directors and supervisors were to "periodically" review the contents of their office files and "destroy them as promptly as possible"—supervisors every 90 days and assistant directors every six months.[9]

Hoover himself did not honor his 1953 order to destroy the contents of his two office files. He did order his administrative assistant, Helen Gandy, to destroy one of his secret office files, his Personal and Confidential File, in the event of his death. Gandy did so in the month after his death in May 1972; the second, the Official and Confidential File, remained extant and was subsequently incorporated into the FBI's central records system.

During congressional testimony in 1975, Gandy claimed that Hoover's Personal and Confidential File contained only personal records—Hoover's personal correspondence and tax returns. There are good reasons to doubt her account, however, based on an examination of the contents of six folders that had originally been filed in his Personal and Confidential File but were transferred to his Official and Confidential File in 1971.[10] Internal references in other documents in the extant Official and Confidential File also describe, if elliptically, the character of records in Hoover's Personal File—in one, the FBI director advised Attorney General Mitchell how he safeguarded sensitive records from being publicly compromised by maintaining them in "a Personal and Confidential file in my office and not in the main Bureau [files]." One of the six folders that Hoover transferred from his Personal and Confidential File in 1971 in point of fact described the Do Not File procedure governing break-in records, another Hoover's planned but controversial testimony before the Senate Internal Security Subcommittee in November 1953, and a third the controversial 1966 case of lobbyist Fred Black. These clearly were not personal but official business.

The contents of the 164 folders composing Hoover's Official and Confidential File, although undeniably very sensitive in that they record his interest in derogatory information about prominent Americans and FBI policy governing illegal investigative techniques, suggest that even more explosive records had been assigned to the Personal and Confidential File. This is indirectly confirmed by the fact that the six transferred folders—relating whether to the Do Not File procedure, Hoover's willing assistance to a Republican-orchestrated attack on President Harry Truman's handling of FBI reports, or to Hoover's attempt to subvert the authority of Attorney General Nicholas Katzenbach—had originally been filed in his Personal and Confidential File. Furthermore, the timing of his decision to transfer these six folders, particularly the folders pertaining to the Do Not File procedure and the Black case, is significant in that he did so at the time when his continued tenure as FBI director was in doubt. Hoover had reached the mandatory retirement age of seventy for federal officials in 1965, but President Lyndon Johnson had waived this requirement by a special order. Given the changed political climate of the late 1960s, particularly captured in hearings conducted by the so-called Long Subcommittee over abusive investigative practices (wiretaps, break-ins, bugs, mail opening) and the Supreme Court's ruling in the Black case, Hoover had an interest in preserving records confirming his decisions to terminate break-ins or that the attorney general had authorized FBI wiretapping and bugging practices. Preservation of the Do Not File and Black folders, via transferring them from his Personal and Confidential File, would advance these objectives, given that Hoover's order "no more such techniques be used" was recorded on the bottom of a 1966 memorandum describing in detail the Do Not File procedure. Ironically, in preserving a record of his order terminating this practice, Hoover preserved a record that described an intended fail-safe system to avert discovery of FBI break-in policy. Gandy's destruction of the contents of the Personal and Confidential File foreclosed an assessment of its contents, soon the subject of conflicting characterizations of the size of this destroyed file, as alleged by Gandy and Justice Department officials and by the truck driver who had physically transported this file to Hoover's home (where Gandy reviewed and destroyed the contents).[11]

A second office file, this one maintained by former FBI Assistant Director Nichols, also escaped destruction, as did portions (significantly covering the years 1965–1972) of FBI Associate Director Clyde Tolson's Personal File. Nichols's and Tolson's extant office files contained documents as sensitive as those in Hoover's Official and Confidential File. Their contents included records of FBI wiretapping policy, monitoring of the personal and political activities of prominent Americans (notably Dwight Eisenhower), and the willing promotion of the political interests of the White House.[12]

Nichols's office file apparently was not subject to Hoover's 1953 regular destruction order and was inherited by his successor, Cartha DeLoach, following his retirement in 1957. Like Nichols, DeLoach also maintained his own "Confidential File," confirmed by a reference in one of the records in the Nichols File. DeLoach's separate file, however, is not extant.

In 1975, senior FBI officials unexpectedly discovered the continued existence of the incompletely preserved Tolson File. Tolson had abruptly resigned as FBI associate director following Hoover's death and had made no plans for the disposition of his office records. His extant file was first discovered by FBI officials in the course of their having to honor Senate Majority Leader Mike Mansfield's 1975 request that the FBI (as well as the other intelligence agencies whose activities were being reviewed by the so-called Church Committee) cease any regular-record destruction during the duration of the Church Committee's investigation. A surprised FBI Assistant Director John McDermott observed that the Tolson File records "should have been destroyed" pursuant to Hoover's March 1953 order, "since they were never intended for inclusion in the Bureau's permanent records collection." The Tolson File records were unintentionally revealing about some of the FBI's more abusive practices—confirmed by a preserved November 1970 memorandum that recorded Hoover's willingness to service a particularly sensitive request of the Nixon White House for a list of "homosexuals" and "any other stuff" about members of the Washington press corps. Recognizing the political repercussions should FBI officials then destroy this file, McDermott recommended its retention "in the [FBI's] Special File Room . . . until at least the Senate hearings are concluded." The changed political climate effected by these hearings precluded FBI officials thereafter from destroying this file after the Committee was dissolved in 1976.[13]

The ability to maintain (and destroy) sensitive records emboldened senior FBI officials (at least Nichols and FBI Acting Associate Director W. Mark Felt) to retain possession of created records after leaving the bureau. Their actions were only inadvertently discovered. Nichols's action was discovered when his son granted popular writer Anthony Summers access to his father's papers, which included numerous sensitive FBI records. In Felt's case, the former FBI official confirmed that he had taken FBI files with him when reprinting a particularly sensitive FBI memorandum in his published memoir.[14]

Hoover, however, had not always anticipated that certain records maintained in the FBI's central records system could prove to be politically embarrassing—and thus in 1949 he was embarrassed by the public disclosure of FBI records during the trial of Coplon that confirmed that the FBI wiretapped extensively and monitored the personal and political activities of prominent Americans. The wily FBI director thereupon responded proactively by instituting two relatively sophisticated special records procedures to address this unanticipated problem: administrative pages and June Mail.

An employee of the Justice Department's alien-registration section, Coplon was apprehended in March 1949 as she was planning to deliver twenty-eight FBI reports to a Soviet agent employed by the United Nations, Valentin Gubitchev. Coplon was indicted in Washington, D.C., on the charge of unauthorized possession of classified government records and in New York for intent to deliver classified records to a foreign agent. For FBI officials, her Washington and New York trials posed serious problems by highlighting their inability to maintain control over potentially explosive records. The specific threat involved a successful motion by Coplon's attorney to require submission as evidence of the twenty-eight FBI reports, the defense having successfully argued that they should have the right to review them to challenge the national-security classified claim. FBI officials had privately opposed honoring this ruling, preferring that the case be dropped rather than having to release these reports. The released reports did not reveal sensitive secrets (as FBI officials had claimed when opposing their release) but proved to be deeply embarrassing, confirming that FBI agents had monitored the political activities of American citizens (actors Edward G. Robinson and Fredric March, the author of a master's thesis on the New Deal in New Zealand, and a supporter of former Vice President Henry Wallace's 1948 presidential campaign) and that fifteen of the twenty-eight reports contained information obtained through wiretaps. The presiding judge, Albert Reeves, however, rebuffed Coplon's attorney's follow-up request for a pretrial hearing to ascertain whether Coplon had been tapped, agreeing with the U.S. attorney prosecuting the case that this request was an unwarranted "fishing expedition." The presiding judge in Coplon's New York trial, however, honored the defense motion, and the released reports confirmed that Coplon had been tapped before and after her arrest (in the latter case possibly intercepting her privileged conversations with her attorney), that the FBI agent who originally denied knowing whether Coplon had been tapped had regularly received the logs of the Coplon taps, and that FBI officials had ordered the destruction of these logs in view of the "imminence" of her trial.

Combined, the revelations suggested extensive FBI monitoring of political activities, extensive FBI wiretapping, and, further, that FBI officials (and agents) had purposely misled the Justice Department and the court about FBI wiretapping and then attempted to cover up this deception by false testimony and record destruction.[15]

FBI Director Hoover quickly acted to preclude the recurrence of this unexpected series of embarrassments. On July 8, 1949, within weeks after the furor precipitated by the public release of the twenty-eight FBI reports, Hoover instituted a new administrative-pages procedure. Henceforth, whenever agents reported "gossip, rumors or any information that could unjustifiably embarrass" a person or organization, any "verified or unverified" information that was not pertinent to the investigation, any "unconfirmed or uncorroborated" information about the associations of a targeted subject, or "facts and information which are considered of a nature not expedient to disseminate, or which would cause embarrassment to the Bureau, if distributed," they were not to include this information in the text but in separate "administrative pages" appended to the back of their reports. Thus, should FBI officials have to submit agents' reports (whether in response to a congressional subpoena or court-ordered discovery motion), the administrative pages could be withheld (without disclosing that information was being withheld). Hoover listed a series of examples of the type of information that should be reported on administrative pages. His first example: "An anonymous complaint alleges A . . . is a member of the Communist Party, and further that A is a man of loose morals, a heavy drinker living with a known prostitute. . . . The allegation of Communist Party membership should be included in the investigative section while the allegation concerning loose morals should be included in the administrative section." Hoover's seventh example: "During the legal search of a white slave traffic act [prostitution] investigation there is found an address book containing data identifying prominent public officials. Unless the names appearing therein are material to the investigation, this information should be placed in the administrative section."

This special records procedure was reassessed in March 1951, senior FBI officials having concluded that the requirement was time consuming and could adversely affect future investigations in cases where the segregated information might be pertinent. More important, they questioned the underlying premise of this special procedure: to confine production to "only the investigative section." A court order "for the entire file," they now concluded, would "of course" require the FBI to "make available both the investigative and administrative sections." Accordingly, the administrative-pages proposal was rescinded but on the "understanding that should it be necessary in any case [for an agent] to advise [FBI headquarters] of any information which should not be included in the regular investigative report, that such information should be submitted by letter," particularly "if placed in a report [it] might cause embarrassment."[16]

The Coplon case, moreover, posed a further problem—that government officials having access to FBI records (whether employees of the FBI, the Justice Department, or the White House) could leak damaging information to the media or Congress. Accordingly, on June 29, 1949, Hoover instituted a second special records procedure, June Mail. Agents and SACs were to employ the caption "JUNE" whenever reporting information obtained through "highly confidential sources" (i.e., wiretaps, bugs, mail opening, break-ins) or from "most secretive sources, such as Governors, secretaries to high officials who may be discussing such officials and their attitude." Such reports were to be sent by "letter, which will be forwarded to the Director under personal and confidential cover . . . sealed in an envelope bearing the code word 'June.'" On receipt at FBI headquarters, June Mail would be kept "in a special confidential file under lock and key" in the FBI's Special File Room, with access limited to a "need to know" basis.

The June Mail procedure was further refined in December 1949, this time triggered by an embarrassing series of revelations in Coplon's New York trial: first when an agent originally denied any knowledge of the FBI's wiretap of Coplon and then that FBI officials had ordered the destruction of the wiretap logs in view of the imminence of her trial. Henceforth, Hoover ordered, every agent, supervisor, or SAC should not "engage in any searches, physical surveillances or other types of work which may make him a competent witness in the event . . . it should be decided to prosecute. Thus, the Agents who might in these instances be competent witnesses would have no specific testifiable knowledge of the existence of a technical surveillance [wiretap] in that particular case." SACs were further ordered telephonically (and not in writing) that all "microphone surveillance[s] [bugs] which involved trespass were to be considered June mail" and that all future instructions regarding June Mail would be "transmitted orally."[17]

Because FBI officials not only wanted to avoid disclosing that FBI agents were employing illegal investigative techniques and were monitoring prominent Americans but also had then sought to exploit the acquired information by leaking it to favored reporters and members of Congress, in 1955 Hoover devised yet another special records procedure, "blind" memoranda. Blind memoranda were to be "used in those instances where the Bureau's identity must not be revealed as the source." Blind memoranda would disguise the FBI as the source of the reported information, as they would be typed on "plain white bond unwatermarked paper" containing no identification of the writer or the recipient.[18]

The FBI director, moreover, developed another ingenious system to disguise the FBI's politically inspired leaking activities, a practice that was inadvertently discovered. Kenneth O'Reilly, during a research trip to the Mundt Library in Madison, South Dakota, came across a trove of letters from Congressman (and subsequently Senator) Karl Mundt to Hoover in each of which Mundt had requested FBI files on named individuals. Mundt's letters were accompanied by Hoover's replies, in which he denied the requests on the grounds of the confidentiality of FBI files. Puzzled by Mundt's persistence, O'Reilly, in an interview with Robert McCaughey (at the time the director of the Mundt Library and formerly Mundt's administrative assistant from 1945–1974), asked about Mundt's apparent obtuseness. Mundt had persisted, McCaughey responded, because Hoover's letter of denial was hand-delivered by an FBI agent who had brought with him the requested file (or files) and was fully prepared to answer any question about the contents. Mundt's creation of an official record of his requests impelled Hoover to create a written record of his denials, in the process disguising the contrary reality of the FBI's covert assistance.[19]

FBI Director Hoover's sophisticated records procedures succeeded in immunizing the bureau's abusive practices from critical scrutiny. This success was abetted as well by the national-security consensus of the cold war era and Congress's and the media's willingness to forego oversight. The latter situation, however, changed in 1974–1975: first as the consequence of Congress's enactment of a series of amendments to the 1966 Freedom of Information Act (FOIA; which made it possible for journalists, academics, and interested citizens to obtain FBI records) and then with the establishment of special House and Senate committees (the so-called Pike and Church Committees) empowered to investigate (and obtain access to the records of) the U.S. intelligence agencies.

Confronted for the first time by their loss of complete control over access to FBI records, senior FBI officials then sought to purge the contents of the FBI's massive field office and headquarters files. Under the Federal Records Act of 1950, all federal agencies and departments were required to obtain the approval of the National Archives before disposing of their records in the course of depositing them in the National Archives. In contrast to other federal agencies and departments, until 1975, FBI officials had not turned over a single page of the bureau's massive files to the National Archives, dating from the bureau's creation in 1908. Indeed, at one time, in 1944, FBI officials had sought Archives approval to destroy "superfluous" records relating to the bureau's White Slave Traffic Act (prostitution) investigations of 1912–1919. The massive increase in FBI records over the years had by then created a major housekeeping problem. Archives officials, however, rejected this request, citing the rich research value of such records for historians and sociologists. Instead, they proposed that the FBI turn these records over to the Archives to be available for research, subject to the FBI director's "explicit" approval. Rather than deliver the records to Archives, decrying that to do so "could be suicidal," FBI officials withdrew this request. FBI Supervisor Richard Cartwright articulated the rationale for this decision: "There is, undoubtedly, considerable information [in these files] of a very personal nature and potentially derogatory to the character of persons still living." Continuing, Cartwright observed that, because the vast majority of the FBI's White Slave Traffic Act investigations had not resulted in prosecution, public access to these case files would put the FBI "in an embarrassing position without even the defense of an indictment or authorized complaint." Then, in 1950, Hoover explicitly banned the transfer of any FBI records to the National Archives or to any other agency.[20]

The FBI's 1944 proposal, moreover, was unique in that FBI officials did not always seek Archives approval before destroying records that had been serialized and indexed in the FBI's central records system (apart from their regular destruction of Do Not File memoranda and the contents of office files). Instead, on their own (and without seeking Archives clearance), they periodically reviewed and approved requests from SACs and officials at FBI headquarters to destroy specific files, a practice recorded in the FBI's massive Record Destruction File 66-3286. Ironically, the FBI's Record Destruction File does not contain all records of approved record destruction, a practice inadvertently confirmed by two known instances of proposed and approved record destruction.

During the early 1960s, FBI agents had intensively investigated Black, a Washington, D.C.–based lobbyist and influence peddler. Their investigation eventually led to Black's indictment and conviction for income-tax evasion. Black, however, appealed this verdict, and the Supreme Court eventually considered this case, at which time Solicitor General Thurgood Marshall (at the direction of senior Justice Department officials) disclosed to the Court that FBI agents had bugged Black's residence and office during the course of this investigation. The justices thereupon demanded that the solicitor general submit a brief outlining the legal authority for these installations. During the internal deliberations in drafting this brief, Attorney General Katzenbach became embroiled in a bitter conflict with FBI Director Hoover over Katzenbach's refusal to stipulate that Justice Department officials had explicitly authorized this and other FBI microphone installations. The frustrated FBI director immediately ordered a cutback in FBI microphone and wiretap installations. At the same time, lower-level FBI officials initiated a review of past wiretapping and bugging activities to determine whether to destroy any of the records of these practices.[21]

As part of this records review, the Washington, D.C., SAC in August 1966 requested Hoover's authorization to destroy "the tesurs [technical surveillances—i.e., wiretaps] logs more than 20 years old in designated cases." Included among these records were the logs of twenty wiretaps installed during an FBI investigation of the allegations of Elizabeth Bentley. Bentley had served as a courier for two Soviet espionage rings during World War II and in November 1945 had defected, at which time she identified to FBI agents more than 150 federal employees in various wartime agencies and departments as her sources. A massive FBI investigation, which included wiretapping twenty of the individuals whom she had named, was then launched to corroborate her allegations.

Hoover rejected the SAC's record destruction request in 1966 "due to the unsettled positions the courts were taking on information emanating from, or connected with, technical surveillances." "If, at a later date, you feel the original information in the logs . . . will not be the subject of court inquiry in the future," the FBI director advised the Washington SAC, "you should resubmit your recommendation for destruction of such records." This request was resubmitted in March 1970. The Washington SAC then asserted that, despite having intensively investigated Bentley's allegations "over and over again" since 1945, FBI agents had been unable to "substantiate and corroborate" them. This "case has now disintegrated to such an extent," he argued, "that there appears to be no possibility of any prosecution or court inquiry at any time."

Hoover commended the SAC's record-destruction request as "well researched." Nonetheless, he pointed out, one of the twenty, Alger Hiss, had a pending court case challenging a statute denying him a federal pension. It was not, Hoover pointed out, "an opportune time to destroy the technical surveillance logs and others listed in" the SAC's letter. Should this matter be finally resolved, the SAC could "resubmit [this] request." The FBI director might have denied this request, but had he approved it, as recorded in the memorandum relating to these deliberations, not only would the wiretap logs of the twenty targets have been destroyed but so too would have been the SAC's memorandum requesting Hoover's approval to destroy these logs. The happenstance preservation of this correspondence thus indirectly confirms that the extant contents of the FBI's Records Destruction File do not comprehensively record all approved record destructions.[22]

A court suit that Stephen Salant initiated in 1978 further confirms this reality. In his suit, Salant argued that the FBI had not fully complied with his FOIA request for all FBI records pertaining to the Hiss case. Salant based his challenge on depositions of FBI agent Martin Wood and Justice Department attorney E. Ross Buckley, who, when responding to his attorney's queries during discovery proceedings, admitted that the FBI's Baltimore field office had destroyed a letter and accompanying check from Whittaker Chambers to Henry Julian Wadleigh. (Wadleigh more than likely had been the target of this FBI mail-intercept operation.)[23] A December 1950 memorandum of the Baltimore SAC and an inventory of the contents of the Baltimore office's "Bulky Matter File" on the Chambers investigation recorded that Chambers's letter and check had been destroyed. According to the inventory, FBI agent Bernard Norton had destroyed on June 4, 1958, "two photostatic copies of a letter dated 12-5-50 to Julian Wadleigh from Whitaker [sic] Chambers, 2 photostatic copies of check payable to Henry Julian Wadleigh signed by Whitaker [sic] Chambers and film."[24] The FBI's Records Destruction File, however, contains no record of the Baltimore SAC's request and FBI headquarters approval to destroy these records.

Salant's suit, moreover, highlights what FBI officials came to perceive in the 1970s as a serious problem—the ability of outsiders to obtain FBI records by filing FOIA requests. In response to the explosion in the number of such requests, in 1975 FBI officials reassessed Hoover's 1950 order and sought Archives approval of a record-disposition plan, in this case to destroy all closed

FBI field-office files. As justification, they claimed that the contents of field-office files were duplicated in FBI headquarters files. Submitted at the time of Senate Majority Leader Mansfield's request that all the U.S. intelligence agencies subject to the proposed review of the so-called Church Committee cease all record destruction, this record-disposition plan was temporarily held in abeyance. Following the termination of the Church Committee's investigation, in 1976 FBI officials resubmitted this plan to the National Archives. Archives officials approved the proposed destruction without independently ascertaining whether the contents were duplicated. Then, in 1978, FBI officials submitted for Archives approval a second record-disposition plan, in this case to purge closed FBI headquarters files and retain only "thick" case files—that is, retention would be based on the size of the file. Archives officials, however, deferred acting on this proposal.

In the interim, during a meeting with the counsel of the House Subcommittee on Government Operations, I had learned of Archives approval of the field-office destruction plan. I cited this discovery in an October 22, 1977, *Nation* article in which I reviewed FBI record-destruction practices. This disclosure eventually triggered a court case brought by the American Friends Service Committee and other public-interest organizations against the FBI and National Archives for violating the record-retention requirements of the Federal Records Act of 1950. The plaintiffs eventually prevailed, as Judge Harold Greene, in a January 1980 ruling on this case, *American Friends Service Committee et al. v. William Webster et al.*, ordered FBI and Archives officials to develop a plan, subject to his approval, to ensure the preservation of FBI records of "historical value." Judge Greene approved the resultant revised plan in 1985, but by the time of his 1980 ruling, FBI field-office files had already been massively purged.[25]

In the interim, in 1977, FBI officials had obtained Archives approval to destroy three specified FBI headquarters files: 105-34074 (Sex Offenders Foreign Intelligence), 105-12198 (Sex Perverts in Government Service), and 94-4-980 (Sex Degenerates and Sex Offenders). This request, and Archives approval, was inadvertently discovered in 1991.

In 1990, Seth Rosenfeld, a reporter for the *San Francisco Examiner*, solicited my assistance for an article he was researching on FBI surveillance of homosexuals. I alerted Rosenfeld to a code-named FBI Sex Deviate program, having learned of this program from a brief reference in the minutes of an October 1953 FBI Executives Conference. (These were regular meetings of senior FBI officials at FBI headquarters at which important policy matters were discussed and proposed actions recommended for the approval of the FBI director.) The minutes in this instance recorded the conferees' review of various FBI programs (cited and briefly described in the minutes) involving the dissemination of FBI information outside the executive branch, one of which was the Sex Deviate program. The minutes described this 1951 program as involving the "furnishing" of information concerning "allegations" of homosexuality on the part of "present and past [federal] employees" to executive, legislative, and judicial officials. I further alerted Rosenfeld to my additional discovery of an index card in the Adlai Stevenson folder in Hoover's Official and Confidential File. Captioned "Sex Deviate," this index card cited Stevenson's name and the specific FBI document upon which this listing had been based.

Forewarned through these extant records, Rosenfeld requested the FBI's Sex Deviate files. All such records (the FBI files identified above), FBI officials responded, had been destroyed in 1978 with National Archives approval. Rosenfeld thereupon contacted the National Archives, and Archives officials released to him copies of the memoranda that they had created during their review and approval of this FBI record-disposition plan. These memoranda record that the destroyed files totaled ninety-nine cubic feet (approximately 330,000 pages) and consisted of index cards, abstracts, and related FBI records created during the period 1937–1977. One of the memoranda records why Archives officials approved this request, in the process confirming that the destroyed files contained "massive amounts of information that relates to matters of individual sexual conduct" and "infringe[s] on personal privacy" and that most of the reported information "involved unsubstantiated accusations and allegations." The Archives official who had conducted this review conceded that these files had "some evidential value by documenting the FBI's interest and activities" but nonetheless recommended destruction. The reported information, he concluded, could not be "made available for research purposes without threatening damage to the reputations of numerous private citizens," while the volume of the records lessened their "value" "in terms of systematic use for research purposes."[26]

FBI officials' belated interest in disposing of their files underpinned their response as well to a new phenomenon: rigorous congressional oversight. The establishment of the Church Committee in 1975 reflected this shift from deference to aggressive oversight. Required to honor the Church Committee's request for specified records, FBI officials remained committed nonetheless to minimizing the exposure of the extent of their predecessor's past abuses. In one instance, they cynically counted on the requirements under the Do Not File procedure for the regular destruction of break-in request and authorization records to mislead the Senate Committee, and thus the public, about the extent and targets of past FBI break-ins.

Having learned of the FBI's Do Not File procedure from their review of the "Black Bag" Jobs folder in Hoover's Official and Confidential File, Church Committee investigators on September 22, 1975, solicited from the FBI an account of the "specific targets" and the number of break-ins that FBI agents conducted against "domestic targets" during the years 1942 and 1966.[27] Responding to this query on September 23, 1975, FBI officials contended that accurate statistics could not be provided, since "no central index, file or document" listing break-ins remained extant. Instead and by drawing on the "recollections" of agents, they admitted that "at least" 242 break-ins had been conducted against "at least" eighteen targets. They further professed their willingness to discuss with the Church Committee's chair and co-chair a list of the "specific targets," emphasizing that "domestic security" break-ins had been "utilized by the FBI on a highly selective basis" but had been terminated in July 1966 pursuant to the former FBI director's order.[28]

This response was misleading in several respects. It had been based, ironically, on what proved to be an unfounded premise—that pursuant to the Hoover-instituted Do Not File procedure, all break-in records would have been destroyed. Their misleading response avoided disclosing that FBI agents, at least during 1970–1972, had conducted numerous break-ins during their investigation of members of the radical Weather Underground. Their list, furthermore, did not include FBI break-ins of the Socialist Workers Party (SWP), currently plaintiffs in a suit charging the FBI with violating their constitutional rights, and then when FBI records relating to the SWP break-ins were first uncovered in March 1976, they understated by 112 the number of such FBI break-ins conducted during the years 1958–1966.

The misleading response of FBI officials in 1975 implied that Hoover's order had terminated this practice. The subsequent discovery that FBI agents had during the years 1970–1972 conducted break-ins involving the Weather Underground raised another question: Had Hoover's hand-written order of 1966 banning future break-ins been intended to create a false written record of his disapproval, or had other senior FBI officials insubordinately ignored his ban?

This intriguing question was triggered by the discovery during the early 1970s of FBI records documenting that senior FBI officials (Acting FBI Director L. Patrick Gray, Acting FBI Associate Director Felt, and FBI Assistant Director Edward Miller) deliberately camouflaged their authorization of break-ins through the resort to euphemism.[29] For example, in a December 1, 1972, memo, Felt demanded that the SACs in the FBI's New York, Chicago, Cleveland, Detroit, Milwaukee, San Francisco, and Seattle field offices "intensify" their investigations of the "Weatherman fugitive cases" by employing "innovative techniques." Still other extant memoranda refer to the use of "special investigative techniques." The same euphemism—"innovative techniques"—was repeated in memoranda relating to another FBI investigation of the 1970s involving the Marxist Revolutionary Communist Party.[30]

Justice Department officials also admitted during a Chicago court case that between 1948 and 1966, FBI agents had conducted "at least 500" break-ins in the Chicago area alone. This number, they further conceded, might actually understate the number of FBI break-ins, as it had been based on "documentation [which] still exists. There may have been additional black bag jobs, the documentation of which has been destroyed or cannot be located."

Furthermore, contrary to the response of FBI officials to the Church Committee in September 1975, the FBI currently maintained a numbered, indexed file on break-ins, described by FBI Director William Webster as "a symbol number sensitive source index maintained in the Intelligence Division."

In a February 1980 report to Attorney General Benjamin Civiletti, Webster confirmed that the FBI maintained a "symbol number sensitive source index"[31] (now formally titled the National Security Electronic Surveillance Card File).[32] Based on Webster's confirmation (that the FBI currently maintained an index listing at least some break-ins), in February 1981, I filed a FOIA request for all break-in records filed under the 66 (Administrative Matters) category. I based this request first on former Acting FBI Director Gray's pretrial discovery motion of May 1978. Gray (along with Felt and FBI Assistant Director Miller) had been indicted the previous month for having authorized illegal break-ins against the Weather Underground fugitives (Gray in 1972 and Felt and Miller in 1970–1972). Gray denied having authorized the illegal break-ins and in one of his pretrial discovery motions sought all FBI records "marked either 'June' and/or 'Do Not File' from the period January 1, 1960, to the present" as well as "F.B.I. files designated as '66-1686' (the 'June' file)." I had, moreover, come across three released FBI records that seemingly confirmed that break-in policy documents (as opposed to the records of the targeted individuals or organizations that FBI agents had photocopied during the break-in) were filed in the 66 category. The first, a Chicago agent's transmittal memorandum of July 23, 1950, accompanying the photocopies of the membership list and correspondence of the National Lawyers Guild obtained through a break-in, bore the classification number 66 (the rest of the serial having been redacted on "national-security" grounds). The second, two memoranda dated December 1, 1975, and March 22, 1976, referred to an October 1963 break-in of the office of the Fair Play for Cuba Committee that New York City agents had conducted. These memoranda bore the full serial number 66-8160.

Responding to my FOIA request on May 7, 1981, FBI officials specified the charges I would have to pay in advance for processing my FOIA request: $33,000. As the standard FOIA processing fee is ten cents per page, this sum meant that the FBI currently held 330,000 pages of break-in records. However, when the news of my discovery (that the FBI had a file, an index, and more than three hundred thousand pages of break-in records) got out, FBI officials quickly advised me that there had been an "error." The 330,000 pages were an "informants" file, only "a minute part of which are actual 'break-in' documents, which irregularly appear throughout the file." The 66-1686 file cited by

Gray, they further claimed, had been destroyed in 1951, and Gray had mis-identified the "June" file (the correct file number for which is 66-1372).[33]

I eventually obtained the contents of a specially created Surreptitious Entries file, FBI 62-117166. Created that year (in 1981), this file consists of the break-in records that FBI Assistant Director John Malone maintained in his office safe covering the years 1954–1973 and that, inexplicably, he had failed to destroy as required under the Do Not File procedure. The existence of these records had been discovered in March 1976.

My subsequent review of this massive file (numbering more than ten thousand pages) confirmed that agents in New York alone had conducted at least 433 break-ins during the years 1954–1973 and had targeted two hundred fifty to three hundred different individuals and organizations. The Surreptitious Entries file further documents that New York agents conducted twenty-eight break-ins after 1968—three of which targeted the Student Non-Violent Coordinating Committee, two the Vietnam Veterans against the War, six the Students for a Democratic Society, and seventeen the Weather Underground. FBI break-ins, moreover, were not confined to claimed "intelligence" (or "domestic-security") investigations but had been employed during criminal investigations (ranging from the Smith Act, the Mann Act, bribery, and interstate theft to gambling investigations).[34]

Those targeted, based on a review of the released Surreptitious Entries file as well as other extant FBI records that I had received in response to FOIA requests and that had escaped destruction, confirm break-ins had been employed extensively (far more than the admitted 242) and had moved beyond even broadly defined "national-security" investigations (implicit in the eighteen figure, which implied that only suspect organizations, such as the U.S. Communist Party and its leadership, had been targeted) to include a host of radical and liberal activists and organizations. Known targets included, at minimum, the American Youth Congress; Washington Committee for Democratic Action; American Peace Mobilization; Fair Play for Cuba Committee; National Lawyers Guild; Chicago Committee to Defend the Bill of Rights; Vietnam Veterans against the War; International Workers Order; Nation of Islam; American Labor Party; *Amerasia*; Students for a Democratic Society; National Emergency Civil Liberties Committee; Student Non-Violent Coordinating Committee; National Committee to Abolish HUAC; American Association of Scientific Workers; Joint Anti-Fascist Refugee Committee; Federation of American Scientists; Russian War Relief; Independent Citizens Committee of the Arts, Sciences and Professions; Veterans of the Abraham Lincoln Brigade; League of American Writers; American Slav Congress; Nationalist Party of Puerto Rico; China Hand Laundry Alliance; Hellenic American Brotherhood; National Mobilization to End the War in Vietnam; Emma Lazarus Federation; *Progressive Labor*; American Association for Democratic

Germany; Jewish Cultural Society; Civil Rights Congress; National Commission to Secure Justice for Morton Sobell; Carol King; Theodore Hall; Saville Sax; Steve Nelson; Nathan Silvermaster; Stanley Levison; William Remington; Thomas Emerson; Inga Arvad; Mark Gayn; Emmanuel Larsen; Kate Mitchell; Philip Jaffe; Dorothy Parker; W.E.B. DuBois; C. Wright Mills; Ursula Wasserman; Jane Keeney; Gerhart Eisler; Bertolt Brecht; Ruth Berlau; Leonhard Frank; Erwin Picator; Ludwig Renn; and Anna Seghers.[35]

The FBI, moreover, was not the sole intelligence agency to adopt special records procedures to preclude discovery of particularly sensitive and illegal programs and other abuses of power. Central Intelligence Agency (CIA) officials had also instituted separate records and record-destruction procedures. We know, however, of only some of these practices.

In January 1973, for example, before leaving office to become U.S. ambassador to Iran, CIA Director Richard Helms ordered his secretary to destroy his office files, which included transcripts of his telephone and room conversations. The catalyst to Helms's order stemmed from a request of Senate Majority Leader Mansfield that month that the CIA (as well as other intelligence agencies) maintain all records that could have bearing on the pending Senate investigation of the so-called Watergate Affair. Helms concurrently ordered the destruction of all CIA records pertaining to the agency's drug-testing program, code-named MKULTRA.

Helms's actions were not unique. At various times, other sensitive CIA records were destroyed. These included the working papers of and interviews conducted by the agency's inspector general when preparing a 1967 report on the agency's various assassination plans, the agency's file on Chilean Police Chief Manuel Contreras, and records of the CIA's covert operation to overthrow the Mossadegh government. Then, following CIA Director William Colby's dismissal of James Angleton as the agency's counterintelligence chief, agency official George Kalaris discovered that Angleton had maintained an office file containing official records that had not been serialized in the agency's official records system. Kalaris further discovered that Angleton had also maintained three vaults containing reams of sensitive files (some pertaining to the agency's illegal mail program HTLINGUAL, others executive files that Angleton and his key aides had created, and still others sensitive counterintelligence files).

In addition, during Senate testimony, Acting CIA Director John Blake admitted that CIA officials had also devised a special records procedure, "soft files," which he described as "files of convenience" and thus "not official records and they are not indexed as such." CIA officials, moreover, adopted still other records procedures to handle the mail of "Elected or Appointed Federal and Senior State Officials (e.g., Governors, Lt. Governors, etc.)" that had been intercepted under the agency's illegal mail-intercept program, code-named HTLINGUAL. Such intercepted mail was not to be included in the agency's top-secret HTLINGUAL file but "filed in a separate file titled 'Special Category Items.'" Furthermore, all correspondence pertaining to the HTLINGUAL program was to be "slugged" to confine distribution to the agency's counterintelligence staff or to low-level CIA officers on an "eyes only basis." In 1962, CIA Director John McCone instituted yet another special records procedure, "Background Use Only," to "preclude the inclusion of the [acquired] information in any other discussion or publication."

As in the case of Helms's office files, Duane Clarridge, the head of the agency's European Division in the 1980s, responded to a pending congressional investigation of the Iran-Contra affair in 1987 by destroying a particular sensitive communication pertaining to a November 1985 transhipment of HAWK missiles from Israel through Portugal to Iran. This communication had originally been sent through "privacy channels," another special records procedure employed for records that were to be maintained temporarily and destroyed after action had been taken. In this case, Clarridge had not destroyed this November 1985 communication and instead had maintained it in a "shadow file" in his desk.[36]

National Security Agency (NSA) officials similarly instituted a special records procedure to preclude discovery of the agency's interception of the international communications of American citizens targeted at the request of FBI and CIA officials. All such NSA-intercepted communications were to be hand-delivered to the requesting agency, were classified "Top Secret," included no identification that they originated in the NSA, and were neither assigned a serial number nor filed with other NSA reports. Then, when refining this interception program in 1969, NSA officials "restrict[ed] knowledge that such information is being collected and processed by the National Security Agency" by directing the recipients of the intercepted communications either to destroy or to return them within two weeks to the NSA.[37]

And I have uncovered at least two occasions when National Security Council (NSC) officials devised special records and record-destruction procedures. The first, which former NSC Executive Secretary James Lay disclosed during September 1975 testimony before the Church Committee, involved the NSC's most "highly sensitive" decisions and discussions. Such decisions and discussions, Lay testified, were not recorded in NSC minutes. "If extremely sensitive matters were discussed at a meeting," Lay elaborated, "it was sometimes the practice that the official NSC minutes would record only the general subject discussed without identifying the specially sensitive subject of the discussion. In highly sensitive cases, no reference would be made in the NSC minutes." The second such practice, inadvertently discovered in 1987 during the joint House-Senate Committee investigation of the Iran-Contra affair, involved a variation of Hoover's Do Not File system. In this instance, NSC aide Oliver

North captioned his sensitive communications to his superior at the NSC, John Poindexter, "do not log." Communications bearing this caption would not be logged in the NSC's central records system, thereby permitting their undiscoverable destruction. Indeed, when the Iran-Contra program was compromised in November 1986, North sought to subvert pending Justice Department and congressional investigations by destroying these communications. His ignorance that the NSC computer system possessed a backup memory (as a safeguard against accidental destruction), however, enabled congressional investigators to reconstruct many of the destroyed messages.[38]

5

The Limits of Counterintelligence

President Franklin Roosevelt's purpose when authorizing Federal Bureau of Intelligence (FBI) intelligence investigations and wiretapping was to enable FBI agents to anticipate and thus hopefully prevent espionage and sabotage operations that could undermine the nation's security. Roosevelt's willingness to bypass the attorney general when authorizing intelligence investigations or drafting the 1940 wiretapping directive (combined with Attorney General Robert Jackson's purposeful decision not to maintain records of approved FBI wiretaps) emboldened the ambitious, if cautious, FBI director to pursue his own more conservative political agenda and at the same time avoid critical scrutiny of the targets and the results of the FBI's noncriminal investigations. On his own, and without even seeking the prior approval or review of the attorney general or the president, J. Edgar Hoover authorized FBI agents to bug, open the mail, and break into the offices and residences of suspected subversives. That the resultant investigations lacked legal authority or that the techniques employed were illegal did not mean Hoover's actions were purposeless—the objective, after all, was not to prosecute spies and saboteurs but to contain the influence of suspected "subversives" as well as to prevent planned espionage and sabotage operations.

The FBI's expanded authority and the latitude granted to the increasingly independent FBI director to initiate investigations based on his assumptions about potential subversive threats did not ensure that the FBI anticipated or deterred Soviet espionage operations (a major problem, as it turns out, during the late 1930s and 1940s). Nor did President Roosevelt suspect that the FBI director had purposefully moved beyond legitimate counterintelligence objectives to monitor political activists. The FBI director, in fact, assured Roosevelt that the FBI had the security situation well in hand. Indeed, in reports of October 31, 1940, and May 23, 1941, Hoover privately and unqualifiedly informed the White House that the FBI was fully cognizant of Soviet, German, French, and Italian "espionage and counterespionage operations" through "constant observation and surveillance . . . of known and suspected Agents of the German, Russian, French, and Italian Secret Services." FBI agents, Hoover continued, maintained "a careful check upon the channels of communication, the sources of information, the methods of finance and other data relating to these agents." The "identities of all major representatives" of these governments, Hoover added, "are known and their activities are under constant scrutiny."[1]

With one exception (disclosed below), however, FBI agents failed to uncover the Soviet Union's most successful espionage operations. FBI reports to the White House based on agents' surveillance of Soviet officials and American Communists invariably reflected that the FBI's intelligence operations focused on political activities and suspected Communist influence in the labor-union and civil-rights movements. Indeed, Hoover's periodic reports to the White House and his monthly "General Intelligence Survey in the United States" during the World War II era offered a relatively benign description of Soviet and American Communist initiatives. On the one hand, the FBI director recounted only that the Soviet Union was funding the American Communist Party and that Soviet officials were concerned about U.S. development of higher-octane gasoline. On the other hand, his descriptions of the actions of American Communists were that they had established a secret branch in a Congress of Industrial Organizations (CIO) union in Butte, Montana, plant producing munitions and war materials; closely monitored the deportation proceedings against the International Longshoremen's and Warehousemen's leader, Harry Bridges; sought to recruit more members and promote Soviet foreign-policy interests; and were involved in civil rights and labor organizing.[2]

The exception (and even this success was a qualified one) involved the FBI's simple discovery of planned Soviet atomic and industrial espionage operations that involved the recruitment of Communist activists. In 1943, forewarned about these plans, Hoover established two massive surveillance programs, code-named CINRAD (Communist Infiltration of the Radiation Laboratory at the University of California–Berkeley) and COMRAP (Comintern Apparatus). In both of these massive investigations, FBI agents extensively employed wiretaps, bugs, break-ins, and mail opening as well as physically monitored suspected Soviet agents and American Communist activists.

The FBI's uncovering of these planned espionage operations stemmed from a wiretap of the New York headquarters of the Communist Party. FBI agents in late 1942 had learned that Communist Party leader Earl Browder had approved Steve Nelson's[3] participation in a sensitive assignment (the specifics remaining unknown at the time). Then, through a bug installed in the party's Oakland office, FBI agents intercepted Nelson's conversation with Giovanni Lomanitz, in which Lomanitz described the secret experiments being conducted at the Radiation Laboratory at the University of California–Berkeley. Through a second bug in Nelson's residence, FBI agents subsequently intercepted Nelson's meeting with Joseph Weinberg, another scientist employed in the Radiation Laboratory. Weinberg had then informed Nelson that the "secret work" currently being conducted at the Radiation Laboratory was about to be moved to Los Alamos, New Mexico. Agents subsequently monitored Nelson's meeting with Peter Ivanov, a Soviet official assigned to that government's San Francisco consulate. They concluded that Nelson had given Ivanov the information about this highly secret project to develop the atomic bomb that Weinberg had described to him earlier.

More dramatically, the FBI's bug of Nelson's residence intercepted another of Nelson's meetings on April 10, 1943, this time with Vassili Zubilin, the third secretary of the Soviet embassy in Washington, D.C. The bug recorded Nelson's receipt of a large sum of money from Zubilin, with both joking about the amount to place "Communist Party members and Comintern agents in industries engaged in secret war production for the United States Government so that information could be obtained for transmittal to the Soviet Union." Concurrently, four months later in August 1943, FBI Director Hoover received an anonymous letter, written in Russian and postmarked Washington, D.C., that identified Zubilin and eight other Soviet officials (Soviet consular officers Gregory Kheifets and Pavel Klarin, Amtorg employees Semen Semenov and Leonard Kvasnikov, Soviet embassy employees Vassili Dalgov and Vassili Mironov, and Soviet Government Purchasing Commission officials Andrei Schevchenko and Serghi Lukianov) and Communist Party officials Browder and Boris Morros as spies.[4]

FBI officials immediately launched the two referenced highly sensitive but separate investigations, CINRAD and COMRAP. Under delimitation agreements of 1940–1941, the Army's Military Intelligence Division (MID) commanded the exclusive responsibility over security investigations at Los Alamos and the Radiation Laboratory, as these facilities were engaged in the production of military weapons. MID officials had by then already requested the FBI to cease investigating individuals employed at these facilities but to "conduct all necessary investigations regarding Communist activities and the activities of individuals not employed" at the Radiation Laboratory "who interested themselves in the project" (the Los Alamos facility not having as yet become fully operational). FBI and MID agents did over time conduct a total of 201 joint and separate investigations under the CINRAD program of individuals employed at the laboratory, based on suspicions that they might be "Communist Party sympathizers, contacts, or persons having actual Communist Party membership." FBI agents, in addition, conducted at the request of MID officials name checks (that is, checking FBI files for information about a named individual) of individuals who required security clearances prior to their employment at these facilities. In return for this assistance, MID officials agreed to notify their FBI counterparts whenever an employee left the project, regardless of whether that employee was suspected of Communist associations. In actuality, MID officials did not always notify their FBI counterparts of these departures or often delayed doing so. In contrast to these limitations on the bureau's authority governing CINRAD, FBI investigations under COMRAP were "broader in scope and . . . conducted without any jurisdictional limitation imposed by the Military Intelligence Section."[5]

FBI officials did fully brief MID about the Nelson-Weinberg meeting and the plan to place Communist Party members in the Radiation Laboratory for the purpose of obtaining information for "transmission to the U.S.S.R." They also reported their interception of Nelson's conversation with Weinberg in which the two men criticized the eminent physicist J. Robert Oppenheimer for not being sympathetic any longer to Communist interests. The latter report heightened MID security officials' suspicions about Oppenheimer, as they had already uncovered information about the eminent physicist's past Communist associations. They had, in fact, recommended that Oppenheimer not be appointed to head the Los Alamos project on security grounds, a recommendation that General Leslie Groves, the head of the Manhattan Project, had rejected.

MID security officers nonetheless remained wary about Oppenheimer and some of the other physicists employed at the Radiation Laboratory. Based on the FBI report about Weinberg's contacts with Nelson and similar other FBI reports, the chief of MID's security detail at Los Alamos, Colonel Boris Pash, denied clearance to Lomanitz, Mark Friedman, and David Bohm (other identified Communists) to work at Los Alamos while acting to have Weinberg assigned to an army post in Alaska.

FBI officials thereafter regularly briefed MID officials about any discoveries they uncovered about possible Communist associations, and specifically about Oppenheimer. One of the subsequent FBI reports raising their doubts about Oppenheimer's loyalty described his September 1943 meeting with Jean Tatlock, his former mistress. Based on this report, Colonel Pash once again urged Groves to fire Oppenheimer as head of the Los Alamos project. Valuing Oppenheimer's scientific and administrative skills, Groves again rejected this recommendation.[6]

While suspicious of Oppenheimer, MID and FBI officials failed to apprehend the Communist adherents employed at Los Alamos and Oak Ridge, Tennessee, who actually engaged in atomic espionage in 1944–1945: David Greenglass, Theodore Hall, Klaus Fuchs, and their couriers Julius Rosenberg, Saville Sax, Lona Cohen, and Harry Gold at Los Alamos and Russell McNutt and George Koval at Oak Ridge. FBI and MID officials, in fact, first learned of some of these espionage activities in 1949–1950.

Their belated discovery was not the product of their own surveillance operations but a highly secret interception program that U.S. military intelligence had initiated in 1940.[7] Only then did they learn that Julius Rosenberg had recruited his brother-in-law (Greenglass) to transmit information about his work as a military recruit assigned to Los Alamos to Soviet courier Gold, that Fuchs had similarly passed classified information to Gold, and that Hall had agreed to spy on behalf of the Soviets at the suggestion of his college friend Sax. The intercepted messages also confirmed that the Soviets had recruited another scientist (McNutt),[8] who was employed in the K-25 gaseous diffusion plant at Oak Ridge. Last, Koval's espionage activities were first discovered in early 1950, when he fled the United States to return to the Soviet Union. An American citizen, Koval had traveled with his family to Moscow in the 1930s. After training in espionage, he returned to the United States in 1940 and subsequently, as a military recruit, was assigned to Oak Ridge, where he stole information about research involving bomb fuels.

This serious counterintelligence failure was not the primary fault of the FBI, as MID was responsible for granting clearance and continued employment at Los Alamos and Oak Ridge. FBI agents, nonetheless, failed to uncover and then share with MID information about the suspect past of three individuals: Rosenberg, Joel Barr, and Alfred Sarant. Rosenberg, Barr, and Sarant during the years 1941–1945 were variously employed performing defense-related work at the Army's Signal Corps Laboratory, Western Electric, and Emerson Radio and Phonograph Corporation and through this work stole and promptly transmitted to the Soviets critical information about sensitive military technology. The pilfered information included radar systems, engine designs, analog fire-control computers, and the proximity fuse. Indeed, Barr and Sarant copied and transmitted nine thousand pages of secret documents relating to more than one hundred weapons programs and the entire twelve thousand–page design for a jet fighter plane. Although clearance for Rosenberg's, Barr's, and Sarant's defense employment, as in the case of the Los Alamos and Oak Ridge appointments, was MID's principal responsibility, FBI agents had failed to follow up upon discovering Barr's and Sarant's Communist associations when both switched jobs to Western Electric after having been denied security clearances at the Signal Corps Laboratory. FBI agents did not even launch an espionage investigation upon discovering that

Barr, Sarant, and Rosenberg were employed in plants performing defense-related work.[9]

FBI officials' belated discovery of Greenglass/Rosenberg's, Hall/Sax's, and Koval's atomic espionage activities[10] was in any event the product of good luck and owed little to the radical expansion of the FBI's investigative authority. In 1940, the Army Security Agency (ASA, the predecessor to the National Security Agency [NSA]) began intercepting the telegraphic messages sent by Soviet consular and embassy officials in New York and Washington to Moscow under the code-named Venona Project. Because the messages were transmitted in code, ASA officials established a special unit in 1943 to attempt to decipher them. ASA analysts achieved a major breakthrough in 1946, discovering that although Soviet agents were to transmit these messages by using one-time pads, they had reused the pads. This indifference to security requirements made it possible for ASA analysts to begin to decrypt these messages in 1946 that, otherwise, would have been undecipherable. By 1949–1950, and over the succeeding years, military analysts deciphered in whole or in part 2,900 of the intercepted messages. Soviet sloppiness, in short, had made this breakthrough possible. Soviet agents, moreover, had not always assigned code names to disguise the identity of their recruited sources in these communications, at times citing actual names (in Hall's and Sax's cases) and at other times providing sufficient background information that ASA/NSA analysts, working closely with their FBI liaisons, successfully identified those assigned code names (Greenglass, Rosenberg, and Fuchs).[11]

The limitations of FBI counterintelligence operations are further confirmed by the contrasting records of their successes and failures following the virtually simultaneous discovery (through the Venona Project) of Greenglass/Rosenberg's and Hall/Sax's atomic espionage activities in 1944–1945. Greenglass and Rosenberg were indicted and convicted in 1950–1951 for having participated in a conspiracy to steal atomic-bomb secrets; Hall and Sax, in contrast, were not even indicted.

The Venona Project source of these discoveries was not revealed in both of these cases at the time, as intelligence officials sought to protect their successful interception and decryption of the Soviet communications. In the Rosenberg/Greenglass case, FBI agents successfully broke Gold and Greenglass, in the process securing Greenglass's admission and agreement to testify against his brother-in-law. The FBI's limited contribution to effecting Rosenberg's conviction involved the acquisition of circumstantial evidence to corroborate Greenglass's testimony about his brother-in-law's purchase of a console and attempts to secure passport photographs in preparation for a planned defection. Rosenberg's attorney, moreover, made a critical error at trial when deciding not to demand an examination of the information that Greenglass admitted providing to the Soviets. His inaction conveyed the impression that this material was crucial to the Soviets' success in developing an atomic bomb—thereby foregoing raising questions about the importance of Greenglass's work at Los Alamos (given the fact that he had only a high-school education).

In contrast, Hall was a brilliant nineteen-year-old graduate of Harvard College with a degree in physics who had been highly recommended by his professors for the Los Alamos appointment. Hall's work at Los Alamos, conducting implosion experiments, played a crucial role in the development of an atomic weapon, with the intercepted Soviet messages recording that Soviet scientists had found this information to be of "great interest."

Based on the Venona revelations, FBI officials also launched an intensive investigation of Hall and Sax in 1950–1951 that included checking the records of past FBI investigations of Communists during the 1930s and 1940s; checking MID records relating to Hall's employment and MID agents' interception of his correspondence while stationed at Los Alamos; and in 1950–1951 breaking into Hall's and Sax's residences, reading their mail, and monitoring their political and social activities. Because Hall had already been denied a security clearance in 1946, he was not at the time performing classified work and thus was not a current security threat.

The FBI's intensive investigation, however, failed to corroborate Hall's and Sax's earlier involvement in espionage activities. As a final resort, FBI agents in Chicago were authorized to conduct separate interrogations of Hall and Sax in 1951, based on the hope that they would break one or both to admit their earlier espionage activities and testify against the other. This strategy failed—owing particularly to Sax's brazen confidence. FBI agents had hoped to blindside him when questioning him about two discoveries documented in the intercepted Soviet messages. Thus, they pointedly asked about his visit to the Soviet consulate in New York in 1944 and travel to Albuquerque, New Mexico, later that year. An unfazed Sax responded that he had visited the Soviet consulate out of interest in assisting relatives in the Soviet Union, citing his mother's work for Russian War Relief. He explained his travel to Albuquerque by claiming that at the time, he had considered applying for admission to the University of New Mexico to pursue a major in anthropology. The failure of the Chicago agents to break Hall or Sax led to the closing of this investigation in 1952 without seeking any charges: "All outstanding leaks have been exhausted" and the "only indications we have" of Hall's and Sax's "espionage activities" came from the Venona Project, but such information "cannot be disseminated outside the Bureau."[12]

As important, despite the advance intelligence acquired through the intercepted Zubilin-Nelson meeting, the FBI's COMRAP investigation also failed to apprehend the participants in planned industrial espionage. When conducting the resultant massive investigation, FBI agents closely monitored Nelson and his various contacts as he traveled around the country from Oakland to

New York and back, with various interim stops. Agents also closely monitored Zubilin and the other Soviet agents identified in the anonymous letter to Hoover. Those targeted during this intensive investigation were not only physically followed but also subjected to wiretaps, bugs, break-ins, and mail opening. The COMRAP investigation, which eventually monitored forty-six suspects based on Nelson's and Zubilin's contacts, was eventually terminated in 1945.

No arrests or indictments were obtained, no advance intelligence having been developed about planned or attempted espionage operations. The failure was captured in a CIA report of 1948 based on a review of the FBI's COMRAP file and a December 1944 FBI report summarizing the result of the to-date seventeen-month investigation of a "vast, illegal and conspirative Russian-controlled and dominated International Communist Organization, 'Comintern Apparatus.'" This latter summary cited no example of planned espionage activity and merely recounted that the targeted forty-six subjects had sought to "influence" the American public to accept Soviet foreign-policy interests, had distributed "pro-Russian propaganda," had operated an "illegal courier system, based on American Communist seaman," had promoted "Soviet Russia's goal of world domination," had collected "political information of value" for the Soviet Union, and had attempted to promote Communist infiltration of the federal bureaucracy to "secure information of value" for the American Communist Party or to ensure the employment of other Communists in federal positions.[13] In essence, FBI agents had discovered that American Communists were Communists interested in promoting Communist (and Soviet) political and policy interests. The COMRAP investigation, because of its focus on prominent Communist Party activists, had in the process missed either sympathizers (like Hall and Sax) or low-level party members holding no leadership position or who currently were not active in the party (Rosenberg, Greenglass, and McNutt) or who had no direct affiliation with the Communist Party (Koval).

FBI agents were no more successful in uncovering the espionage activities of the Soviet agents whom they targeted under the COMRAP program. Indeed, a 1948 Central Intelligence Agency (CIA) report that summarized the findings of an agency official's review that year of the FBI's COMRAP file concluded that the FBI had been unable to substantiate that any of the identified Soviet agents had engaged in espionage with one exception, and even that involved a mail-drop operation in New York that related to the earlier assassination of Leon Trotsky.[14]

While FBI agents had focused on the wrong American Communists, their failure to uncover the espionage activities of Soviet agents derived from the safeguards these agents had adopted to avert FBI discovery. As well-trained, highly disciplined spies, they had suspected that they were being monitored by the FBI and their telephone conversations were intercepted. The intercepted Venona messages confirm this information. In their reports to their superiors in Moscow, the Soviet agents acknowledged that their movements were being monitored by FBI agents but evinced no concern and described the safeguards they had adopted to preclude discovery. These included ensuring that their American recruits were reliable and trustworthy, were well trained in "conspiracy" (i.e., how to evade discovery), and met "only with reliable undercover contacts" of the American Communist Party whom FBI agents would not suspect were involved in espionage. Soviet agents were directed not to use their recruits' "real surnames" and to limit knowledge of their work by other Soviet officials to a need-to-know basis. Last, to counter FBI physical surveillance and wiretapping operations, the Soviet agents did not communicate by telephone at Soviet consular or embassy offices, used automobiles when arranging secret meetings, and suspended meetings whenever suspecting that the FBI was monitoring them.[15]

FBI agents, moreover, failed to follow up on a potentially crucial lead that could have led to the uncovering of two Soviet espionage rings involving Communist federal employees who during World War II pilfered and then gave classified information to a courier, Elizabeth Bentley, for transmission to the Soviet Union. In the course of their surveillance of one of the COMRAP subjects, Louise Bransten, FBI agents had uncovered her meeting with Nathan Silvermaster and Charles Flato in Washington, D.C., in October 1944. Silvermaster and Flato were federal employees and were, at the time, providing classified information to Bentley—Silvermaster as head of one of the two spy rings and Flato as a ring member. (Silvermaster, moreover, at the time was the subject of a Hatch Act investigation to ascertain whether he was a member of the Communist Party.) Bransten's meeting triggered a rather perfunctory FBI investigation of Silvermaster and Flato but did not lead to their being targeted under COMRAP. FBI agents had then uncovered only that both were involved in radical political and labor-union activities.[16]

FBI agents belatedly discovered Silvermaster's and Flato's espionage activities one year later as the result of Bentley's unsolicited defection in November 1945.[17] Bentley then told FBI agents of her role as a courier for two Washington-based spy rings in her November and subsequent interviews and eventually identified 150 federal employees from whom she claimed to have received classified information for transmission to the Soviet Union. An intensive FBI investigation was immediately launched (involving the participation of 200 agents) to confirm her allegations. Agents physically monitored the identified suspects and, as well, wiretapped at least 20 of those whom she identified, opened the mail of 15, and conducted at least three break-ins. No evidence was uncovered through this intensive investigation that any of those identified had been or were currently engaged in espionage—a failure due, in part, to bad luck. The British liaison to U.S. intelligence, Kim Philby (who, it turns out, was a Soviet spy) had immediately informed his Soviet contacts about Bentley's defection. KGB agents in Washington and New York were thereupon immediately instructed to cease all contacts with Bentley and to advise "all persons known to Bentley in our work" about her betrayal. The Soviet KGB agents were recalled to Moscow (to avert their being interrogated by the FBI) but before departing advised their American recruits that, if interviewed by the FBI, they should deny any involvement in espionage but not that they did not know Bentley (as the FBI might have already monitored such meetings). Furthermore, all "documents from American government institutions [and] other documents and notes which could compromise agents and their sources" were "destroyed immediately."

These preventive measures ensured that FBI agents would not uncover what had been an ongoing espionage operation. This failure was potentially embarrassing for Hoover, as he had immediately alerted President Harry Truman, Attorney General Tom Clark, and Secretary of State James Byrnes about Bentley's uncorroborated allegations. A follow-up FBI report to the White House of October 1946 summarizing the results of the intensive FBI investigation sought to justify the FBI's failure to confirm the earlier reports. Owing to the "time element," since the alleged espionage activities had dated "back several years," the FBI author of this report noted, "the reader must consider the difficulty of actually proving these activities by investigation at this later date." The summary lamely maintained that "the facts are strong in many instances and circumstantial in others primarily because of the disparity in time between the date of the activities and the actual report on these activities to the authorities."

Privately, FBI officials recognized their failure. Indeed, in January 1947, FBI agent Edward Morgan counseled Hoover not to seek indictments in this case. "We have no evidence from which 'intent or reason to believe' can be proved or reasonably inferred," Morgan maintained. At this point, he continued, "the evidence very definitely is insufficient to sustain a successful prosecution under the espionage statutes." Justice Department officials arrogantly ignored this assessment and instead convened a grand jury on what proved to be an unsuccessful strategy based on the hope that one of those that Bentley named would break and corroborate her. FBI officials nonetheless continued thereafter to develop information that could justify indictments, even attempting to exploit the 1954 Compulsory Testimony Act granting immunity from prosecution for testimony before a grand jury (thereby subverting a Fifth Amendment claim) to pressure one of the identified participants, Edward Fitzgerald, to testify against the others. This effort failed, as Fitzgerald refused to testify and went to jail. By 1970, the Washington Special Agent in Charge (SAC) conceded, if reluctantly, that FBI agents, despite having investigated

Bentley's allegations "over and over again" since 1945, had been unable to "substantiate and corroborate" them.[18]

This was not a unique failure for the FBI's World War II and cold war counterintelligence operations. It was replicated in the case of another suspected Soviet spy, Alger Hiss. FBI officials first became seriously interested in Hiss in 1942, triggered by an earlier uncorroborated allegation about his loyalty. In September 1940, an FBI informer, Ludwig Lore,[19] advised his FBI contact that he knew an individual who had been a "high [Soviet intelligence] officer for eight years abroad and for seven years in this country." After several unsuccessful attempts to meet Lore to learn more about this matter, FBI agent George Starr finally met him in May 1941. Lore then acknowledged knowing this Soviet agent but refused at the time to disclose the alleged spy's identity, claiming that this individual "is afraid to reveal the true story of his OGPU [the predecessor to the KGB] activities in the United States, believing he will encounter serious trouble," as he might be prosecuted. This unnamed individual, Lore elaborated, had supervised approximately seventy Soviet agents and others who worked under his supervision, and his sources included two "private secretaries to Assistant Secretaries of State" from whom he received typed copies of all the Roosevelt administration's "confidential correspondence" and another secretary employed by "one of the higher officials of the Department of Commerce" from whom he obtained "all necessary statistical data." Lore added that if his friend "could get a promise of immunity he would reveal the whole [O]GPU set-up in this country." He further claimed that this unnamed individual had recently expressed his willingness to identify to the FBI director the federal employees "who were Communists or possessed pro-Russian political sympathies" if granted immunity but that Hoover had rejected his demand for this guarantee. Briefed on this information, Hoover denied having ever been informed about this matter. Starr was directed to recontact Lore to have him identify this unnamed former OGPU agent. Starr did so, and this time Lore, "in strictest confidence," named Whittaker Chambers and repeated his earlier allegations that "until fairly recently" Chambers had "held an important position in the OGPU" that involved "placing agents in the Government service at Washington or for making contacts through which the OGPU agents could obtain information at Washington."[20]

FBI officials inexplicably delayed interviewing Chambers until May 1942. At this time, Chambers contradicted Lore's description of his role as an OGPU agent and supervisor. Chambers denied having been "directly connected with the OGPU but that on the contrary his real position was with the Underground Movement of the Communist Party U.S.A." Chambers did name twenty individuals (including Hiss), affirming only that their purpose was to influence government policy. The interviewing FBI agents failed to press Chambers about the contradictions between his and Lore's accounts, specifically that Chambers had headed an espionage operation and had recruited secretaries of prominent State and Commerce Department officials to obtain classified information. Briefed on this interview, FBI Director Hoover dismissed Chambers's account as "either history, hypothesis, or deduction."[21]

Hiss soon commanded the keen interest of senior FBI officials, an interest triggered by two separate developments—the defections in October 1945 of Soviet cipher clerk Igor Gouzenko, stationed in Ottawa, Canada, and in November 1945 of Bentley.

When defecting, Gouzenko had described in detail to Canadian security officials Soviet espionage activities in Canada during World War II, adding that Canadian Communist Party members had actively supported these activities. Gouzenko further claimed that the Soviets had "more agents in the United States," one of whom was "an assistant to [Secretary of State Edward] Stettinius." Briefed on this allegation, Hoover concluded that the referenced assistant was Hiss, although he conceded that "there was no evidence to sustain this suspicion." The FBI director had based his suspicion on Chambers's 1942 interview (in which he had named Hiss) and a September 1939 report of Assistant Secretary of State Adolf Berle (which Berle had belatedly forwarded to the FBI) in which Chambers named Hiss among eighteen others whom he claimed were members of a Communist underground. Hoover's suspicions about Hiss intensified in light of Bentley's vague reference to Hiss's having attempted to recruit Harold Glasser away from the Silvermaster–Victor Perlo rings to one that he headed.[22]

An intensive FBI investigation of Hiss was immediately launched that included wiretapping his office and home phones, reviewing his telephone toll-call records for 1943 and 1944, and intercepting his telegrams and mail. This FBI investigation uncovered no evidence that Hiss was currently involved (or had been involved) in espionage. In March 1946, convinced nonetheless that Hiss was a security risk, FBI officials opted for another strategy to force Hiss's removal from his post as director of the State Department's Office of Political Affairs. Accordingly, FBI Director Hoover urged Secretary of State Byrnes to leak derogatory information about Hiss's suspected disloyalty to influential members of Congress—Senators Tom Connally and Arthur Vandenberg (the chair and ranking Republican on the Foreign Relations Committee), House Speaker Sam Rayburn, and House Majority Leader John McCormack—as their public protest could force Hiss to resign. Byrnes, however, claimed not to have the time "to contact anyone on [the] Hill" owing to the demands of preparing for a forthcoming UN Security Council meeting and instead confronted Hiss directly. Hiss rebuffed these allegations about his disloyalty and agreed to seek an appointment with the FBI to repeat his denial. He did so and was received politely, if unconvincingly, by FBI officials.[23]

Byrnes's decision left FBI officials with one alternative: to convene a Civil Service hearing to have Hiss fired for violating the Hatch Act (membership in the Communist Party), an initiative that relied on a consistent allegation of Chambers. Having developed no other evidence to support such a hearing, FBI officials ordered FBI agent Thomas Spencer to reinterview Chambers about his earlier claims that Hiss had been a member of a Communist "underground organization." Chambers, however, denied knowing whether Hiss was a current party member, pointing out to Spencer that he had defected in 1937 but believed that Hiss was "favorably impressed with the Communist movement." Spencer then asked directly whether Chambers possessed any documentary evidence confirming Hiss's party membership. Stating that he did not, Chambers added that he had "never purposefully held out any information and had always been forthright in relaying any information that he had in which the Bureau had shown an interest." When Spencer then inquired whether he would be willing to appear as a witness in a security dismissal hearing, Chambers demurred and expressed his preference that he neither be identified nor asked to testify. Chambers's claim to have no evidence and his unwillingness to testify forced FBI officials to abort the convening of a security dismissal hearing.[24]

Thus, when Chambers in November–December 1948 produced typed, hand-written, and microfilmed copies of classified State Department documents that he claimed to have received from Hiss in 1938 for transmission to the Soviet Union, his dramatic disclosures blindsided not only Hiss but FBI officials as well. Chambers's production of these documents in 1948, which he claimed to have stored in a dumbwaiter in his nephew's residence, led to Hiss's perjury indictment in 1948 (his denial to a grand jury that he had given State Department documents to Chambers in 1938) and eventual conviction in 1950. Yet, this exposure of Hiss's espionage activities owed little to FBI counterintelligence operations and more to extraordinary good luck: Chambers's retention ten years after his defection of documents that he had not disclosed to FBI agents during interviews of 1942, 1945, and 1946. Although Chambers had purposefully misled the FBI, it was the case that FBI agents had not pressured him in 1942 to explain Lore's account of his OGPU activities and then again in 1946 to ask about his own and Hiss's espionage activities.

FBI officials also did not follow up in another case of 1944–1945 about potentially significant information that could advance U.S. security interests. This occasion involved the defection in April 1944 of Victor Kravchenko, a Soviet engineer who since 1943 had been assigned to the Soviet Government Purchasing Commission (SGPC) in Washington, D.C., and whose defection offered the opportunity to learn about ongoing Soviet espionage operations and procedures.

Soviet officials in Moscow and Washington were deeply troubled by

Kravchenko's public defection on April 3, 1944. Their concerns are recorded in the intercepted Soviet consular messages (although military-intelligence analysts did not successfully decipher these coded messages until years after Kravchenko's defection) and FBI wiretaps of the Soviet embassy and SGPC office. On the one hand, Soviet intelligence agents stationed in the United States contacted their sources in the American Trotskyite community (as leading Trotskyites had been instrumental in promoting Kravchenko's defection and then in providing him with a safe haven after his defection) to learn where Kravchenko was hiding following his defection. These contacts were unsuccessful in learning of his hiding places and thus in their efforts to meet him (whether to pressure him to redefect). The concerns of Soviet officials heightened on learning of his plans to write articles and a book in which he sharply criticized Soviet policy, methods, and postwar objectives. Soviet intelligence agents, moreover, took a particular interest in reports that Kravchenko believed that he was being followed by Soviet agents and feared that they intended to assassinate him.[25]

FBI officials almost immediately learned of the concerns of Soviet intelligence operatives over Kravchenko's defection. Their knowledge stemmed from a variety of sources: FBI wiretaps of the Soviet embassy and the SGPC office, FBI contacts in the State Department (who relayed to their bureau counterparts that Soviet officials had demanded Kravchenko's return, claiming that he was a military deserter), and Soviet press releases protesting this defection. The FBI wiretaps, for example, intercepted Zubilin's[26] surprise over Kravchenko's defection, attempts to ascertain from SGPC officials Kravchenko's employment status, and discussions with other Soviet officials over the ramifications of this defection. FBI wiretaps also recorded that SGPC officials were particularly alarmed by this defection, with "many people . . . questioned and . . . much 'cursing.'" FBI officials also knew that Soviet officials, after first downplaying Kravchenko's status (claiming that he did not lead the SGPC's metal division, as he had claimed, but was a lowly clerk on temporary assignment), subsequently pressured the State Department to deport him as a deserter from the Soviet Army.[27]

FBI officials were also aware that Kravchenko, after defecting, had bitterly criticized Soviet foreign-policy objectives, trustworthiness, and repression of dissent. They also were fully aware that American activists holding militant anti-Soviet views had collaborated with him to ensure the publication of these criticisms in a variety of publications: *Cosmopolitan*, *American Mercury*, *Reader's Digest*, the *Saturday Evening Post*, and his memoir, *I Chose Freedom*, published by Scribner's in 1946. Kravchenko's collaborators, a virtual "Who's Who" of prominent American critics of the Soviet Union, ranged from former U.S. ambassador to the Soviet Union William Bullitt and *New York Times* reporter Joseph Shaplen to an impressive cast of disgruntled former Marxists and Trotskyites—David Dallin, Max Eastman, Isaac Don Levine, Sol Levitas, William Chamberlain, and Eugene Lyons.[28] FBI agents learned of Kravchenko's collaboration with these prominent critics through monitoring his movements, bugging his room at the Park Crescent Hotel, and intercepting and reading his mail and telegrams. On the basis of their discovery of these contacts, FBI agents wiretapped and intercepted the mail of Dallin, wiretapped Herman Judey, and wiretapped and intercepted the mail of Charles Malamuth (during the period when Kravchenko stayed at his home in Ithaca, New York).[29]

Moreover, FBI officials first became interested in Kravchenko and his associates before his public defection. On February 15, 1944, Bullitt (the former U.S. ambassador to the Soviet Union) advised Attorney General Francis Biddle that Dallin (a leading anti-Soviet critic in the Russian émigré community) knew "a Russian who wanted asylum in the United States." The attorney general immediately briefed FBI Director Hoover, who thereupon had two experienced FBI agents interview Dallin. During his initial interview, Dallin did not identify Kravchenko as this interested defector but did so in a subsequent interview, at which time he agreed to put the agents in contact with Kravchenko. The agents thereupon interviewed Kravchenko over three days in March 1944 (25, 26, and 29). In the interim between the first Dallin interview and the subsequent Kravchenko interviews, however, Hoover solicited Biddle's and President Roosevelt's approval to pursue this matter "in view of the delicate international aspects arising out of it." After first consulting the president, Biddle assured the FBI director that Roosevelt "had stated that whatever arrangements the Director made relative to the use of the Russian would be entirely agreeable and approved by the President."[30]

During his March interviews, Kravchenko offered to brief the FBI, once he had formally defected, on (1) the "espionage activity on the part of Soviet representatives in the United States," (2) the SGPC's "illegal conspiracies" with U.S. firms, (3) the "activities" of NKVD (the Soviet intelligence agency, successor to OGPU) agents in the United States, (4) the organization and plans of the Soviet Communist Party, and (5) the organization of the NKVD. In return, Kravchenko demanded personal protection (including transportation to a safe hiding place, a permit to carry a gun, a change of identity, and medical care for six months) and financial assistance (specifying "no monetary worries for about a year and a half").[31]

Apprised of this offer and Kravchenko's conditions, Hoover again solicited Biddle's guidance. FBI agents, he assured the attorney general, had made no "offers or promises" to Kravchenko. Before pursuing the matter further, he asked Biddle to resubmit the question to the president for his determination "whether he desire[d] the Federal Bureau of Investigation to go forward in this situation." "No steps" would be taken, Hoover emphasized, "which might prove embarrassing to him [the president] or to the foreign relations."[32]

Because the president had "already cleared the matter," Biddle instead briefed Secretary of State Cordell Hull about Kravchenko's pending defection. At first disinclined to "approve further steps taken by the Bureau," Hull relented based on Biddle's assurances that the Justice Department would not arrest or seek indictments of any Soviet officials without first obtaining his approval. Characterizing Kravchenko's defection as "purely an internal intelligence matter," Biddle informed Hull that the Justice Department considered this to be a "matter of internal security and might involve sabotage." He further assured the secretary of state that the FBI would handle Kravchenko's defection "discreetly," adding, "No one but Hoover and myself know about the situation." A relieved Hull thereupon welcomed this opportunity to learn "what the Russians are doing here," adding that Kravchenko's defection could very well be a "convenient card" that he could use "when he next conferred" with Soviet officials. Hoover was thereupon instructed that the FBI "might proceed with the Kravchenko case as the Bureau desires."[33]

Following Kravchenko's defection on April 3, FBI agents from the New York and Washington field offices immediately interviewed him on April 4, 5, and 6 and again on April 17, 1944. During these interviews, Kravchenko supplied information "along the lines indicated" in his earlier predefection interviews. But when FBI agents declined offering assurances of protection and monetary assistance, Kravchenko "urgently" requested that "the interviews be stopped so that he could look to his own affairs."[34]

Because of the extensive redactions in the released FBI files, it is impossible to ascertain what information Kravchenko had provided FBI agents during the predefection (March) and the postdefection (April) interviews, particularly whether he had identified any NKVD agent by name or had provided any useful information about Soviet espionage activities in the United States.[35]

It might seem puzzling that FBI officials passively accepted Kravchenko's decision to cease cooperating and further, given Biddle's assurances (supported by President Roosevelt), were unwilling to meet Kravchenko's security and monetary demands. Their disinterest stemmed from their initial response to Dallin's interview when Kravchenko was identified as the pending defector. Rather than welcoming this opportunity to learn about Soviet intelligence operations, they feared that Kravchenko "may be an agent" of the NKVD and that his proposed defection and contacts with the FBI might be "part of a NKVD scheme to check on the Bureau's activities and attempt to lay some predication for possible embarrassment of the Bureau." Suspecting Kravchenko's bona fides and suspicious about the politics of his American associates (Trotskyites and former Communists), FBI officials instructed agents to take precautions and to be aware of a "double tail" (i.e., that NKVD agents might be following those who were following Kravchenko). Furthermore, because of these suspicions, they ordered agents to monitor Kravchenko's mail, bug his room at the Park Crescent Hotel (where he moved after staying briefly with Dallin and Levine), wiretap Dallin and Judey, intercept Dallin's mail, and wiretap Malamuth and intercept his mail (during the period when Kravchenko was staying with him). In addition, FBI agents checked the COMRAP and CINRAD files for any information relating to Kravchenko and his associates, checked Dallin's "toll-call" records dating from September 18, 1943 (the date when Kravchenko entered the United States), checked all phone calls that the FBI's New York field office intercepted (to ascertain whether any referred to Kravchenko by first or last name), and checked all the FBI's Washington field office's wiretap intercepts of Soviet officials and of the Soviet embassy.[36]

Because of their suspicions about Kravchenko, FBI officials failed to exploit his undoubtedly limited knowledge of Soviet espionage operations. Their handling of Kravchenko's defection (and, as well, their other failures, whether to corroborate Bentley's detailed account of her role as a courier for two spy rings or to break Chambers, in 1942 or 1946, to exact his admission to having also served as a Soviet espionage courier) raises questions about the effectiveness of FBI counterintelligence operations but also about the misdirected domestic political debate about Soviet espionage operations of the early cold war years.[37] The McCarthyite phenomenon, with the attendant criticisms that the Roosevelt and Truman administrations' alleged "softness toward Communism" had undermined the nation's security, seems surreal in light of both administrations' willingness to accord a free hand to the FBI and, even more important, the FBI's failure to apprehend Soviet spies and their American recruits.

FBI officials, however, were never subject to criticism or censure at this time, ironically the by-product of the secrecy surrounding FBI operations. Secrecy benefitted senior FBI officials in that it foreclosed an understanding of the FBI's counterintelligence limitations. Ironically, this very secrecy had another far-reaching consequence during the so-called McCarthy era. FBI officials were able to divert attention from their own failures and through a series of orchestrated leaks (whether to conservative activists in Congress—the chair, chief counsel, and members of the House Committee on Un-American Activities, J. Parnell Thomas, Robert Stripling, Richard Nixon, and Karl Mundt; the chairs and counsel of the Senate Internal Security Subcommittee, Pat McCarran, William Jenner, Robert Morris; and Senator Joseph McCarthy—or in the media—Don Whitehead, Ray McHugh, Walter Trohan, William Hutchinson, Courtney Ryley Cooper, Fulton Oursler, Frederick Woltman, and George Sokolsky) to promote politics that attributed Soviet espionage successes and expansionism to the inaction and Communistic sympathies of the Democratic administrations of Roosevelt and Truman.

6
The Politics of
Counterintelligence

The Federal Bureau of Investigation's (FBI's) failure to have uncovered Soviet espionage activities during World War II was not due to the lack of authority or legal restrictions precluding the use of intrusive investigative techniques. A key source of these failures stemmed from the political assumptions of senior FBI officials, assumptions that determined whom agents should target and that were based on essentially political conceptions of the nature of the "subversive" threat. Thus, FBI investigations not only focused on identifying prominent Communist activists suspecting that they were potential spies or saboteurs and intensively monitored their activities through wiretaps, bugs, mail opening, and break-ins (and the recruitment of informers who infiltrated the Communist Party). As important, the underlying objective of these investigations was to contain Communist influence in American society (whether in the labor or civil-rights movements or in the popular media). The COMRAP and CINRAD investigations, for example, indirectly confirm this misdirected focus, as FBI investigations targeted not only known Communist leaders Earl Browder, Steve Nelson, Boris Morros, and Louise Bransten but also suspected Communist sympathizers Harry Bridges and J. Robert Oppenheimer. In the process, agents missed the actual spies who had either severed direct contact or were peripherally associated with the Communist Party, such as Elizabeth Bentley, Nathan Silvermaster, Theodore Hall, Saville Sax, George Koval, Russell McNutt, Julius Rosenberg, Joel Barr, and Alfred Sarant. Even in the cases when they had monitored Silvermaster, Rosenberg, Barr, and Sarant (not to mention Soviet KGB officer Vassili Zubilin), FBI agents failed to uncover their espionage activities. Equating militancy with a proclivity to commit espionage or sabotage, FBI officials were not dissuaded when the resultant intensive investigations uncovered no evidence of espionage or sabotage. FBI agents were directed to continue to monitor Communists, and, in time, their acquired information about a target's personal and political activities was purposefully leaked to FBI officials' cooperative allies in Congress and in the media.

The most dramatic example of this shift from counterintelligence to political surveillance and containment involved the covert relationship FBI officials forged in 1947 with the House Committee on Un-American Activities (HUAC). Through this relationship, FBI officials sought to exploit information that FBI agents had accumulated earlier under a code-named COMPIC program (the acronym for a formal program of investigating Communist Infiltration of the Motion Picture Industry).

Senior FBI officials first became concerned about suspected Communist influence in Hollywood in the mid-1930s, based on their belief in the subversive character of the organized labor-union movement. The militancy of those active in the Screen Actors Guild and the sharp increase in strikes and organizing activities in Hollywood led FBI Director J. Edgar Hoover to order the Los Angeles field office to investigate those active in strike and organizing activities and then the roles of Hollywood artists and their left-wing allies in the so-called Popular Front of the mid-1930s. Hoover's interest shifted in 1942 from militant labor-union and left-wing political activism to focus as well on those involved in the production of popular films. The FBI director that year authorized the code-named COMPIC program to ascertain the extent of Communist influence in making films. Ironically, Hoover's concern occurred at the very time of the World War II U.S.-Soviet alliance and when American Communists (including those employed in the film industry) enthusiastically supported the U.S. war effort.

Hoover's request of November 1942 was honored three months later. The resultant report of the Los Angeles field office reiterated what had been FBI officials' earlier concerns and thus cited how Communists had assumed leadership roles in Hollywood's thirty-nine labor unions and had set up "many Communist controlled front organizations." The report, however, identified a new threat, one posed by a "cultural group" of actors, actresses, and writers who "appear to be under the control and direction of the Communist Party and follow the Communist Party line in all details and revise their positions without difficulty when the Communist Party changes its policy." At the time, however, the Los Angeles office had developed limited sources, and its report relied on press accounts (whether Los Angeles newspapers or trade publications), the names of prominent supporters listed on the letterhead stationery of Popular Front organizations, or the uncorroborated allegations of informers who had infiltrated the local Communist Party and Popular Front organizations or were employed in the film industry. It had been unable, the Los Angeles office accordingly conceded, to positively identify all Hollywood Communists owing to the fact that the Communist Party leadership had intentionally created "closed" units for actors, actresses, writers, and directors (for the express purpose of precluding other Communist Party members from learning of these artists' "official connection" with the party). Furthermore, Communist Party officials, allegedly and on a regular basis, destroyed all membership, dues payment, and "other documentary" evidence. His office, the Los Angeles Special Agent in Charge (SAC) assured Hoover, would continue to "compile information showing the Communist connections of many of the influential personages in the motion picture industry" and would further identify the "large number of books, pamphlets, scenarios, plays, newsreels, speeches, letters and other material . . . which indicate the enormous effort that has been made and is now being made by the Communist Party to get complete control of the motion picture business and use it for propaganda purpose."[1]

The examples of Communist influence cited in the Los Angeles report did not, however, diverge fundamentally from the Franklin Roosevelt administration's wartime foreign- and domestic-policy goals. Yet FBI Director Hoover remained convinced that a serious internal security existed and, four months later, demanded an "up to date" report on "significant developments." His request was triggered by "recent events"—the release of a pro-Soviet film *Mission to Moscow* (based on the memoir of the former U.S. ambassador Joseph Davies) and the forthcoming release of a number of anti-Fascist films (notably *For Whom the Bell Tolls*, based on Ernest Hemingway's novel about the Spanish Civil War), which, the FBI director contended, "have demonstrated the extent of influence of the Communist Party has been felt in Hollywood."[2]

The resultant report of the FBI's Los Angeles field office identified seven released films as containing "Communist propaganda"[3] and nine other films that "have been made or are now in the process of being made but have not been released" as containing "information of a propaganda nature."[4] The report's claimed evidence, however, was again ideological; its sources were primarily conservatives employed in the film industry who made these charges publicly or volunteered this information in confidence to the Los Angeles office.[5]

The FBI director's renewed demand, however, produced a significant breakthrough. On July 23, 1943, two weeks after submitting the requested report, Los Angeles agents broke into the Communist Party's local office and photocopied the membership records of the Los Angeles section. The identified Communist members employed in the film industry were then linked with specific films, and in two reports to Hoover (the first sent in August 1943 and the second in February 1944) the names and affiliated films were listed in a "complete memo of influence of Communists in motion pictures."[6]

Through this break-in, the FBI's Los Angeles office could now confidently report that Hollywood Communists had exploited the "present apparent patriotic position of the party to recruit new members and control fellow travelers and sympathizers." Hollywood Communists, the Los Angeles office unqualifiedly charged, "bore within" the film industry's labor unions; "spread propaganda within and without unions to create sympathy for the Soviet Union and their system of government"; "browbeat and terrorize public officials by such tactics as demonstrations, letter-writing campaigns, slander campaigns, and personal attacks"; "force the making of motion pictures delineating the Negro race in most favorable terms as part of the general line of the Communist Party"; and propagandize un-American themes.[7] The Los Angeles office promised to continue to "observe the production of motion pictures having a propaganda effect favorable to Communist ideology" and to "obtain evidence of activities of directors, producers, writers, actors, and distributors engaged in producing and distributing pictures of a propaganda nature."[8]

Not content with these assurances, the FBI director demanded regular reports on "all developments indicating Communist infiltration of motion picture field." In their efforts to meet this demand, Los Angeles agents repeatedly broke into the local Communist Party's office to photocopy its membership records—doing so in November 1943, August 1944, January 1945, February 1945, November 1945, February 1947, and May 1947. Through these break-ins, FBI agents identified 47 actors, 45 actresses, 127 writers, 8 producers, and 15 directors either as having been or continuing to be Communist Party members.[9]

The Los Angeles office never uncovered any evidence that the identified Hollywood Communists engaged in espionage or violated any federal laws. This was never a concern, as FBI officials were fearful that Communists might influence the popular culture. Accordingly, the original assessment of the serious nature of the Communist threat was never reassessed even when Los Angeles agents concluded in August 1944 that Hollywood Communists only "injected small portions of propaganda into pictures" and "almost completely abandoned the idea of putting over any pictures filled with propaganda and are just as active to see to it that propaganda pictures favorable to America are kept to a minimum." Thereafter, the Los Angeles office continued to update a "ready reference" of all Hollywood employees "who are members of the Communist Party or of Communist front organizations," breaking down this list by categories of "producers, directors, writers, actors, labor union figures and miscellaneous."[10]

Hoover briefed Attorney General Francis Biddle about this perceived

Communist threat for the first time in October 1944. "No direct investigation" of the movie industry had been conducted, the FBI director claimed (a claim that misrepresented the intensity of the FBI's efforts, including the resort to illegal investigative techniques). He thought the attorney general would be interested in "the attached data relating to the growing Communist influence in that industry, which industry is recognized not only as a great medium for propaganda but also as one of the most influential agencies of education."[11] As Hoover's report cited no evidence of criminal conduct and simply reflected the FBI director's ideological conception of subversive threats, Biddle did not even respond.

Undaunted by the attorney general's indifference and his own inability to exploit the acquired information for legitimate law-enforcement purposes,[12] the FBI director in time adopted another strategy to exploit this information: through a series of carefully orchestrated leaks to the chairman of HUAC, J. Parnell Thomas, in the critical months May–September 1947. His action marked a reversal in what had heretofore been his policy of distancing the FBI from HUAC.

Two years earlier, upon learning that HUAC planned to investigate Communist influence in Hollywood and given that committee's infamous reputation, Hoover ensured that the FBI would not be linked with the proposed investigation.[13] This distancing policy was reaffirmed in March 1947, when Hoover explained to Attorney General Tom Clark why he would not honor HUAC's request that month for "certain summaries of [FBI] files on subversive activities." Stressing the need to preserve the confidentiality of FBI files, the FBI director pointed out that compliance with this request would inevitably lead to the committee's publicizing this information, and then "our sources of information will dry up and we will not be able to obtain the coverage that we now have." The FBI's interest in confidentiality had to be balanced against the need to maintain "harmonious relations with members of Congress and Committees thereof," Hoover conceded, adding that congressional investigations have "powers broader than those of the Bureau . . . [to] compel witnesses to appear and testify and also compel the production of records and documents which this Bureau cannot do unless there is a case pending in a court of law." These advantages, Hoover added, had to be counterbalanced against the public's antipathy toward Congress's "irresponsible" investigations, a situation that "has been particularly true of the Committee on Un-American Activities." "If now that committee," he continued, "can put in a 'pipe-line' to the files of this Bureau, even though it be in the form of a synopsis of our files, I think there is going to be a very bad public reaction ultimately."[14]

In May 1947, however, HUAC Chair Thomas, accompanied by HUAC Counsel Robert Stripling and unaware of Hoover's reservations, traveled to Los Angeles to conduct a preliminary investigation of Communist influence in the film industry. Almost immediately, Thomas and Stripling recognized their own inadequacies and requested Los Angeles SAC Richard Hood's appearance before their subcommittee. Hood immediately informed Hoover of this request. Fearing that the HUAC chair intended to involve the FBI publicly in HUAC's inquiry, Hoover instructed Hood to advise Thomas that he "could not appear before the Committee in open session because to do so would spotlight the things we are trying to do with respect to keeping in touch with the Communist situation." Hood, however, should assure Thomas of the FBI's desire to "cooperate but that a public hearing would necessarily disclose confidential information and would make it more difficult for us to do our work." The FBI could not provide "any confidential information in our files," Hoover added, but "if any" Hollywood personalities "had been the subject of publicity which is available to anyone, there would be no objection to pointing out [to Thomas] such instances."[15]

In his meeting with Hood the next day, Thomas quickly allayed what had been Hoover's principal concern—that the HUAC chair intended to involve the FBI publicly in HUAC's investigation. "Information in the Bureau's files," Thomas pleaded, "ought to be made available to [Thomas and Stripling] in order that they might better put the spotlight of public opinion on the Communist movement." HUAC, Thomas assured Hood, would do nothing "that might in any way interfere with any Bureau activity." He then explained the reason for his request—that during their interrogation of Hanns Eisler (a suspected Communist film writer), he and Stripling had been "severely handicapped" by their lack of information to "question him further along this line" (after Eisler admitted only to a one-time attendance at a Communist Party meeting). This difficulty, Thomas emphasized, could submarine their ability, upon returning to Washington, to convince the full committee, at a scheduled June 16 meeting, to "send investigators" to Los Angeles. Thomas then identified by name nine individuals and asked Hood to check FBI files for "any data that might be of assistance to them concerning these persons." He did not want anything that "might embarrass our Sources of Information or interfere with our investigations," but only "background and other definite data" that could be of "assistance."

Relieved upon learning of Thomas's specific request, Hoover agreed on a plan to assist Thomas and Stripling: He would "furnish" to them the names of "known Communists who have some basis for knowledge of Communist activities, the known Communist front groups and officers whom the Committee might investigate" and prepare "summary" memoranda based on FBI files on the nine "individuals about whom [Thomas] has requested specific information." The Los Angeles office was thereupon ordered to "Expedite. I want to extend *every* assistance to this Committee."[16]

Hood personally delivered the requested summary memoranda to Thomas the very next day, but on eleven, not nine, individuals.[17] One memorandum listed their Communist Party "membership book number" and was provided on the understanding that "the disclosure of this data will not in any way embarrass the Bureau." Thomas was also given a lengthy summary memorandum, captioned "Re: Communist Activities in Hollywood," which identified nine "non-Communists" (including Ronald Reagan, Robert Montgomery, Richard Arlen, Leila Rogers, Jack Warner) who would "probably be cooperative and friendly witnesses" and twenty-four "hostile witnesses and uncooperative" who were "identified with the Communist movement, together with positions and activities" about which they could be questioned. This assistance was rendered on the condition that Thomas and Stripling agreed that the information "is furnished strictly for their confidential information and . . . under no circumstances will the FBI source of this information be disclosed." The Los Angeles SAC reported back that Thomas and Stripling were "very friendly and appreciative of this cooperation."[18]

Returning to Washington, Thomas and Stripling convinced the full committee to approve a thorough investigation. Thomas thereupon sought a personal meeting with Hoover, at which time, after conceding that HUAC might not have "worked harmoniously" with the FBI in the past, he promised to "work even closer." The committee, he advised Hoover, would hold public hearings in September, adding that the preliminary hearings of May–June had failed to develop the "necessary information," as many potential witnesses had been pressured not to cooperate. Thomas then solicited Hoover's counsel about former FBI agent H. Allen Smith, whom he was considering hiring as a committee investigator (and was immediately assured of his excellent record). After recounting his appreciation of the need to preserve the confidentiality of FBI files, which contained "vast knowledge of subversive activities," Thomas asked Hoover "entirely off the record and with absolute assurance that it would not pass beyond him as Chairman of the Committee for leads and information of value to the Committee to be furnished to the Committee." Hoover agreed to be "as helpful to the Committee as we could" and promised to initiate a search of FBI files to "see what help we might be able to be to the Committee insofar as submitting leads and material that might be used as a basis of interrogation." This assistance was conditioned on Thomas's agreement that "the Bureau could not be publicly drawn into the investigation nor be called to appear in any capacity." Thomas readily agreed to this condition and to the specific arrangement whereby he alone would relay any committee request through FBI Assistant Director Louis Nichols.

When briefing his key aides about his decision to be as "helpful to this Committee as I can," the FBI director articulated his underlying political objective:

We will not be able to disclose the confidential sources of our information and no doubt in some instances by reason of the extreme confidential character of information . . . may not be able to divulge some
of the information we have, but I do think that it is long overdue for
the Communist infiltration in Hollywood to be exposed, and as there
is no medium at the present time through which this Bureau can bring
that about on its own motion I think it is entirely proper and desirable
that we assist the Committee in Congress that is intent on bringing to
light the true facts in the situation.[19]

Assisting HUAC became an FBI priority. FBI files (in Los Angeles, New
York, and Washington) were scoured, and summary memoranda were prepared about the "leading Communists and pro-Communists" in Hollywood
and "all the motion pictures in which Communists and Communist sympathizers have participated" for HUAC's "utilization." Great care, nonetheless,
was taken to ensure that no information was reported that could compromise
the FBI's confidential sources (break-ins, wiretaps, and informers).[20]

By mid-August 1947, HUAC investigators had identified forty unfriendly
individuals whom the committee was considering subpoenaing to testify during hearings then scheduled for September 24. When submitting these names,
Stripling specifically asked Nichols "unofficially" for "blind memoranda[21]
giving [their] background, associations, Communist Party membership, etc."
Hoover immediately ordered FBI Assistant Directors Edward Tamm and D.
Milton Ladd to "get to work on the list."[22]

Before acting on this request, Ladd briefed Hoover on how the requested
memoranda would be prepared. Each would "1. Include all pertinent public
source data; 2. Exclude all data received from technical [wiretap] and microphone surveillances, as well as from other highly delicate media [break-ins,
informers]; and 3. If the public data alone does not suffice, the memoranda
will have included therein on a selected basis information received from live
confidential informants which will be prepared in such a fashion to obviate
the possibility of jeopardizing our informants." Ladd was thereupon ordered
to seek Hoover's or FBI Associate Director Clyde Tolson's advance "approval"
before giving the completed memoranda to Thomas. The time-consuming
process of first culling FBI files and then ensuring that the FBI's sources would
not be compromised delayed completion of this task. Indeed, the first ten
memoranda were not completed until September 12, twenty more the next
day, and the last ten on September 16. Each memorandum listed background
information on the individual's membership in, affiliation with, or attendance
at meetings sponsored by various Communist or left-wing organizations but
also proposed specific questions that committee members could ask the individual during the hearings.[23]

When originally prepared, the blind memoranda did not include information obtained through wiretaps, bugs, and break-ins. Almost immediately, however, Hoover partially relented on his earlier order to withhold such information from the committee. On September 13 and 17, the Los Angeles SAC was ordered to forward to FBI headquarters the photostats of the "Communist Party membership cards" of twenty-five named individuals (the twenty-five included eight of the so-called Hollywood Ten,[24] such information about the other two, Edward Dmytryk and Adrian Scott, having already been given to Thomas and Stripling in May 1947).[25]

The blind memoranda in effect undermined the First Amendment strategy that the Hollywood Ten adopted during their October 1947 HUAC testimony. Thus, after each refused to answer the committee's questions on First Amendment grounds, HUAC Counsel Louis Russell took the stand to introduce into the record photostats of their Communist Party membership cards while Stripling read into the record information about their Communist activities (meetings attended or affiliations with Communist-front organizations). The committee members then voted to cite the Ten for contempt of Congress. The House subsequently approved their recommendation, with a grand jury returning indictments. Immediately following the conclusion of the hearings, Thomas telephoned Nichols to convey his "heartfelt appreciation" for the FBI's covert assistance and to emphasize that Hoover "more than any other person is responsible for the Committee not being put out of business." Thomas specifically cited the committee's ability to exploit the information about the Ten's Communist membership cards and Communist affiliations.[26]

FBI officials did not cease their political containment efforts with HUAC's citation of the Ten for contempt of Congress. They continued to monitor the actions of the indicted Ten and their supporters to avert first their indictments and then their convictions on the contempt charge. The FBI's efforts extended to wiretapping two of the Hollywood Ten's attorneys (Bartley Crum and Martin Popper, with the Popper tap being the most valuable, since his office operated as the clearing house for the various attorneys handling aspects of the defense work). These wiretaps provided invaluable intelligence about the strategies of the attorneys and their politically connected allies to avert their indictment and conviction.[27]

Between November 26, 1947, and May 7, 1948, FBI Director Hoover regularly forwarded detailed reports based on these wiretaps to Attorney General Clark and Assistant Attorney General T. Vincent Quinn (the head of the Justice Department's Criminal Division and supervisor of the government's prosecution of the Hollywood Ten). The reported information was masked as having been obtained from a "highly confidential source."[28]

Clark and Quinn as a result were alerted to Crum's and Popper's plans to convince Clark and U.S. Attorney George Fay not to present Congress's contempt of Congress citation to a federal grand jury (and the legal grounds for not doing so); Popper's (and another attorney's) plan to convince Clark to delay arraigning the Hollywood Ten until the Supreme Court ruled on another contempt case; the plans of defense attorneys to have Senator Claude Pepper intercede with Clark and Crum to contact the White House to secure its support for a continuance; and Popper's claim that Clark, during his meeting with Pepper, had expressed an interest in making a "deal" and that the Hollywood Ten also hoped to exploit Pepper's connections with President Harry Truman. In addition, Clark and Quinn were the recipients of detailed information about the defense's trial strategies: having Methodist Bishop G. Bromley Oxnam file an amicus brief; subpoenaing all of John Lawson's films (Lawson was the first of the Ten to be tried), seven of Dalton Trumbo's films (the second to be tried), and identified HUAC records; subpoenaing actors Burgess Meredith and John Huston; hiring Irving Pichel, Lewis Milestone, and Howard Koch as expert witnesses on the film industry; having actors and actresses Lena Horne, Marsha Hunt, Fredric March, Florence Eldridge, and John Garfield testify that HUAC's investigation was unjustified; recruiting Paul Dwyer as a trial attorney; and hiring prominent black attorney Charles Houston as co-counsel (on the premise that his presence might influence black jurors and thereby enhance the chances of a hung jury). Justice Department officials were further alerted to the divisions among the defense attorneys over Clark's proposal to delay the trials of the remaining eight until the Supreme Court had ruled on the Trumbo and Lawson verdicts, and that some of the defense attorneys had wanted to condition acceptance on Clark's agreement to urge the executives of the film industry to abolish the blacklist. Last, Clark and Quinn were briefed about the Hollywood Ten's strategies to influence public opinion, whether by hiring John Stone, Irving Lichtenstein, or Jack McManus to formulate a public-relations strategy; bringing "big-name" people to Washington in an effort to focus public attention on the trials' civil-liberties issues; or obtaining the support of labor unions (on the premise that compelling congressional testimony could compromise labor's organizing efforts).

Neither Clark nor Quinn ever inquired about the identity of the FBI's "highly confidential" source. Their indifference is troubling, since the confidential nature of the reported information confirmed that the source was either a wiretap, a bug, or an informer employed on the defense team. Ironically, their only known response involved Quinn's request that the FBI investigate the "April and May panels of petit jurors to be called in connection with the trial" and to check "indices, credit reports, and other available sources" "for the purpose of ascertaining the background of members of the panels." This investigation, Quinn insisted, should be completed "at your earliest convenience after the names of the jurors are made available" in view of the "importance of these contempt cases."[29]

The FBI's political-containment efforts in assisting HUAC were not a one-time action. FBI officials continued to assist the committee until its members' carelessness in revealing the FBI as a source led the agency to sever relations with this infamous committee in the mid-1950s. FBI officials, moreover, also sought to contain the influence of popular authors, particularly those writing about the FBI. In this case, FBI officials sought to discredit those authors who criticized the FBI or, conversely, to assist those sympathetic toward the bureau as part of their broader agenda of shaping public opinion and sustaining a militant anti-Communist politics.

In 1960, for example, FBI Director Hoover outlined for FBI agents the criteria for listing individuals in a renamed Reserve Index. His purpose was to ensure that those who "represent a greater threat in time of emergency than do others" would be so listed. Individuals meeting a higher standard of danger-ousness (that they were "in a position to influence others against the national interest") were to be listed in this index's Section A. As examples, Hoover cited "writers,[30] lecturers, newsmen, entertainers, and others in the mass media field," and specifically "Norman Mailer, a novelist and author of *The Naked and the Dead* and an admitted 'leftist.'"[31] Hoover's concern about subversive authors intensified when he learned of the imminent publication of Max Lowenthal's critical history of the FBI.[32]

A former congressional aide and low-level federal bureaucrat, Lowenthal began research on this history in the mid-1930s. Learning of the pending publication of his critical history, titled *The Federal Bureau of Investigation*, Hoover moved quickly first to prevent its publication and then to discredit the book and its author. The FBI director accordingly asked Morris Ernst, an American Civil Liberties Union attorney with whom he had developed a close relationship, to intercede with Lowenthal's publisher, William Sloane Associates, not to publish the book, adding that although he was "perfectly willing to leave everything to [Ernst's] judgment," some action had to be taken. Ernst, however, was reluctant to "contact the publishers as he is fearful that they might seize upon any contact and issue a statement that the Director, through his attorney, had approached them on the book." Hoover thereupon urged Ernst to call to Sloane's "attention that the book was filled with distortions, half-truths, and incomplete details, as well as false statements," confirming that the FBI had somehow illicitly obtained an advance copy of the book.

Ernst instead proposed a more devious strategy: Hoover's aides should inquire whether "somebody at the Library of Congress might not write to [Sloane] merely indicating that they know a book is coming out through adver-tisements and then asking if the publisher knows they have indexed a writing under a similar title and that considerable confusion on the public might occur unless the title is changed." Should Hoover decide not to approach the Library of Congress, Ernst added, "the FBI itself should write to the publisher but in doing so, make clear that even the change of the title should not be construed as putting a blessing on the book in any form."[33]

Unwilling to operate openly, Hoover instead exploited the FBI's contacts with HUAC. Sympathetic to the FBI director's concerns, HUAC staff members interviewed Lowenthal and his publisher twice in August and September 1950. The committee then subpoenaed Lowenthal to testify on September 15 about his past "subversive" associations and, immediately following publication of his history, publicly released Lowenthal's testimony.

FBI Director Hoover concurrently alerted all SACs about the pending publication of Lowenthal's history, instructing them that "book salesmen of [Sloane] are endeavoring to secure advance orders at a reduced price, and there is some indication they are attempting to sell copies of this book to Chiefs of Police and other law enforcement officials." "It is well known," Hoover continued, that "Lowenthal has been exceedingly active in the past ten years in his attempts to discredit the FBI." To assist in this effort of having SACs exploit their contacts in the local media, Hoover forwarded to them copies of Congressman George Dondero's speech, a speech that FBI officials helped prepare that stressed Lowenthal's "subversive" background, and urged them to ensure extensive press coverage. This initiative failed, with the FBI director privately lamenting that even the *New York Times* and *New York Herald* had made "no mention of Max Lowenthal."

FBI officials considered it "significant" that the media had failed to question Lowenthal's prejudices in light of their own assessment of a book that they found to be "filled with distortions, misrepresentations, erroneous conclusions, and outright falsehoods." Lowenthal's history of the FBI, Hoover nonetheless feared, might impress the "uninformed individual" owing to his extensive "quotes from numerous editorials, Congressional debates, public hearings, etc." and, while advising SACs that the FBI "does not desire to dignify the book with any comment," Hoover nonetheless instructed them that "should any question arise regarding the book from law enforcement officials and friendly sources, there is no objection to your advising them of the true character of the book."

Leaving nothing to chance, Hoover had the FBI's Crime Records Division prepare and plant with sympathetic reporters and other public-opinion leaders (including syndicated columnists Walter Winchell, Fulton Lewis, Jr., and George Sokolsky; reporters Walter Trohan and Frederick Woltman; and Georgetown University Dean Edmund Walsh) critical reviews of the book. Derogatory information about Lowenthal and his publisher was also leaked to these and other sympathetic sources. FBI Assistant Director Nichols even urged an NBC news commentator to report that the press response to Lowenthal's book showed "how stooges do the Communists' work." Last, FBI agents visited bookstores around the country to pressure their managers not to stock the book.[34]

Hoover's vendetta did not stop with the publication of *The Federal Bureau of Investigation*. Following the creation of the Senate Internal Security Sub-committee in 1951, the FBI director ordered his aides to raise with the sub-committee's staff "the possibilities of the Committee looking into the matter of Communist infiltration of the book publishing industry" to "counteract the left-wing element in the publishing business, which has been the source of attacks on the Bureau ... particularly the Max Lowenthal book, William A. Sloan[e] Associates, Merle Miller's *The Sure Thing*, and others." Because of the priority of other matters (its current investigations of the Institute of Pacific Relations and of suspected Communist infiltration of the United Nations and federal agencies), the subcommittee did not honor Hoover's request at the time. In August 1952, the subcommittee requested, and FBI officials duti-fully compiled, a memorandum on Lowenthal. Then, when the subcommittee finally had the time, in February 1953, to launch the suggested inquiry, Hoover decided not to provide assistance, observing, "A year ago we had more time. Now we haven't."[35]

In the case of authors who could be expected to praise Hoover and the FBI, FBI officials willingly provided every assistance. In the process, one such favored reporter, Donald Whitehead, reaped a personal fortune that allowed him to retire as a working journalist and, relying on continued FBI assistance thereafter, to embark on a lucrative career as a freelance writer.

A feature writer for the Associated Press since 1931, Whitehead authored a series of highly favorable articles about Hoover in 1954. Recontacting the FBI director's press liaison Nichols in 1955, Whitehead sought FBI assistance for a proposed article "on the fight against Communism and what the Communists are now doing." His request elicited a wholly unanticipated response.

On Hoover's order, FBI officials closely reviewed Whitehead's writings. Based on their assessment, the FBI director concluded that the reporter "has clearly established his reliability" and should be considered a possible can-didate to write a history of the FBI. Before launching this "special project," however, Hoover ordered a "Special Inquiry type investigation" of Whitehead on "a very discreet basis" and without contacting his current employer. The ensuing intensive investigation convinced Hoover that Whitehead could be trusted. The trustworthy reporter was thereupon informed that he would be granted access to carefully selected FBI records, which he would be allowed to review in a special office at FBI headquarters.

Whitehead accepted this offer with alacrity, along with its condition that he allow Hoover and his aides to review his manuscript prior to publication. FBI officials did subsequently demand specified revisions, with Hoover personally monitoring Whitehead's research and writing (at one time conveying his "pleasure with the first four chapters" and at another insisting on specified revisions to chapter 29). And, when the manuscript was completed, Hoover had Nichols accompany Whitehead to New York to discuss same with White-head's publisher Bennet Cerf. Nichols was to secure Cerf's agreement to an FBI voice in planning the book's publicity to ensure that it was "dignified and [was] passed upon by the Bureau."

Whitehead's history, *The FBI Story*, eulogized Hoover and the FBI, extol-ling in particular the FBI's successful battle against the Communist menace. The book's success was not left to chance, however. The FBI's Recreation Association purchased hundreds of copies of the book to boost sales and dis-tribution. These sales and other FBI promotion efforts helped make *The FBI Story* a best seller and then a popular movie under the same name.[36]

One of these FBI efforts to ensure that Whitehead's history would be favorably reviewed earned Harry Overstreet Hoover's personal thanks: "The encouragement and support which you have rendered Mr. Whitehead and the FBI in connection with his book have been extraordinary, and we are all deeply appreciative." Such helpfulness, in turn, benefitted Overstreet by ensuring favorable FBI assistance for his (1958) anti-Communist diatribe, *What We Must Know about Communism*. As in Whitehead's case, the spark for this book was once again the FBI, with Nichols urging Overstreet the previous year to write a book "against communism directed toward liberals and progressives, et cetera, who would not normally read a book condemn-ing communism." The FBI's assistance to Overstreet (and to his wife and co-author) included FBI Inspector William Sullivan's culling FBI files for public source information and spending "approximately one night each week (7:00 P.M. to about 11:00 P.M.) during the winter months . . . devoted to reading and analyzing the materials the Overstreets were preparing." No passive research assistant, Sullivan ensured that the book conformed with the interests of the FBI director and the FBI. "While working with the Overstreets on this book," Sullivan assured his FBI superiors, "I purposely had them direct 95% of their thinking to the world communist movement believing this would best supple-ment the Director's book [*Masters of Deceit*], which was directed almost 100% to the communist movement in the United States."[37]

In a companion initiative, FBI officials had earlier sought to limit the influ-ence of the so-called isolationist press during the World War II era, in this case willingly promoting the political interests of the Roosevelt administration. Ironically, although FBI officials later targeted liberal and radical journalists during the Vietnam era (most notably Joseph Kraft, Peter Lisagor, Joseph Alsop, Harrison Salisbury, Ben Gilbert, and the so-called underground press), they monitored the articles, columns, and personal character of journalists and publishers of conservative, isolationist newspapers during the 1939–1942 era, such as the *Chicago Tribune*, the *Washington Times-Herald*, and the *New York Daily News*.

The most fully documented of these actions involved a relatively uninfluential columnist, Inga Arvad. Arvad first commanded the attention of senior FBI officials in December 1940, triggered by an unsolicited report from one of her classmates at Columbia University's School of Journalism that she had allegedly boasted to having interviewed prominent Nazi officials Adolf Hitler, Joseph Goebbels, Heinrich Himmler, and Rudolf Hess and that she had abandoned her earlier sympathy for Nazi Germany. Hoover's correspondent conceded that she had no evidence that Arvad had done anything illegal but was worried that Arvad's associations with prospective journalists could "influenc[e] morale in this country for the benefit of the German government."[38]

Hoover promptly ordered the FBI's New York field office to investigate these allegations. The resultant investigation, however, uncovered no evidence of Arvad's "subversive" influence except that at one time she might have expressed anti-Semitic and pro-Hitler comments.[39]

Similar allegations one year later precipitated a far more intensive FBI inquiry. By then, Arvad was employed as a columnist for the *Washington Times-Herald*, a bitter critic of the Roosevelt administration's domestic and foreign policies. Arvad's gossipy column described the activities of low-level federal employees, socialites, and other prominent Washingtonians. Her favored position at this newspaper as a protégé of Publisher Eleanor Patterson and Assistant Editor Frank Waldrop, however, had triggered a hostile response from a jealous colleague.

This colleague (whose name the FBI has withheld) informed FBI Assistant Director Nichols (Hoover's liaison to the media) in mid-November 1941 that Arvad had formerly been "Hitler's publicity agent" in Europe and yet had been "picked up by Patterson and had either hoodwinked Frank Waldrop or Waldrop is working under orders." When briefing Hoover about this allegation, Nichols added that Arvad's husband, Paul Fejos, headed one of Swedish financier (and suspected Nazi agent) Axel Wenner-Gren's expeditions to South America.[40]

Arvad's jealous rival had concurrently circulated this rumor within the newspaper's office. Learning of her accusations within a month, Arvad protested to Patterson who, fearful that "it might reflect unfavorably upon the *Times-Herald*, an isolationist paper, if it became known that they had employed a person suspected of being a spy," directed Waldrop to arrange FBI interviews of Arvad and her accuser. Waldrop complied.

During her FBI interview, Arvad's accuser called attention to a photograph of "Arvad taken with Hitler at the [1936] Olympic games" that carried a caption that she was working for the German propaganda ministry. This

photograph, the reporter contended, "combined with Arvad's strong isolationist viewpoint, which [Arvad] openly expresses, has caused her to become
suspicious." In her separate interview, Arvad rebuffed these allegations,
explaining that, before immigrating to the United States in 1940, she had
been employed as a reporter for a Danish newspaper and in this professional
capacity had interviewed Hitler, Hermann Goering, and Goebbels during the
1936 Olympic Games and had also covered Goebbels's wedding.[41] Another
woman (whose name the FBI has also withheld) concurrently contacted the
FBI to report that Wenner-Gren "is trying to get a woman a certain position
that in this position she would be in a good spot to make trouble and put
[name withheld] in a predicament."[42]

In light of Arvad's alleged influence at the *Washington Times-Herald* and
her husband's association with Wenner-Gren, Hoover responded to these
unsupported allegations by ordering the Washington, D.C., SAC, Sam McKee,
to initiate a "discreet" investigation to determine the "truth." A report should
be submitted "in the near future," and, when soliciting the assistance of other
FBI field offices, the Washington SAC was to advise them of the "discreet
nature of the investigation."[43]

Having concluded that a wiretap could prove invaluable in uncovering
Arvad's activities, Hoover requested Attorney General Biddle's approval. As
justification, he cited her estranged husband's employment with Wenner-
Gren, her employment with the *Times-Herald*, and the photograph of Arvad
captioned "Meet Miss Inga Arvad, Danish beauty, who so captivated Chan-
cellor Adolf Hitler during a visit that he made her Chief of Nazi Publicity in
Denmark." In addition, Hoover continued, "in the short period she has been
in Washington, she has established close social and professional contacts
with persons holding important positions in the Government departments
and bureaus vitally concerned with the national defense, . . . is carrying on
an affair with one such Naval officer . . . [and] another man in a similarly
commissioned position [then naval ensign John F. Kennedy] has indicated
he is engaged to her. . . . The combination of these facts indicates a definite
possibility that she may be engaged in a most subtle type of espionage activity
against the United States." Convinced by Hoover's "facts," Biddle authorized
the wiretap.[44]

Hoover had misled the attorney general. By then, FBI agents had uncovered no evidence that Arvad had sought or relayed to Germany classified
information obtained through her interviews of government officials. She had
contacted these officials (as her other contacts in the Washington community) only to interview them for her column, which (the FBI agent reviewing
her columns conceded) contained "nothing" to "reflect pro-Axis or anti-Axis
viewpoint." Her views were those of a "strong isolationist," and her relationships with several navy ensigns were strictly sexual. Arvad's intercepted phone

conversations and her private correspondence and records obtained through a break-in of her apartment further confirmed her innocence.[45]

The Arvad wiretap nonetheless heightened FBI officials' concerns for secrecy. Having learned through this tap that Kennedy had somehow discovered (and had then alerted Arvad to this discovery) that the FBI was monitoring his contact with Arvad, FBI officials further learned that Arvad suspected that the FBI had tapped her phone and that she intended to seek an appointment with Hoover to ascertain if this were true. Hoover thereupon terminated the Arvad tap "for the time being."[46]

Unwilling to reinstate the tap on his own or to seek Biddle's approval again, Hoover instead shrewdly exploited President Roosevelt's suspicions about the isolationist press. In an unsolicited report to the White House, the FBI director hinted at the sinister character of the Wenner-Gren archaeological expedition to South America, pointing out that neither of the expedition's leaders, Fejos and G. K. Lowther, "could be classified as competent archaeologists." He added that Fejos's "wife, who is presently divorcing him is reported to be a former favorite of Hitler. . . . At present she writes a column for the *Times-Herald* under the name of Inga Arvad." Then, in a companion briefing of Biddle, Hoover reported that (former U.S. ambassador) Joseph Kennedy's daughter Kathleen "is private secretary to Frank Waldrop who writes the column for the *Times-Herald*" and that Inga Arvad "writes profiles in the *Times-Herald* and is intimate with [*Times-Herald* publisher] Cissy Patterson. It is also alleged that she [Arvad] is also intimate with Joe Kennedy's eldest son."[47] (John was actually the second-oldest son.)

Hoover's distorted briefings succeeded—by then, he knew that Arvad had broken off all contact with Fejos except to arrange a divorce, that she wrote her column under her maiden name and not to mask her association with Fejos or Wenner-Gren, and that her affair with John Kennedy was strictly amorous and that Joseph Kennedy opposed it. Hoover's briefings nonetheless succeeded. On May 4, President Roosevelt concluded, "In view of the connection of Inga Arvad, who writes for the *Times-Herald*, and in view of certain other circumstances which have been brought to my attention, I think it would be just as well to have her specially watched."[48]

The wiretap was reinstated, and FBI agents continued monitoring Arvad and her contacts. This investigation uncovered no evidence of espionage—only that Arvad and John Kennedy had ended their affair, that she continued to arrange interviews for her column, and that she had resumed an earlier romance with another Danish immigrant, Nils Bloch.[49]

The FBI investigation of Arvad was unique only in its vindictiveness (FBI officials found her lifestyle immoral) and in its creation of a detailed written record, which remains extant.[50] Nonetheless, the Arvad investigation conformed with a more general pattern of FBI monitoring of journalists who either criticized the Roosevelt and subsequent administrations' foreign-policy initiatives or the FBI's competence. The monitoring of these journalists was either responsive to White House demands or was initiated on Hoover's order.

In April 1942, for example, President Roosevelt demanded that Attorney General Biddle move vigorously against "publishers of seditious matter." Biddle thereupon informed the president that the Justice Department already had a "program of moving against seditious magazines through grand juries," had garnered "wide publicity" in some of these cases, and had "stopped delivery" by an express company of Charles Coughlin's *Social Justice*. Then, when the president complained about *Times-Herald* publisher "Cissy Patterson's subversive mind," Biddle assured him that the Justice Department had "put a surveillance on her and on [*New York Daily News* publisher] Colonel [Joseph Medill] Patterson, which we have done."[51] (Neither the holdings of the Roosevelt Presidential Library nor released FBI files contain any records of this surveillance. A blind memorandum, dated March 19, 1940, maintained in FBI Assistant Director Nichols's secret office file nonetheless confirms that the FBI was already monitoring Joseph Patterson's editorials and editorial decisions.)[52]

Indeed, long before U.S. military involvement in World War II, the FBI began monitoring the Roosevelt administration's media critics. In July 1940, for example, Hoover solicited Secretary of the Treasury Henry Morgenthau's assistance for an investigation of Vomenico Trombetta, the publisher of the Italian-language newspaper *Grido Della Stirpe*. Hoover was responding to New York Mayor Fiorello LaGuardia's complaint about Trombetta's "pro-Fascist" attitude in his paper's editorials. LaGuardia had then recommended that President Roosevelt have the FBI investigate "Trombetta's financial status and activities, with a view of determining the source of the funds used in operating the newspaper," as he was convinced that the Italian consulate was funding Trombetta. The publisher, LaGuardia argued, "should be made to change his editorial policies," since his paper "does tend to excite the Italian element." The New York mayor also urged Hoover to investigate another Italian American newspaper publisher, Generoso Pope, owing to his "similar pro-Fascist attitude." In response, Hoover secured the treasury secretary's assistance to access the bank records of these two publishers by citing President Roosevelt's interest in both investigations. FBI agents, however, were unable to document that either publisher had received Italian funding or had violated the internal-revenue laws. The FBI investigation did succeed nonetheless in pressuring Pope to cooperate with prominent anti-Fascist Italian refugee Max Ascoli. Under this arrangement, Pope agreed to "start an aggressive campaign to inculcate loyalty among Italian Americans for the internal and foreign policies" of the Roosevelt administration and to turn his newspaper into an "uncompromising and militant champion of the present Administration."[53]

President Roosevelt also solicited Hoover's assistance to influence press coverage of the devastating Japanese attack on Pearl Harbor. Briefed about *Orlando (FL) Sentinel* publisher Martin Andersen's query whether to publish Drew Pearson's and Robert Allen's syndicated column describing the scale of losses resulting from this attack, Roosevelt directed Hoover to "say to Pearson and Allen that if they continue to print such inaccurate and unpatriotic statements,"[54] the administration "will be compelled to appeal directly to their [Pearson and Allen] subscribers and to bar them from all privileges that go with the relationships between the Press and the Government." When contacting Pearson, Hoover denied that this was a threat, claiming to be only "acting in my official capacity as temporary coordinator of censorship arrangements."[55] Reporting back on this contact, the FBI director disclosed that Pearson had agreed to "eliminate from the article those portions giving the details of the losses in Hawaii."[56]

In a companion initiative, Roosevelt solicited from the FBI director any derogatory information on another of the administration's media critics, radio commentator Upton Close. Hoover thereupon reported that in 1931 Close "had brought a Chinese girl into the United States and was engaging in immoral acts with her, possibly in violation of the White Slave Traffic Act" and that in 1942 he was in "possible violation of the Sedition Statutes." The Justice Department in neither case sought indictments, deeming the FBI's evidence to be insufficient.[57]

Hoover could readily service this presidential request about Close, as FBI agents were already monitoring the political activities, writing plans, and personal conduct of the nation's mainstream journalists. As important, the FBI director had devised an efficient system to retrieve all derogatory information that agents had accumulated about journalists. Thus, when learning in 1970 that *Los Angeles Times* reporter Jack Nelson planned to write a critical article about Hoover and the FBI, Hoover met with that paper's vice president and general manager Robert Nelson and Washington bureau chief David Kraslow to protest this assignment. During this meeting, Hoover read from an FBI report detailing reporter Nelson's "heavy drinking." In an even more sensitive action later that year, Hoover willingly honored a request from President Richard Nixon conveyed by White House aide H. R. Haldeman for an FBI "run down on the homosexuals known and suspected in the Washington press corps" that "also [asked] whether we [FBI] had any other stuff; [saying] that he, the President, had an interest in what, if anything else we knew." The requested report was hand-delivered by special courier to the White House in two days. Significantly, when making this request, Haldeman had volunteered that the president thought that Hoover "would have it pretty much on hand so there would be no special investigation." Nixon assumed correctly, as the FBI not only collected such personal derogatory information but also could link this information by professional occupation.[58]

The Roosevelt and Nixon administrations, moreover, were not alone in turning to the FBI to discredit their media critics. Dwight Eisenhower and Lyndon Johnson did so as well.

For one, FBI Director Hoover learned in April 1957 of syndicated columnist Joseph Alsop's "incurable" homosexuality, having been briefed by CIA Director Allen Dulles that Alsop had been compromised by a KGB sting operation in Moscow. Alsop had volunteered this information to the FBI and CIA directors at the time, intending to disarm any future Soviet attempt to blackmail him into supporting Soviet interests. The syndicated columnist nonetheless had requested that Dulles and Hoover keep this information "out of the general file and in a special file." Unwilling to honor this request, Hoover immediately shared Alsop's admission, along with other information that the FBI had independently collected about Alsop's sexuality, with Attorney General Herbert Brownell and White House aide Sherman Adams.[59]

An ardent anti-Communist, Alsop continued to criticize Soviet defense and foreign-policy decisions and, consistent with his advocacy of a militant anti-Soviet foreign policy, emerged in 1958–1959 as a strident critic of the Eisenhower administration's defense-spending cuts as contributing to a "missile gap" that favored the Soviets and as "playing Russian roulette with the whole course of human history at stake."[60]

Incensed by Alsop's criticisms, all the more so given the syndicated columnist's influence, Attorney General William Rogers (Brownell's successor) asked Hoover in April 1959 to "get together what we [FBI] have on Alsop as he [Rogers] believed very few people knew about" Alsop's homosexuality, possibly including President Eisenhower. He intended to brief the president, Secretary of Defense Neil McElroy, Under Secretary of State Christian Herter, White House aide Wilton Persons, and Secretary to the Cabinet Robert Gray about Alsop's homosexuality and the Moscow incident, Rogers told Hoover, but he would not "take the responsibility for such information going any further."[61]

One of those briefed, General Nathan Twining, the chairman of the Joint Chiefs of Staff, reacted bitterly by "wonder[ing] how Alsop could be trusted" and asserted that administration officials had "an obligation to let some of the [newspaper] publishers [who carried Alsop's column] know of this incident." In addition, President Eisenhower and White House Press Secretary James Hagerty purposefully circulated this information about Alsop's "moral character," with Hagerty describing Alsop to another journalist as a "fag" and threatening to "lift his White House pass."[62]

President Johnson, in contrast, confronted a more serious political problem, as by 1966–1967, his administration's Vietnam War policy increasingly encountered public opposition, opposition that was strengthened by critical press reports that challenged the president's positive characterization of the progress of the war. In a concerted attempt to discredit his militant critics, Johnson turned to the FBI (and also the Central Intelligence Agency [CIA]) to develop evidence linking antiwar dissent with international Communism, showing that militant activists were acting at the direction and control of the Soviet Union and Communist China. In a companion initiative, President Johnson solicited FBI "name checks" (that is, checks of FBI files for all information about identified individuals) on his prominent media critics: NBC commentator David Brinkley, AP reporter Peter Arnett, *New York Times* reporter Salisbury, syndicated columnist Kraft, *Life* magazine Washington Bureau Chief Richard Stolley, *Chicago Daily News* Washington Bureau Chief Lisagor, and *Washington Post* executive Gilbert.[63]

FBI officials, moreover, did not simply respond to White House requests but, in addition, sought administration support to silence their own media critics.[64] In February 1941, for example, Hoover alerted the White House to the influence of *New York Daily News* reporter John O'Donnell over his paper's editorial policy. The FBI director cited O'Donnell's stories describing Roosevelt as "a war monger," Hoover as emulating the tactics of former Attorney General A. Mitchell Palmer, the FBI as "preparing to go on a 'witch hunt' against subversive elements," and the American people as "becoming aware of the fact that they are being 'sold down the river.'" O'Donnell, Hoover added, wrote that "Hitler should be permitted to do as he pleases" and that the United States "should mind its own business and stop meddling in Europe and Latin America."[65]

Emboldened by the changed political climate brought about by the devastating Japanese surprise attack on Pearl Harbor, President Roosevelt and FBI Director Hoover sought to settle scores with their mutual media critic, the *Chicago Tribune*. One week prior to the attack, the *Tribune* and its sister paper, the *Washington Times-Herald*, had obtained and then on December 1, 1941, published a copy of the Joint Army and Navy Board's contingency war plans. As the United States was not a military participant, the *Tribune*'s publication of these plans precipitated congressional and public inquiries as to why the administration was preparing for war. These criticisms were silenced with the Pearl Harbor attack and the German declaration of war. Nonetheless, an infuriated Roosevelt demanded that the FBI identify the source of this leak. FBI agents were unable to identify the source, with Hoover citing as the reason the carelessness of army officials when distributing seventy-five copies of this plan. Hoover nonetheless concluded that the source was a "high army officer" (General Albert Wedemeyer) and that the administration's isolationist critics had access to this officer and to an army "group" that was "bitterly opposed to the President's Lend Lease program, anti-Nazi" policy.[66]

FBI officials thereupon sought to exploit the administration's concerns to settle a score with the *Chicago Tribune*, having become incensed over *Tribune* reporter Chesly Manly's article reporting that the FBI's inept surveillance of Japanese consular officials in Hawaii had enabled the successful Japanese attack on Pearl Harbor. Dismissing these criticisms as "gross fabrications" and a "malicious tissue of lies," the FBI director urged Attorney General Biddle to convene "a Grand Jury proceeding" over the *Tribune*'s publication of the war-plans article. During these grand-jury proceedings, Hoover emphasized, department attorneys could question Manly, as well as other staff members of the *Chicago Tribune*, *New York Daily News*, and *Washington Times-Herald*, "under oath as to their utterly inexcusable actions in securing and publishing" the war-plans document and at the same time question Manly about his Pearl Harbor article. "Some measure" must be taken to "curb such 'smear' tactics," the FBI director protested, adding that Manly's Pearl Harbor article, and other articles critical of the FBI, were "a well planned 'smear' campaign" that would "continue and no doubt become intensified unless it is met and exposed for what it is."[67]

Justice Department officials eventually decided to forego seeking an indictment in the war-plans case. They did attempt, however, to indict *Tribune* officials for publishing, and reporter Stanley Johnson for writing, another article in June 1942 containing "secret" information about Japanese Naval strength in the Pacific. The grand jury, however, refused to return an indictment in this case, as the jurors demanded that the government specify "what harm the publication [of the article] had done." The U.S. Navy Department refused to provide such evidence, fearing that disclosure even in a secret grand-jury session could compromise "intelligence methods and the inferences that the Japs could draw" from the *Tribune*'s publication (that the United States had broken the Japanese code). This refusal forced the Justice Department to abandon this effort. Hoover, nonetheless, attempted to exploit this opportunity by poisoning the president's mind about reporter Johnson's character and loyalty. In a four-page report, the FBI director first recounted the history of the published article and then portrayed the Australian immigrant as a "heavy drinker" who had falsely claimed to have been an Australian Army officer and who, prior to immigrating to the United States and while a correspondent in Europe, had close ties with German officials.[68]

Hoover further attempted to heighten President Roosevelt's antipathy toward the *Tribune* in this case by recounting the contents of a telegram that the *Tribune*'s publisher Robert McCormick sent to his paper's Washington-based reporter Arthur Henning.[69] In this telegram, McCormick advised Henning that President Roosevelt had intervened to settle a "violent disagreement" between the U.S. and British Army staffs over the dispatch of U.S. troops to "various foreign ports." McCormick further promised to send Henning a follow-up letter "relative to this entire plan." If McCormick did send the promised follow-up letter, the FBI director apparently was unable to obtain a copy.[70]

President Roosevelt in any event welcomed such intelligence. Personally offended by the criticisms of the isolationist and Fascist press, he frequently queried upon receipt of copies of these publications, "Is anything being done about this?" or "I think that the FBI can run down things like this." Criticizing "some" of the statements of pro-Fascist activists William Pelley and Albert Kahn as "pretty close to being seditious," he contended that "now that we are at war," "it looks like a good chance to clean up a number of these vile publications."[71]

Because Justice Department officials hesitated to prosecute the offending publications and their publishers, Hoover solicited the intercession of the White House by exploiting a March 1942 White House request for "action taken against publishers of seditious matter." Although "much seditious writing and publishing is going on in the country," Hoover advised White House aide Stephen Early that "his hands were tied by the Attorney General" and that "until some of the Attorney General's instructions were changed his agents could not operate." The FBI director then cited "case after case" where FBI agents "had been blocked by the Attorney General time and time again." Early reaffirmed the president's "insistence" on "action on seditious cases" and instructed Hoover to inform the attorney general of Roosevelt's "desires." Agreeing to "do this immediately," Hoover cautioned that "it would be necessary for the President to talk to the Attorney General before he [Hoover] would be permitted to act in these cases." Within the week, Roosevelt asked Biddle to "speak to me" about the matter of "seditious publications in the United States—the clear and present danger."[72]

The attorney general did authorize prosecution, but only of pro-Fascist publications. Nonetheless, bowing to this pressure, he ordered Justice Department attorneys to conduct a "content analysis" of "selected" *Chicago Tribune*, *New York Daily News*, and *New York Journal American* editorials published since U.S. military involvement in World War II "in terms of consistency and contradictions of manifest statements with respect to 16 major Nazi radio themes." The completed study concluded only that these newspapers were "critical" of some of the administration's or its allies' war policies and that "too few of the themes" in the sixteen selected Nazi radio broadcasts "occur" in the editorials.[73]

A concern over the influence of press critics of his domestic- and foreign-policy decisions also underpinned an earlier, and politically explosive, request of Roosevelt's of July 1940. In this case, in an attempt to discredit an influential critic of the president's recent foreign-policy initiatives, former Republican President Herbert Hoover, Assistant Secretary of State Adolf Berle on July 2, 1940, requested an FBI investigation of the former president. President Roosevelt had learned from reporter Marquis Childs, Berle confided, "that while Mr. Herbert Hoover and his former secretary, Larry Ritchey

[Richey] were attending the Republican National Convention in Chicago they addressed certain cablegrams to former Premier [Pierre] Laval of France." After describing Laval as "the Fascist Leader in France," Berle claimed that Herbert Hoover's and Richey's purpose was "to endeavor to obtain some statement from Laval indicating that President Roosevelt had made definite commitments to send men to France to fight for France in the present war." The alleged overture to Laval, Berle continued, was "subject to official inquiry," because Herbert Hoover and Richey had "injected themselves into international entre [sic] . . . and so related to the operation of the Federal Government." FBI Director Hoover was thereupon asked to "determine what messages, if any, of the type were sent by Mr. Hoover and Mr. Ritchey [sic] and what replies were received."

Hoover honored this request and immediately specified how the investigation was to be conducted. FBI agents checked "various trans-Atlantic communications" but were unable to "disclose that any such messages were sent." Berle was immediately "advised" of this failure.[74]

FBI officials, however, were not blind servants of the White House. Indeed, their intelligence investigations reflected their own far more conservative conceptions of "subversive" threats, which extended even to monitoring the political activities and associations of First Lady Eleanor Roosevelt. The political sensitivity of such operations, given the adverse consequences for Hoover's tenure as FBI director, necessitated great caution to avert discovery. FBI officials, nonetheless, directly and indirectly, sought to learn about Mrs. Roosevelt's political objectives and associations and, as important, to acquire derogatory personal information about the First Lady, and, when appropriate and safe to do so, to utilize the accumulated information (really misinformation) to besmirch her personal character.

One such indirect effort involved an FBI break-in of the New York City headquarters of the American Youth Congress (AYC). Formed in 1934 to lobby for legislation helpful to young Americans, the AYC eventually came to be dominated by radical activists. The idealism of its membership commanded Mrs. Roosevelt's financial and moral support dating from the organization's formation until mid-1940 (when the First Lady broke with the AYC leadership over its strident opposition to her husband's interventionist foreign policy). Thus, when HUAC launched an investigation of the AYC in 1939, Mrs. Roosevelt personally attended its hearings to demonstrate her belief in the loyalty of the organization's leaders. At times, she even invited AYC members to the White House to meet the president.

Mrs. Roosevelt's relations with the AYC leadership became strained in the late 1940s owing to the AYC's attacks on her husband's foreign policy as promoting "war hysteria" and the organization's opposition to the peacetime draft as an attempt to "Hitlerize" America. She nonetheless continued to support the AYC financially until May 1941, when AYC leaders ignored her advice to denounce Stalin as well as Hitler. By July 1941, she severed all ties with the organization.

Worried about her continued contact with AYC leaders, FBI officials approved a break-in in January 1942 of the AYC's New York City headquarters. Mrs. Roosevelt's extensive correspondence with the organization's leadership was photocopied and duly forwarded to FBI headquarters in Washington, where, on receipt, FBI Director Hoover demanded, "These should be carefully reviewed & analyzed." FBI officials complied, subsequently advising the FBI director that "the pertinent information [is] set forth in a blue memorandum for you."[75] When reporting this analysis to Hoover, FBI Assistant Director Ladd remarked, "The attached material is identical with much of the previously received material," confirming that this was not the first FBI break-in of AYC headquarters.[76]

FBI officials, again indirectly, willingly accepted from Military Intelligence Division (MID) officials politically explosive, if wholly inaccurate, information about Mrs. Roosevelt's alleged affair with Joseph Lash. MID officials had acquired this misinformation in the course of an investigation of Lash, an army recruit at the time and radical activist who during the 1930s as an AYC leader had developed and sustained a close personal relationship with Mrs. Roosevelt. An MID counterintelligence unit intensively monitored Lash's current activities and associations during his assignment as an army trainee at Chanute Field (near Urbana, Illinois). This investigation, which began in February 1943, intercepted his personal correspondence with Mrs. Roosevelt and his wife-to-be, Trude Pratt; wiretapped at least one of his conversations with Mrs. Roosevelt; monitored his March 5–7, 1943, meetings with Mrs. Roosevelt at the Urbana-Lincoln Hotel; monitored and bugged his meetings with Pratt on March 12–14, 1943, at the Urbana-Lincoln Hotel, including photocopying their personal papers; and monitored his meeting with Mrs. Roosevelt at the Chicago Blackstone Hotel on March 27–28, 1943.

The MID unit's interception of Lash's correspondence with Mrs. Roosevelt and Pratt in February–March 1943 only intensified the concerns of MID officials. On the basis of this intercepted correspondence, Colonel Paul Boyer, who headed the Chanute counterintelligence unit that monitored Lash, advised his superior, Colonel John Bissell, of his concern over Lash's "subversive" objectives, his interest in securing an officer's commission, and Mrs. Roosevelt's support for such a commission. The Chanute Field commander, Boyer further advised Bissell, was "anxious to remove" Lash from the military base to forestall this promotion and "would cooperate in any way to get [Lash] another assignment," adding that another district assistant chief of staff would also "cooperate to the fullest extent with this office in any handling of the case." Unfortunately, Boyer continued, his and Bissell's plan to have Lash arrested on a "morals" charge (given their earlier discoveries of his sexual relations with Pratt during their weekend tryst of March 12–14 and Pratt's existing marriage to another man, although she was in the process of obtaining a divorce) had been aborted. Boyer had learned that Lash planned to meet Pratt in Chicago over the weekend of April 3 and intended to arrange for the Chicago police to arrest him "with no complications whatever and in such a manner that there would be no publicity [about the military's role]" and further that "it might be thought advisable to give the arrest sufficient publicity that E.R. [Eleanor Roosevelt] would not care to intercede in the matter." Boyer then detailed the reason for this plan—Lash's intercepted correspondence with Mrs. Roosevelt indicated "a gigantic conspiracy participated by not only [Lash] and Trude Pratt but also by E.R., [Vice President Henry] Wallace, [Treasury Secretary] Morgenthau, etc." Boyer's proposed plan was first aborted when Lash's April visit with Pratt was delayed, but then it was not revived, as General George Marshall disbanded the Boyer unit.

Marshall's order disbanding this unit had been triggered by Mrs. Roosevelt's inadvertent discovery, on leaving the Blackstone Hotel in late March 1943, that MID agents had monitored her stay (having been so advised by hotel officials). Upon returning to Washington, Mrs. Roosevelt protested this invasion of her privacy (having rejected even Secret Service protection) to White House aide Harry Hopkins, who, in turn, contacted General Marshall. The general's decision to disband this unit centered on its violation of MID's delimitation agreement with the FBI (under which MID agents were barred from monitoring civilian political activities). In addition, Marshall ordered the destruction of this unit's surveillance records.

Rather than destroying the records of the unit's surveillance of Lash, and thus Mrs. Roosevelt, in December 1943, Colonel Edgar Kibler (at the time the head of MID's counterintelligence corps) advised George Burton (the FBI liaison to MID) that "powerful elements within or near the War Department" had dismembered the military's counterintelligence corps. President Roosevelt, Kibler explained, had been told that a military counterintelligence unit had bugged Mrs. Roosevelt's hotel room in Chicago, recording her sexual affair with Lash, and had immediately ordered that the corps be "wrecked"; that "anyone who knew about this case should be immediately relieved of his duties and sent to the South Pacific for action against the Japs until they were killed"; that Lash be sent "within ten hours" to an overseas combat post, and that Colonel Bissell (Kibler's predecessor as head of the counterintelligence corps) be blackballed from promotion to lieutenant general.[77] Burton readily accepted from Kibler the unit's surveillance records as well as Kibler's misinformation (reported in his Do Not File memorandum to FBI Assistant Director Ladd) concerning a Lash-Roosevelt affair. Burton's Do Not File memorandum on this meeting and the MID surveillance reports were immediately forwarded to Hoover and were maintained in the FBI director's secret office file.[78]

Because the reports were kept in nonrecord records (that is, neither serialized nor indexed in the FBI's central records system), FBI officials were in a position to exploit this misinformation when it was safe to do so. Thus, when FBI Assistant Director Nichols was approached by Waldrop (the editor of the militantly anti–New Deal *Washington Times-Herald*) in 1949 with the news that he was "on the trail of certain recordings that allegedly show an illicit relationship between Lash and Mrs. Roosevelt" (MID officials had been quietly circulating this rumor), Nichols purposely did not confirm the rumor; doing so would have required disclosing the FBI's possession of the MID surveillance records. Again, in late 1950, Jack Anderson, an assistant to syndicated columnist Pearson, based on a rumor that conservative Republican Senator Arthur Watkins circulated, asked Nichols whether the FBI had ever investigated the "Roosevelt-Lash incident." "It is obvious," Nichols then concluded, "that Anderson probably has learned of the file from G-2 [MID] sources and from rumors which had been circulated in Washington." Nichols immediately directed FBI Assistant Director Stanley Tracy to ensure that the FBI's possession of the military-surveillance records could not be discovered. After confirming that no such information was included in the FBI's "main files" and that all FBI personnel knowledgeable about the receipt of the Lash material (including secretaries in Nichols's and Hoover's offices) were trustworthy, Tracy was instructed to inform Senator Watkins, and to have the senator so inform Anderson, that he "had checked at the FBI and FBI files do not contain[79] any such information."[80]

Nichols's wariness in 1949–1950 stemmed from the fact that the current president, Truman, was a New Deal Democrat. FBI officials abandoned this caution, however, following Eisenhower's election to the presidency in November 1952. The first opportunity to exploit this derogatory information occurred in early January 1953. At this time, George Murphy and Francis Alstock, two of Eisenhower's campaign advisers, secured a meeting with Nichols to brief the FBI assistant director about the president-elect's intended senior appointments and interest in forging a cooperative relationship with the FBI. During this briefing, they advised the FBI assistant director that "the General [President-elect Eisenhower] has a thorough distrust, distaste and dislike for Eleanor [Roosevelt] and told [Secretary of State–designate John Foster] Dulles several times to get her out of the picture [as U.S. ambassador to the United Nations]."

Nichols responded by confidentially advising Murphy and Alstock about the alleged Roosevelt-Lash affair. Conceding that "as long as Eleanor was in the picture, she would not become the object of any Congressional investigation," Alstock observed, "sooner or later there was going to be an investigation of her affair with Joe Lash."[81]

Mrs. Roosevelt might have been gotten "out of the picture," but FBI officials nonetheless continued to monitor her political activities during the 1950s (and report their findings to the Eisenhower White House). Then, on February 2, 1954, Nichols pointed out to FBI Director Hoover that President Eisenhower might not "know of the furor that was caused in G-2 some years ago as the result of G-2's investigation of Joe Lash and his connections with Mrs. Roosevelt." After summarizing the misinformation about the Lash-Roosevelt affair (based on Burton's Do Not File memo), Nichols urged the FBI director to "consider mentioning this incident" to President Eisenhower and explained why this might be timely: "Joe Lash is a close friend of [New York Post editor] Jimmy Wechsler and the last word I had was that Joe Lash was working for the New York Post which has been exceedingly critical of the President as well as of us. Wechsler, of course, is a kingpin in the Americans for Democratic Action along with Mrs. Roosevelt."[82]

FBI officials, moreover, on their own sought to confirm the rumors of the Lash-Roosevelt affair (and another rumor about her alleged affair with her bodyguard and driver, Earl Miller). On the one hand, FBI agent Thomas Spencer was directed to confirm Mrs. Roosevelt's affair with Lash. Spencer thereupon monitored Mrs. Roosevelt's townhouse in New York City, discreetly inquiring of the doorman about Mrs. Roosevelt's relationship with Lash. A second FBI agent was assigned to verify the rumor of Mrs. Roosevelt's affair with Miller. Wearing the uniform of a milk driver and driving the route in upstate New York where Mrs. Roosevelt resided, the disguised FBI agent brashly entered the residence to discover Mrs. Roosevelt in her housecoat having breakfast with Miller. FBI officials concluded in both cases that they had uncovered Mrs. Roosevelt's sexual affairs.[83]

FBI officials sought similar information (or misinformation) about other liberal politicians, extending even to Democratic presidential nominee and Illinois Governor Adlai Stevenson.

Senior FBI officials first became interested in Stevenson in the late 1930s and early 1940s through agent reports about the young attorney and New Deal Democrat's membership in or associations with various Popular Front and other organizations considered to be "subversive." That interest peaked in April 1952, triggered by an uncorroborated report about his alleged homosexuality, an interest that continued for decades and that led to the retention of such misinformation in Hoover's secret office file.

When the folder recording all derogatory personal and political information about Stevenson was first incorporated in Hoover's secret office file in April 1952, the Illinois governor had disavowed any interest in being considered for the 1952 Democratic presidential nomination (his name having circulated after President Truman's February 1952 announcement disavowing any interest in being renominated). No clear choice emerged during the ensuing primaries and state conventions, ensuring an open convention when the Democratic delegates assembled in Chicago in July. Stevenson's welcoming speech (as governor) electrified the convention, and a combination of liberal activists and the Chicago Democratic machine orchestrated a successful campaign to draft him as the Democratic nominee. Agreeing to be formally nominated on July 24, Stevenson won the support of a majority of the delegates the next day.

Stevenson's name had first surfaced in April as a possible Democratic presidential nominee. Immediately Hoover's aides—in what by then was a standard practice—prepared a "summary memorandum" recording whatever derogatory personal and political information that FBI agents had already compiled about the prominent Democrat. An updated "summary" was once again prepared in July, on the very day that Stevenson won the Democratic nomination. This summary, however, included the homosexual allegation that had first been reported on April 17 (two weeks after the preparation of the April summary).

Hoover's folder on Stevenson continued to burgeon thereafter, particularly when FBI officials either welcomed or sought to confirm allegations of Stevenson's homosexuality. In late November 1952, for example, former FBI agent C. Robert Love, in an unsolicited letter, informed Hoover that Stevenson "was homosexual." Personally thanking Love for his thoughtfulness in providing this intelligence, the FBI director added his letter to his ever-increasing file on Stevenson. This file expanded in 1956, when the 1952 "summary" memorandum on Stevenson was updated following the Illinois governor's renomination as the Democratic presidential nominee. Then, when Kennedy won election to the presidency in 1960 and appointed Stevenson as UN ambassador, FBI officials briefed key White House aides about Stevenson's alleged homosexuality. In December 1961, the derogatory comments about Stevenson's alleged homosexuality were supplemented by a report that the then UN ambassador, during a visit to Lima, Peru, had taken a particular interest in the Peruvian Museum of Archeology's "collection of highly pornographic Inca statuettes."[84]

Because the contents of Hoover's office file were not serialized or indexed in the FBI's central records system, the FBI director (and his key aides) could truthfully deny that the FBI had investigated Stevenson and maintained files containing derogatory information on his personal character, political views, and associations. This system proved essential at least on five occasions.

Thus, when Democratic National Committee officials learned in August 1952 that Guy Hottel, the FBI's Washington SAC, was "spreading word that Stevenson was a 'queer' [and] that the FBI had a file on him," FBI officials squelched this story by formally interviewing Hottel and then preparing a report of his categorical denials of any knowledge of any FBI "file" on Stevenson[85] and of having been present at the time and place when the rumored remark had been made. This report was immediately forwarded to Attorney General James McGranery.[86]

The second and third occasions were potentially more serious. On January 19, 1953, the last day of Truman's presidency, White House aide Donald Dawson contacted the FBI's White House liaison and reported having "heard that the Bureau had investigated Adlai E. Stevenson and desired to obtain copies of the reports." On Hoover's direct order, Dawson was told that "the Bureau had not conducted an investigation [of Stevenson] in recent years and that, if it was desired, a further check would be made into old records."[87] Dawson did not press the issue and merely thanked the FBI liaison for "checking into this matter." However, had he requested the further check, the FBI liaison would have told him that the FBI had investigated Stevenson in 1937 at the time of his application for an appointment in the Justice Department.[88]

Earlier, on August 29, 1952, FBI Assistant Director Nichols briefed Hoover about his recent meeting with Milt Hill, a former Washington-based reporter who had been hired by Arthur Summerfield, the chair of the Republican National Committee, to (in Nichols's phrasing) "do the official Republican biography of Governor Stevenson." Hill at this time briefed Nichols about his recent meeting with Orval Yarger, a former FBI agent who, after retiring from the FBI, obtained employment in the purchasing department of the State of Illinois.

Yarger had told him, Hill informed Nichols, about derogatory information about Stevenson on the condition that he would not disclose his former association with the FBI. Nichols and Hill then discussed how this information about alleged corruption and sexual "deviance" could be exploited. On the one hand, Nichols dismissed Hill's suggestion that the FBI investigate the corruption charges, pointing out that the U.S. attorneys "are Democrats." They then discussed Hill's report and solicitation of FBI confirmation that "some years ago . . . Stevenson was arrested on a morals charge [in New York City], put up bond, and elected to forfeit," and for this reason his wife had divorced him. Already aware of Stevenson's alleged homosexuality, Nichols apparently assured Hill of the reasonableness of this rumor.[89]

Following Eisenhower's election, FBI officials, moreover, were more willing to directly assist Republican political operatives. Thus, during the 1956 presidential election, Deputy Attorney General Rogers asked Nichols in September whether the FBI had a "criminal record" about an individual, whose name the FBI has withheld, who had given a picnic, attended by Stevenson, at his Annandale, Virginia, estate. Nichols honored this request, but, because the FBI has withheld his two-and-a-half page report, it remains unclear what specific information was provided. Then, in late October, Dorothy Donnelly, one of Vice President Nixon's secretaries, asked Nichols (on behalf of the vice president) for background information about two of Stevenson's campaign aides, Nixon having been told that they were or had been Communists. Nichols directed Donnelly to "check with the House Committee on Un-American Activities" but concurrently had his aides prepare summary memoranda detailing whatever derogatory personal and political information that the FBI had compiled on the two individuals, which Nichols apparently provided directly to the vice president (and not to his secretary). Hoover had earlier in December 1953 reported this background information about one of the two individuals, Stevenson speechwriter and later Secretary of Labor Willard Wirtz, to White House aide Adams.[90]

FBI officials' interest in collecting information about suspected homosexuals, in any event, extended beyond prominent personalities, such as Stevenson. This interest intensified during the cold war years, given the prevailing conviction that homosexuals were potential security risks and that, as in the case of suspected Communists, they should be barred from government employment. Significantly, the issue of "homosexuals in Government" first surfaced as a political issue in early 1950 as a by-product of Senator Joseph McCarthy's dramatic emergence to national prominence when accusing the Truman administration of knowingly harboring "Communists in the State Department."

In late February 1950, the Democratic Senate leadership had responded to Senator McCarthy's claim to having evidence that eighty-one Communists were employed in the State Department by appointing a special committee, chaired by Senator Millard Tydings, to investigate his claimed evidence. At the time, Democratic senators were confident that the Wisconsin senator could not substantiate his charges and that this inquiry would not only discredit McCarthy but also in the process subvert a recent strategy of Republican politicians that attributed the "fall" of China and the "loss" of Eastern Europe to the Roosevelt and Truman administrations' "softness toward communism."

Prominent Republicans (notably, Republican National Committee Chair Guy Gabrielson, New York Governor Thomas Dewey, and Senate Minority Whip Kenneth Wherry) did rise to McCarthy's defense in April–May 1950. They did so warily, at the same time seeking to distance the fortunes of the Republican Party from the irresponsible senator (it seemed at the time that McCarthy could not sustain his charges). But they concurrently adopted a parallel line of attack—condemning as well the Truman administration's tolerance of "homosexuals in government." Gabrielson, for one, pointedly claimed that "sex perverts who have infiltrated our government in recent years" were "perhaps as dangerous as the actual communists." The Truman administration, he further charged, had also sought to ensure that radio and newspaper commentators could not "adequately" present to the public "the facts" about this homosexual menace.

The "homosexuals in government" charge was in reality as bogus as McCarthy's "communists in government." The evidence consisted solely of State Department officials' admission that ninety-one "sex perverts" had been fired since the establishment of the Federal Employee Loyalty Program in 1947 and the publicized speculation of a Washington, D.C., vice squad officer. Based on his experience, this officer had projected as a "quick guess," during congressional testimony, that 3,500 "sex perverts" were employed in the federal bureaucracy, of whom 300 to 400 were State Department employees.[91]

To address this alleged security threat, the Senate Democratic leadership in the late spring of 1950 authorized a companion investigation to evaluate this security threat. Chaired by North Carolina Senator Clyde Hoey, this committee conducted its hearings in secret, given the delicacy of the matter, releasing its findings in December 1950. The Hoey Committee's final report decried the dangerous security problem that the employment of "sex perverts" posed, criticized federal officials for having failed to take "adequate steps to get these people out of government," and recommended stricter screening measures to prevent their future employment. The findings, however, were not based on hard evidence. Committee members, in fact, conceded that they could not document the precise number of homosexual federal employees. The statistical section of the Hoey Committee's report, moreover, suggested that the threat was minor at best: Only 574 of the 4,954 "sex perverts" uncovered since the inception of the Federal Employee Loyalty Program in March 1947 held civilian appointments, with the remaining 4,380 employed in the military (the vast majority of whom were inductees). No recent example of betrayal by a homosexual employee was cited. In effect discounting its own findings, the committee uncritically endorsed the unsupported claims of federal intelligence officials who categorically asserted that homosexual employees constituted a serious security threat, their "lack of emotional stability" and "weakness of their moral fiber" rendering them "susceptible to the blandishments of foreign espionage agents."[92]

The Hoey Committee's recommendation of more-effective screening procedures proved to be a godsend for FBI officials. FBI investigations would be required to identify applicant or incumbent homosexual employees. And an instituted screening program would permit FBI officials to use information that FBI agents had already collected but until then could not have been otherwise used, insofar as homosexuality was not a federal crime. Indeed, well before 1950 (in fact, beginning in 1937), FBI agents had begun compiling reports about alleged homosexuals, although FBI officials responded differently, depending on the subjects of the allegations.

In those cases when learning of rumors that FBI Director Hoover was homosexual, FBI agents were required to identify the purveyor of these rumors to their superiors (who, in turn, alerted Hoover), no matter how nebulous or even if the rumor was never publicly disseminated (because, for example, gossipy commentary at private bridge club or dinner parties). FBI agents had to take this reporting requirement seriously. Their failure to do so could result in severe reprimands, should Hoover learn of their derelictions. Agents would then visit Hoover's accuser, demand documentation of the allegation, and adopt intimidation tactics, such as threatening bodily harm or a libel suit.[93]

In contrast, FBI agents automatically reported all other homosexual allegations without establishing their validity, and their uncorroborated reports were incorporated in the individual's case file. No follow-up attempt was generally made to verify the allegation. Moreover, such allegations were routinely cited whenever FBI officials prepared summaries about the individual (for example, for submission to a loyalty review board or in response to a White House inquiry). The exceptional case of Senator Henry Cabot Lodge, Jr., highlights this indifference to accuracy. An incredible November 1950 allegation of Lodge's homosexuality was automatically cited in prepared summaries on Lodge until December 1952. Then, because President-elect Eisenhower had requested an FBI security check on Lodge prior to nominating him as U.S. ambassador to the United Nations, senior FBI officials for the first time evaluated the validity of this allegation included in an FBI summary on Lodge. A cursory inquiry confirmed its falseness, and, in this case, the allegation was not included in the FBI report submitted to Eisenhower. FBI officials could not risk disclosing to the new president that FBI files contained often unsubstantiated or derogatory personal information.[94]

This practice of collecting and maintaining derogatory personal information about suspected homosexuals as a matter of course was not purposeless. FBI officials recognized the value of such information, given the prevailing homophobia. Not surprisingly, then, FBI Director Hoover moved quickly to exploit the publicity that the public release of the Hoey Committee report triggered. In April 1951 testimony before a House appropriations subcommittee, Hoover cited the FBI's expanded investigative responsibilities under the Federal Employee Loyalty Program to justify the FBI's increased funding request. "Derogatory information," he then asserted, had been uncovered on 14,484 of the 3,225,000 incumbent and applicant federal employees, and since April 1950 FBI investigations had identified 406 "sex deviates" in government service.[95]

Then, on June 20, 1951, the FBI director purposefully exploited this new security opportunity and instituted a code-named Sex Deviate program "for forwarding information concerning allegations [of homosexuality] concerning present and past employees of any branch of the United States government." Under this program, FBI officials disseminated information about identified "sex deviates" to the various federal agency loyalty boards; to the White House; to "specific individuals" in both houses of Congress, the Library of Congress, the Government Accounting Office, the Government Printing Office, and the Botanical Gardens; and to "specified individuals" in the judiciary.

To fulfill this dissemination objective, FBI officials devised an efficient retrieval system to ensure that no reported instance of homosexuality would be lost in the FBI's massive case files. A special Sex Deviate index-card file was created that listed all alleged homosexuals, their current occupations, and the file numbers of the reports upon which the listings of the individuals had been based. To ensure that the FBI's interest in and dissemination of information about homosexuality could not be discovered, this special index-card file was maintained separate from official FBI records—permitting FBI officials to deny, truthfully, that the FBI's "central records system" included any record of the FBI's monitoring of illicit but noncriminal sexual activities.

When creating the Sex Deviate program, Hoover's original purpose had been to identify homosexual government employees. The program almost immediately expanded to include compiling and indexing such information about individuals who were not federal employees—such as Illinois Governor Stevenson and Bradley University President David Owen. FBI officials were soon emboldened to use the acquired information. An extant October 28, 1954, FBI memo, for example, records that "in appropriate instances where the best interests of the Bureau is served, information concerning sex deviates employed either by institutions of higher learning or law enforcement agencies is disseminated to proper officials of such organizations." This memo recounts two occasions when Hoover "instructed" his key aides to "confidentially make available to George Washington University information concerning sex deviates or communists employed as teachers there" and "confidentially" to advise a "contact" at New York University "as to sex deviate practices of an instructor who was involved in the Police Training Field."[96]

7

Ignoring the Lessons
of the Cold War

Secrecy had enabled Federal Bureau of Investigation (FBI) officials (and, as well, those of the Central Intelligence Agency [CIA] and the National Security Agency [NSA]) to avoid public scrutiny of their abuses of power throughout the World War II and cold war years. This success in avoiding accountability seemingly ended in the early 1970s. The Lyndon Johnson and Richard Nixon administrations' conduct of the Vietnam War had increased public skepticism about the wisdom of deferring to presidential national-security claims and provoked an attendant questioning about the role of the U.S. intelligence agencies. Then, a cascading series of developments in the early 1970s combined to finally breach the wall of secrecy that had heretofore shrouded White House, FBI, CIA, and NSA operations. The first of these involved the discovery in 1970 that FBI agents had monitored those attending and planning Earth Day rallies, followed by the public release of thousands of pages of FBI records illegally obtained by radical activists through a break-in of the FBI's resident agency in Media, Pennsylvania. The widespread dissemination of these pilfered FBI records in turn led to NBC correspondent Carl Stern's successful Freedom of Information Act (FOIA) suit that brought about the release of the FBI's now-infamous COINTELPRO records. These records confirmed that FBI agents, with the approval of senior officials at FBI headquarters, had harassed and disrupted radical organizations and their adherents. The subsequent special Senate committee inquiry of 1973 into the Watergate break-in and resultant uncovering of the Nixon

White House cover-up added a further dimension—the Nixon White House had secretly exploited the resources of the FBI and the CIA for political purposes, with White House and intelligence-agency officials willingly resorting to illegal investigative techniques. This evolving scandal culminated with the publication in December 1974 of Seymour Hersh's front page *New York Times* expose of the CIA's massive and illegal domestic-surveillance program, Operation MHCHAOS, and then Attorney General Edward Levi's disclosure during February 1975 testimony before a House Judiciary Subcommittee that former FBI Director J. Edgar Hoover had maintained a secret office file containing dossiers on the personal and political activities of prominent Americans, including members of Congress.

In response, in 1975, the House and Senate created special committees (the so-called Church and Pike Committees) to investigate FBI, CIA, and NSA operations and their White House relationships. For the first time, congressional committees obtained unprecedented access to the heretofore secret records of the U.S. intelligence agencies, many of which had been created on the premise that they would forever remain secret. These records documented the FBI's widespread abuses of power dating from the mid-1930s:[1] the extensive use of illegal investigative techniques, the monitoring of the personal and political activities of liberal and radical activists (notably, prominent civil-rights leader Martin Luther King, Jr.), and the implementation of the code-named COINTELPRO program to "harass, disrupt, and discredit" targeted organizations and their members.

The House and Senate committees, however, failed to explore the record of FBI counterintelligence operations (the ostensible reason for the FBI's shift from law enforcement to intelligence and for the secret authorization of illegal investigative techniques). For one, despite having closely monitored Soviet agents stationed in the United States (as consular, embassy, or press officials or employees of the Soviet trading corporation, Amtorg) and having massively monitored members of the U.S. Communist Party (with the use of illegal investigative techniques—wiretaps, bugs, break-ins, and mail opening), FBI agents nonetheless failed to uncover Soviet atomic and industrial espionage operations during World War II. These included the espionage activities of Justice Department employee Judith Coplon; of four individuals employed at the Manhattan atomic bomb project, George Koval and Russell McNutt (at Oak Ridge, Tennessee), David Greenglass and Theodore Hall (at Los Alamos, New Mexico), and their recruiters or collaborators Julius Rosenberg, Harry Gold, Saville Sax, and Lona Cohen; of employees in private defense industries having government military contracts, notably Rosenberg, Joel Barr, and Alfred Sarant; and of employees in sensitive government offices, notably Nathan Silvermaster, Victor Perlo, Harry Dexter White, and Alger Hiss.

The after-the-fact discoveries of these espionage activities in late 1945–

1950, some of which had been conducted during the 1930s and others in 1944–1945 (in Coplon's case, continuing until her arrest in 1949), moreover, was due less to FBI investigations than to simple good luck: in the cases of Silvermaster, Perlo, White, and Hiss, to the defections of former Communist couriers Elizabeth Bentley and Whittaker Chambers; and in the cases of Coplon, Rosenberg, Greenglass, Hall, Sax, Barr, and Sarant, to the skill of military intelligence agents in deciphering intercepted Soviet consular messages.[2]

Despite commanding intrusive and illegal surveillance powers, FBI agents had failed to uncover the above-listed Soviet espionage operations. In part, this failure was due to the professionalism of the Soviet agents, who had adopted well-crafted methods to preclude discovery. After all, spies (and terrorists) assume that they are being closely monitored and their communications intercepted. This failure was also the inevitable consequence of the key premise governing FBI "intelligence" operations—that monitoring the political associations and labor-union and civil-rights activities of liberal and radical activists (suspected as "subversives") could lead to the discovery of potential spies or saboteurs. FBI intelligence investigations predictably focused on prominent Communists (and their liberal and radical associates) because of these activists' public efforts to influence public opinion. In the process, FBI agents missed recruited spies who purposefully distanced themselves from the Communist Party.[3]

More important, FBI intelligence investigations were never confined to Soviet agents and their recruited spies. Instead, FBI agents monitored the personal and political activities of prominent Americans (First Lady Eleanor Roosevelt, Illinois Governor and Democratic presidential nominee Adlai Stevenson, and naval ensign/U.S. Congressman/U.S. Senator/Democratic President John Kennedy). Furthermore, although FBI officials during the World War II and cold war eras might have had a legitimate interest in monitoring employees in defense industries or in the federal bureaucracy whom Soviet agents might attempt to recruit as spies, one of their most intensive investigations of the World War II era centered on the motion-picture industry. Their purpose in investigating suspected "subversive" Hollywood employees was based on the fear that Communists might influence the political culture. This concern also underpinned the FBI's monitoring of reporters and editors (Harrison Salisbury, Inga Arvad, Stanley Johnson, Joseph Patterson) and writers (e.g., Max Lowenthal, purposefully targeted because he authored a critical history of the FBI).

FBI officials, moreover, did not simply amass information about the personal and political activities of suspect Americans. Purposefully establishing informal (or in some cases formal) liaison relations with reliable reporters (Don Whitehead), members of Congress (Senator Joseph McCarthy, Congressman Nixon), governors, and congressional committees (House Committee on

Un-American Activities [HUAC], Senate Internal Security Subcommittee), they leaked derogatory personal and political information to these witting allies. Their purpose was to promote and sustain a militant anti-Communist politics—in extreme cases, they even willingly advanced the partisan interests of conservative Republicans and a liberal Democratic president (in one case, targeting Democratic presidential nominee Stevenson, and in another, former Republican President Herbert Hoover).

The same excesses and political considerations underpinned at least five known CIA and NSA illegal surveillance programs. Under the code-named HTLINGUAL mail program, CIA officers photographed 2,705,726 envelopes and copied the names and addresses from an additional 389,324 envelopes, while opening and photographing the contents of 215,820 letters. The subjects of the intercepted letters included Senators Frank Church and Edward Kennedy, a (name withheld) U.S. congressman, Edward Albee, John Steinbeck, American Friends Service Committee, Federation of American Scientists, Students for a Democratic Society, Student Non-Violent Coordinating Committee, and Americans who frequently traveled to the Soviet Union (including one member of the Rockefeller family). CIA officials then created a database listing the names of 1.5 million suspected "subversives." Under the code-named MHCHAOS domestic-surveillance program, CIA officers compiled files on 7,500 activists and indexed the names of an estimated 300,000 political activists. Under Project Mockingbird, CIA officers monitored, including wiretapping, syndicated columnists Robert Allen and Paul Scott. This program failed to identify the source of the leaked classified information. Nonetheless, CIA officials deemed this operation "very productive" in that the wiretaps intercepted the columnists' conversations with twelve U.S. senators and six U.S. congressmen. Under the NSA's Operation MINARET, the international communications of 1,030 U.S. citizens and organizations and 2,400 foreign citizens were intercepted, and 1,900 reports were prepared for the FBI and the CIA based on these intercepts. A partial list of the subjects of these intercepts includes Jane Fonda; Joan Baez; Dr. Benjamin Spock; the Reverend Martin Luther King, Jr.; the Reverend David Abernathy; Eldridge Cleaver; Abbie Hoffman; and David Dellinger. And although Army Security Agency (ASA) analysts under Operation SHAMROCK had originally intercepted telegrams sent to the Soviet Union and Soviet satellite countries, over time, the NSA (ASA's successor) began to extract as well the telegrams of U.S. citizens. The massive number of the intercepted telegrams necessitated their regular destruction, for housekeeping reasons. Nonetheless, in 1975, NSA officials admitted to the Church Committee that during the last two to three years of this program's operation, NSA analysts had reviewed approximately 150,000 telegrams monthly.[4]

Assessing these widespread abuses of power, the Church Committee concluded that the principal reason for their occurrence was that the "checks

and balances designed by the framers of the Constitution to assure accountability have not been applied." Committee members singled out the exclusive
role of executive branch officials in defining the scope and purpose of FBI
operations and their attendant reliance on secrecy to undermine congressional
oversight and accordingly proposed a series of needed reforms. Their principal recommendations involved enactment of "a comprehensive legislative
charter defining and controlling the domestic security activities of the Federal
Government" and creation of "permanent intelligence oversight" committees. Legislative charters, committee members explained, "should provide the
exclusive legal authority for domestic security activities."[5]

The Senate did enact one of these recommendations, when establishing
in May 1976 a permanent Senate Select Committee on Intelligence (with the
House following suit in July 1977) to oversee the foreign-intelligence and
counterintelligence activities of the U.S. intelligence community. Responsibility to oversee FBI domestic-intelligence operations remained within the prov-
ince of the House and Senate Judiciary Committees and henceforth became a
more important priority.[6]

The Church and Pike Committees' dramatic revelations had seemingly
catalyzed a broad consensus that Congress should enact legislative charters
for the intelligence agencies rather than defer to the executive branch. Nonetheless, this consensus masked fundamental differences between liberals and
conservatives over whether such charters should proscribe the limits of the
authority of the intelligence agencies (specifying what was permissible and
forbidden) or should merely define the parameters of each agency's authority,
leaving to the president or the attorney general the discretion to issue specific
guidelines.

In February 1978, after lengthy deliberations, Senator Walter Huddleston
convened public hearings on a massive bill, S. 2525, that was intended to
impose effective controls over the foreign-intelligence and counterintelligence
operations of the U.S. intelligence agencies and to ensure that Congress could
meet its oversight responsibilities by defining by law the conduct of intelligence investigations within the United States. Senator Kennedy introduced
a companion bill, S. 1612, in July 1979 to define the permissible domestic-
surveillance activities of the FBI and to ensure more-effective executive and
legislative oversight over FBI operations.[7]

Neither S. 2525 nor S. 1612, however, was enacted. The Soviet invasion
of Afghanistan and the seizure of U.S. embassy personnel in Teheran by
Iranian militants in October–November 1979 contributed to a radically different political climate, captured in Republican presidential nominee Ronald
Reagan's 1980 campaign for the presidency. Tapping into widespread public
dissatisfaction over the twin economic problems of high inflation and high
unemployment, candidate Reagan also called for a sharp increase in defense

spending to meet the Soviet threat and the "unleashing" of the intelligence agencies. His election to the presidency in 1980 spelled the death knell for the legislative charter reform initiative. The sole legislative restriction on FBI intelligence operations (as well as those of the NSA) thus became the 1978 Foreign Intelligence Surveillance Act.

The catalyst to this legislation was a series of recent disclosures: first, President Nixon's claimed absolute authority to conduct "national-security" wiretaps (a claim that the Supreme Court struck down in June 1972 in *U.S. v. U.S. District Court*); then, the FBI's wiretapping (at the behest of the Nixon White House) of prominent reporters and White House and NSC aides between 1969–1971; and finally, the NSA's Operation MINARET program. To preclude future abuses, the act specifically distinguished between "domestic-security" and "foreign-intelligence" electronic surveillance and required that any interception during a "foreign-intelligence" investigation of "U.S. persons who are in the United States" must be approved in advance (although in camera) by a specially established court based on the "certification" that the target was either a "foreign power," "an entity directed and controlled by a foreign government," or "an agent of a foreign power." This special court, however, was not empowered to determine either the necessity or the propriety of the proposed interception, only that the government certification established a "foreign" connection. The act, moreover, contained an emergency-exemption exception, permitting such interceptions for twenty-four hours, after which court approval was required.[8]

Despite the furor that the revelations of past widespread abuses of power created, the sole restrictions on FBI "domestic-security" operations (beyond electronic eavesdropping) instituted in the aftermath of the Church and Pike Committees' revelations were imposed (and thus could be rescinded) by the executive branch. Originally intended as a temporary measure until an expected FBI charter law was finally approved, Attorney General Levi in March 1976 issued new FBI investigative guidelines. His guidelines addressed the two recently exposed sources of past FBI abuses—FBI officials' unilateral and broad definition of "subversive" threats and senior Justice Department officials' failure (or unwillingness) to meet their oversight responsibilities. Levi's guidelines thus rejected what had heretofore been the exclusive role of senior FBI officials in defining the targets of FBI "domestic-security" investigations. Such investigations henceforth would be divided into two categories: "preliminary" and "full." FBI officials could initiate "preliminary" investigations based on "allegations or other information that an individual or group may be engaged in activities which involve or will involve the use of force or violence and which involve or will involve the violation of federal law." Such investigations were limited to ninety days in duration and were to be confined to verifying or refuting the allegations. A "full" investigation, in contrast, could be initiated only if, at the onset or during a "preliminary" investigation, information was obtained that met a probable violation of criminal law standard—"on the basis of specific and articulable facts given reason to believe that an individual or group is or may be engaged in activities which involve the use of force or violence and which involve or will involve the violation of federal law."

As important, Attorney General Levi required Justice Department officials to supervise FBI intelligence investigations, reversing the earlier deference of previous attorneys general. Department officials would have to determine that the investigation complied with these standards and had to review "the results of full investigations at least annually and . . . determine in writing whether continued investigation was warranted."[9]

Attorney General Levi concurrently issued secret guidelines to govern FBI "foreign-counterintelligence" investigations.[10] A foreign-intelligence investigation could be initiated only if an agent had "reasonable suspicion" that the intended subject (whether a U.S. citizen or alien resident) "was a conscious member of a hostile foreign intelligence network, and [the FBI agent] could seek approval for electronic surveillance if there was probable cause that the [subject's] activities involved clandestine transmission of information to a hostile intelligence service."[11]

The Levi guidelines, however, immediately encountered studied opposition from FBI officials and leading congressional conservatives. Indeed, in March 1979, the Pittsburgh Special Agent in Charge (SAC) protested that his office's investigation of the radical Revolutionary Communist Party (RCP) had uncovered no evidence of the group's resorting to "force or violence . . . or the violation of Federal Law . . . for the purpose of overthrowing the Government." "Newly surfaced" RCP activities, he argued, citing demonstrations against the Iranian government, underscored the need to modify the Levi guidelines to permit a "domestic-security" investigation of this group. The RCP's recent abstention from violence, the Pittsburgh SAC contended, was likely to be temporary: "Such periods of quiescence followed by acts of violence or other activities which violate U.S. Law or the U.S. Constitution are not uncommon for the Communist Party organizations, and . . . provisions for such activity should be made in the Attorney General's guidelines to cover such situations prior to violent and/or detrimental reactivations of such organizations."[12]

Upon assuming office in 1981, the Reagan administration moved quickly to address this alleged problem. During June 24, 1982, testimony before the Senate Subcommittee on Security and Terrorism, FBI Director William Webster disclosed that the Justice Department was currently reviewing the Levi guidelines. These guidelines required revision, Webster asserted, to enable FBI agents to investigate "terrorist groups" that are "no different from other criminal enterprises." Senator Jeremiah Denton, the chair of the subcommittee, welcomed the forthcoming revisions, confident that FBI agents would be permitted to investigate radical organizations, such as the National Lawyers Guild, Socialist Workers Party, Weather Underground, and Progressive Labor Party.[13]

On March 7, 1983, new, more permissive guidelines were issued to govern FBI "domestic security/terrorism investigations." Abandoning the probable cause standard, Attorney General William French Smith authorized such investigations "when the facts or circumstances reasonably indicate that two or more persons are engaged in an enterprise [to further] political or social goals wholly or in part through activities that involve force or violence and a violation of the criminal laws of the United States." FBI agents should "anticipate or prevent crime" and could initiate investigations based on statements that "advocate criminal activity or indicate an apparent intent to engage in crime, particularly crimes of violence." The FBI director or a designated FBI assistant director could authorize "domestic security/terrorism" investigations for a one-hundred-eighty-day period, which could then be reauthorized every one hundred eighty days. Smith also abandoned Levi's requirement that the Department of Justice review FBI intelligence investigations at least annually and "determine in writing whether continued investigation is warranted." FBI officials only had to "notify" the Justice Department's Office of Intelligence Policy and Review whenever initiating a "domestic security/terrorism" investigation. This office would only review the results of such investigations annually but would not have to determine in writing that continued investigation was warranted. The attorney general's oversight role, moreover, became discretionary—"may, as he deems necessary request the FBI to prepare a report on the status of the investigation."[14]

The institution of executive or legislative changes in the succeeding decades further undermined the limited restrictions that had been imposed during the 1970s. Thus, on the eve of the 9/11 terrorist attack, FBI officials already commanded broad, legal powers to monitor suspected terrorists, whether under the Smith guidelines, the 1968 Crime Control Act and Safe Streets Act, the 1978 Foreign Intelligence Surveillance Act, or the 1996 Anti-Terrorism and Effective Death Penalty Act. Moreover, dating from the 1980s and intensified during the 1990s, counterterrorism became a major FBI priority (confirmed by the establishment of special Radical Fundamentalist and Usama Bin Laden units in 1994 and 1999, respectively). Indeed, in August 2001, the month before the 9/11 attack, the FBI was "currently conducting approximately 70 full field investigations that it considers Bin Laden-related."[15]

Nonetheless, despite these expanded powers, FBI agents failed to meet their counterintelligence responsibilities, in this case to anticipate the 9/11 attack. Rather than confronting the reality of limited capability and the inherently politically motivated character of intelligence investigations, the George W. Bush administration attributed the surprise attack of 9/11 to a failure of resources. As with the Franklin Roosevelt administration in 1936 and subsequent cold war presidents, a perceived internal security threat once again led to the further expansion of the FBI's political-surveillance authority.

At a joint press conference with FBI Director Robert Mueller III in May 2002, Attorney General John Ashcroft publicly announced that the FBI henceforth would adopt a more aggressive approach. His announcement glossed over the reality that FBI agents, since 1936 and reaffirmed under the Smith guidelines, had been conducting noncriminal "intelligence" investigations. His new FBI investigative guidelines, Ashcroft nonetheless claimed, would effect a change in the FBI's culture from that of a law-enforcement and reactive agency to one that would be proactive and preventative (language nearly identical to that privately used fifty years earlier). FBI field offices would have greater leeway to initiate counterterrorism investigations, with specially trained agents becoming more "vigilant in detecting terrorist activities to the full extent permitted by the law with an eye toward early intervention and prosecution of acts of terrorism before they occur" to put "prevention above all else." As FBI agents were already empowered first under Roosevelt's 1936 directive and then under the Smith guidelines to be proactive and preventative, the main changes Ashcroft introduced merely allowed agents to initiate and continue investigations without seeking advance clearance from FBI headquarters and to monitor public meetings (mosques in particular).[16]

An indifference to the history of FBI intelligence investigations underlay the public's and Congress's acceptance of this "new" approach. Capitalizing on this consensus, in late September 2008, Attorney General Michael Mukasey announced new FBI "domestic" operations guidelines. These changes, Mukasey claimed, would address the different reality that the 9/11 terrorist attack exposed by establishing a "consistent policy" and effecting a "more complete integration and harmonization of standards" while remaining "consistent with the Constitution and laws of the United States." Contrary to this benign description, however, FBI agents were explicitly encouraged to move beyond law enforcement to "prevent" or "protect" against crime and national-security threats—in the latter case, to avert as well "violations (or potential violations) of federal criminal laws." In another key provision, FBI officials were invited to resume earlier World War II and cold war practices of serving as the political-intelligence arm of the White House. Indeed, Mukasey demanded that FBI "collection activities become more flexible, more proactive, and more efficient" to increase an administration's acquisition of information about its political critics.

The "expanded" and "better integrated" FBI investigations, Mukasey maintained, would be conducted in a "lawful and reasonable manner" and would avoid "unnecessary intrusions into the lives of law abiding people." The attorney general, however, never defined what would be "reasonable" or "unnecessary," leaving that determination to the discretion of FBI agents and their supervisors. Furthermore, information "incidentally obtained" in the course of an authorized investigation that might fall outside the FBI's "areas of primary investigative responsibility" could be retained and disseminated to "responsible authorities in other agencies or jurisdictions."[17]

Mukasey's directive that FBI agents be "more flexible, more proactive, and more efficient" inevitably invited the adoption once again of ideological criteria, now to identify suspected terrorists based on their militancy or suspect associations—all the more so, given the attorney general's further admonition that collection activities should extend "beyond federal crimes" to include a "broader range of matters relating to foreign powers, organizations, or persons that may be of interest to the conduct of foreign affairs." Mukasey even conceded that such investigations "may concern lawful activities." And although urging FBI agents to employ the "least intrusive methods," the attorney general left the "choice of methods [to be] a matter of judgment," adding that agents "should not hesitate to use all lawful methods consistent with the Guidelines, even if intrusive, where the degree of intrusiveness is warranted in light of the seriousness" of the threat. Agents could launch investigations on the basis of "allegations or other information concerning crimes or threats to the national security," in which case the agent "may engage in otherwise illegal activity that could be authorized" (under the guidelines) "if necessary to meet an immediate threat to the safety of persons or property, or to the national security, or to prevent compromising of an investigation or the loss of a significant investigative opportunity."

Despite the broad scope and permissiveness of his guidelines, the attorney general did not institute strict oversight procedures to deter zealous agents from abusing this authority. Oversight responsibility was instead vested in the heads of FBI field offices (SACs), with senior FBI officials at FBI headquarters playing secondary and senior Justice Department officials peripheral roles (in the latter case confined to reviewing an already conducted investigation). Senior Justice Department officials, moreover, were not required to certify in writing that an investigation was warranted and complied with the guidelines.

Authorized investigations fell into two broad categories: "assessments" and "predicated," with the latter further subdivided into "preliminary" and "full." SACs alone would supervise assessments (to seek information about or to "prevent or protect" against crimes or national-security threats or to identify potential targets or sources). SACs alone would authorize preliminary investigations (initiated on "the basis of information or allegations" of crime or national-security threat). And SACs alone would authorize full investigations (initiated on an "articulable factual basis" of a crime or national-security threat or to acquire foreign-intelligence information) and "notify" FBI head-quarters and the U.S. attorney (or "other appropriate" Justice Department official[s]) only when a "sensitive matter" was involved, in which case the Justice Department's National Security Division would have to be notified "as soon as practicable but no later than 30 days" after the inception of this investigation. Last, FBI headquarters and the Justice Department's National Defense Division would review and approve only those FBI investigations involving "religious or political organizations" that concerned "threats to the national security or foreign intelligence."

The Mukasey guidelines in effect (if not purpose) invited FBI agents to resume monitoring political and personal activities[18] and furthermore encouraged the sharing of information obtained through "foreign-intelligence" investigations with the White House (and other U.S. intelligence agencies), a requirement that seems benign and responsible. Mukasey's further proviso, however, conveys a broader purpose that is reminiscent of the FBI's earlier service as the political-intelligence arm of the White House. "Compromising information concerning domestic officials or political organizations, or information concerning U.S. persons intended to affect the political process in the United States" was to be disseminated to the White House. Mukasey's stipulation that such dissemination would require the "approval of the Attorney General based on a determination that such dissemination is needed for foreign intelligence purposes, for the purpose of protecting against international terrorism, or other threats to the national security, for the conduct of foreign affairs" seems less restrictive in light of the known actions of President Bush's attorneys general (Ashcroft and Alberto Gonzalez) and some of their cold war predecessors as well as the fact that such determinations would be made in secret.[19]

The underlying indifference to the rule of law and the basic premise that FBI surveillance activities need not comply with legislative restrictions had also determined the secret rulings of 2001–2007 of senior Bush White House and Justice Department officials. In sharp contrast to the secret rulings of FBI officials during the World War II and cold war eras when these officials privately conceded that break-ins were "clearly illegal" and that information obtained through wiretaps, bugs, break-ins, and mail opening came from "sources illegal in nature," Justice Department officials (John Yoo, Jay Bybee, Steven Bradbury) in their secret rulings of 2001–2007 offered tendentious interpretations of presidential and congressional powers as permitting interrogation, detention, and electronic-surveillance practices that violated various domestic laws and international treaties. The shoddiness of their legal rulings led attorneys in the Justice Department's Office of Professional Responsibility (OPR) to launch an investigation in 2004 to ascertain whether these Justice Department officials, when rendering these rulings, had violated the ethical and professional standards of the legal profession.[20] This inquiry was temporarily aborted, senior Bush Administration officials having refused to grant OPR attorneys the necessary security clearances to review relevant classified records.

Eventually granted clearance, OPR attorneys completed their investigation in December 2008. Their report, however, was not publicized until May 2009, owing to Attorney General Mukasey's insistence on allowing Bybee and Yoo the right to respond to OPR's findings and recommendations. In their final report of July 29, 2009, OPR attorneys concluded that Bybee and Yoo had "committed professional misconduct" (in Yoo's case "intentional professional misconduct") and had acted in "disregard" (in Bybee's case "reckless disregard") of their duties to "exercise independent legal judgment and render thorough, objective and candid legal advice" when rendering their rulings on interrogation practices. Yoo's and Bybee's rulings, OPR attorneys continued, had ignored legal precedents and were slipshod and "seriously deficient," with aspects constituting "errors, omissions, misstatements, and illogical conclusions." The "cumulative effect" of their legal deficiencies compromised the "thoroughness, objectivity and candor" of their legal advice. Rejecting a defense based on the need to consider the critical situation following the 9/11 terrorist attacks, OPR attorneys instead contended that "situations of great stress, danger, and fear do not relieve departmental attorneys of their duty to provide thorough, objective, and candid legal advice, even if that advice is not what their client wants to hear." OPR attorneys, however, did not recommend prosecution, but rather that their "finding of misconduct" should be referred to state bar associations for possible disciplinary action, even disbarment. In Bradbury's case, OPR attorneys concluded that the "shortcomings" of his legal analysis did not rise to the "level of professional misconduct."

On January 5, 2010, Associate Deputy Attorney General David Margolis rejected OPR's state bar referral recommendation, holding that its conclusion of professional misconduct was not based on "known, unambiguous" standards. Cognizant, however, that Yoo's and Bybee's rulings had been rescinded by Justice Department officials in 2004 when their ruling was leaked, and further that this legal ruling had precipitated sharp criticisms from legal scholars and commentators over their tendentious reasoning,[21] Margolis asserted that his rejection of OPR's recommendation "should not be viewed as an endorsement of [Yoo's and Bybee's] legal work." Indeed, he concluded that Yoo's and Bybee's legal rulings were "flawed," their "errors more than minor," and that Yoo's "loyalty to his own ideology and convictions clouded his view of his obligations to his client, and led him to authorize opinions that reflected his own extreme, albeit sincerely held, views of executive power." Margolis added that Yoo and Bybee had "exercised poor judgment by overstating the certainty of their conclusions and underexposing countervailing arguments."

Margolis's rejection of OPR's recommendations scarcely amounted to a ringing endorsement of Yoo's and Bybee's legal rulings. His critical assessment was repeated in the joint report on the NSA surveillance program that the inspector generals of the Justice and Defense Departments, the CIA, the NSA, and the Office of National Intelligence publicly released in July 2009. This report concluded that Yoo's legal justification for the NSA surveillance program, and that of his colleagues in the Justice Department, was "serious[ly] factual[ly] and legal[ly] flaw[ed]," specifically criticizing its "shoddiness."[22] In any event, in the cold war and post-9/11 eras, secrecy enabled executive-branch officials to avoid accountability for their authorization of illegal conduct and to avert the scrutiny that would otherwise have precluded widespread abuses of power.

CIA officials and Vice President Richard Cheney also repeated this same indifference to the rule of law during the years 2001–2009—in this case, however, responding quite differently to the problem of congressional oversight than FBI officials did during the World War II and cold war eras. In 1942, committed to ensuring that members of Congress could not discover his authorization of "clearly illegal" break-ins, FBI Director Hoover had devised the Do Not File procedure to govern the disposition of break-in request and authorization records. This procedure enabled FBI officials to affirm truthfully, whether during congressional hearings or when honoring congressional subpoenas, that the FBI's "central records system" contained no record that illegal activities had been conducted or authorized. In contrast, in the post-9/11 era, CIA officials, on the order of Vice President Cheney, purposefully did not brief the congressional leadership (the chairs of the House and Senate Judiciary and Intelligence Committees) about a planned sensitive CIA counterterrorism program that involved attempts to assassinate Al Qaeda leaders (including contracting with a private security firm, Blackwater, in 2004 to further this planned effort). Cheney's decision directly violated the requirements of the 1980 Intelligence Oversight Act (an act that had been amended in 1991 to avert the reoccurrence of the Reagan administration's action in the Iran-Contra affair). Under this amendment, the White House would have to "fully and currently" brief Congress about all major CIA covert operations "in a timely fashion."[23]

As in the case of the FBI's World War II and cold war investigations of suspected subversives, the FBI's post-9/11 counterterrorist investigations resulted in very few prosecutions. A 2009 report confirmed one consequence of this obsession to anticipate terrorism—that FBI agents often "chas[ed] shadows" and in the process were unable to meet the FBI's other law-enforcement responsibilities. Indeed, of the 5,500 leads pursued by the FBI's twenty-eight-member special counterterrorism 6 squad, only 5 percent were found to be credible enough to warrant further investigation. Between October 2005 and

June 2006, moreover, Justice Department officials declined to bring charges in 131 of the 150 FBI international terrorism referrals. As revealing, the General Accounting Office concluded that 132 of the Justice Department's claimed 288 international and domestic terrorism convictions of 2002 were wrongly classified, and further that of the sixty-two New Jersey terrorist cases, all but two involved Middle Eastern students who had paid imposters to take their English-proficiency exams.[24]

This paltry prosecution record was not due, as in the World War II and cold war eras, to FBI agents' uses of illegal investigative techniques, thereby negating prosecution. To the contrary, FBI agents after 9/11 commanded broad legal authority to employ intrusive investigative techniques. Despite this expanded legal authority, FBI agents once again focused on perceived "terrorist" activists and organizations based on the targets' militant views and political activities. After 9/11, FBI agents could operate under the even broader and discretionary powers of the USA PATRIOT Act, enacted in October 2001, whenever initiating "anticipatory" investigations. For one, the Patriot Act authorized agents to use National Security Letters (NSLs; issued solely on the authority of FBI officials without court review) if "relevant to an authorized counterterrorism or counterespionage investigation" (a more relaxed standard than the previous requirement of "specific and articulable facts . . . that the person or entity . . . is a foreign power or agent of a foreign power"). The Patriot Act also permitted agents to install roving wiretaps (targeting an individual and not a phone number, whether a land or cell phone); intercept Internet communications (privately owned or library computers); or obtain credit, bank, or other business records. NSLs, moreover, could be used to investigate individuals suspected of "harboring" or "supporting" terrorism.

The Patriot Act also relaxed the restrictions of the 1978 Foreign Intelligence Surveillance Act by extending the "emergency" period (permitting the interception of an electronic communication without an advance court order) from twenty-four to seventy-two hours and changing the requirement that FBI and NSA officials provide evidence of a proposed target's "direct" connection with a foreign power or movement when seeking court approval for claimed "foreign-intelligence" wiretaps to having to prove only that the target had a "significant" connection to a foreign government or movement.[25]

Enacted during a period of intense crisis, the Patriot Act captured the prevailing sentiment that terrorist threats could be averted only through enhanced surveillance powers. Members of Congress at the time, nonetheless, adopted a provision that was intended to permit that such uses would be reviewed in a less-stressful time and accordingly stipulated that the act's most-controversial sections (those governing the use of NSLs) would automatically expire in five years unless explicitly reauthorized. Members of Congress could then evaluate how this authority had been, and was currently being, used after obtaining access to relevant records of such uses. Nonetheless, even though Justice Department officials repeatedly rejected subsequent requests of the House and Senate Judiciary Committees for direct access to relevant records, in 2006 Congress made these powers permanent, with the Republican congressional leadership denying that this legislation would invite abuses.

By then, however, some of the FBI's records (those relating to closed investigations) had been released in response to FOIA requests. In addition, the office of the Justice Department's inspector general released its report evaluating the FBI's monitoring of domestic political advocacy groups. These released records and the inspector general ruling confirmed that the targets of FBI "domestic security/terrorism" investigations included a number of radical and pacifist organizations—the Catholic Workers, Thomas Merton Center, Greenpeace, People for the Ethical Treatment of Animals, and activists protesting the Iraq War. Although the inspector general's office concluded that FBI agents had not intentionally targeted these groups, it nonetheless criticized FBI officials for having made a series of "false and misleading statements to the public and Congress in 2002" about the bureau's surveillance of antiwar groups and for having classified certain nonviolent crimes as terrorism. Other FOIA requests confirmed that Defense Department agents had monitored a "Stop the War Now" rally in Akron, Ohio; the American Friends Service Committee; anti–Iraq War protests at the University of California–Santa Cruz; and various peace and anarchist groups in the Seattle area, and that Immigration Bureau agents, in the midst of the 2004 presidential election, had pointedly questioned more than 2,500 alien residents, predominantly (79 percent) from Muslim majority countries, about their views of the United States, whether they possessed chemical or biological weapons, and whether violence was preached at the mosques that they attended.[26]

These known examples of FBI (and military) monitoring of dissident political activities leaves unresolved whether the FBI, the CIA, and the NSA had once again resumed their earlier practices of the World War II and cold war eras of monitoring political activities and then surreptitiously using the acquired information to further a political agenda. The scope, and possible uses, of such surveillances cannot be conclusively determined at present, since the records of ongoing FBI, CIA, and NSA operations remain classified and are not subject to FOIA requests.[27] Recent revelations of the Bush administration's and CIA special records procedures raise a further worrisome concern—the reinstatement of procedures to destroy particularly sensitive records documenting abusive practices. In 2005, forewarned that Congress would convene hearings that year to examine the CIA's interrogation practices, CIA officers destroyed ninety-two videotapes recording hundreds of hours of harsh CIA interrogations of Al Qaeda detainees Abu Zubaydah and Abd al-Nashiri.[28] In a second known case, Bush White House officials created special e-mail accounts (particularly of their communications with the Republican National Committee), with the subsequent discovery that many of these e-mails had either been destroyed or were missing. Third, OPR attorneys, in the course of their investigation of the legal rulings on interrogation practices of Justice Department attorneys Yoo, Bybee, and Patrick Philbin, discovered that e-mail files relating to these rulings were missing and, specifically, that "most of" Yoo's e-mail records and Philbin's e-mail records covering the period July–August 2002 "had been deleted and were not recoverable."[29]

Further revelations about the general contents of undisclosed FBI records provide an additional reason for concern that the abuses of the cold war years have been repeated. In 2006, although denied direct access to relevant FBI records, Congress nonetheless (as discussed earlier) reauthorized the sections of the USA PATRIOT Act governing the FBI's uses of NSLs. Congress at the time, however, adopted a provision that the Justice Department's inspector general conduct an internal investigation of such uses during the years 2003–2005 and release his report to the appropriate oversight committees of Congress.

Inspector General Glenn Fine's reports on his office's investigation of the FBI's "terrorist" wiretapping practices were released, one in March 2007 and a second in January 2010. Fine's scathing assessment of 2007 precipitated protests from many members of Congress over the scope of the FBI's uses—with the former Republican Chairman of the House Judiciary Committee James Sensenbrenner, ironically, expressing his "outrage." During this three-year period, Fine reported, the FBI had employed 143,074 NSLs. This mind-boggling number, Fine then observed, understated the FBI's actual uses by an estimated 6 percent, basing this estimate on his office's review of a "judgmental sample" of selected files from four of the FBI's fifty-six field offices, a review that had uncovered widespread "inaccuracies" in the FBI's database. An NSL, Fine further pointed out, at times involved more than one target (in one case, one NSL involved seven telephone numbers).

In addition, Fine's inquiry uncovered that FBI agents had made "misleading and serious misuse" of NSLs, that FBI officials had underreported NSL uses to Congress, that NSLs had been illegally used to obtain records, that many of the FBI's claimed "exigent letters" (ostensibly in emergency situations) involved nonemergencies, that NSLs had "most often" been used for "intelligence purposes rather than criminal prosecution," and that 125 FBI reports inaccurately identified the target as a non-U.S. person when the "appropriate memoranda on the investigation indicated that the subject was a U.S. person or a presumed U.S. person." In January 2010, Fine further recounted that of the FBI's claimed "exigent" letters initiatives, agents had obtained 3,500 telephone accounts during the years 2003–2006 without following required legal procedures and in some cases had uploaded call records on FBI databases, which they then reviewed on their computers without determining whether these records were relevant to a claimed terrorist investigation.[30] Furthermore, on four occasions that Fine uncovered, FBI officials had made inaccurate statements to the special court (known colloquially as the FISA court) created under the Foreign Intelligence Surveillance Act to review proposed interception applications concerning how calling records had been obtained and in two other cases had obtained access to call records of reporters during a claimed leak investigation. Not highlighted in Fine's report, NSLs, it was subsequently disclosed, had been used to obtain records relating to *New York Times* reporters Raymond Bonner and Jane Perlez and *Washington Post* reporters Ellen Nakashi and Natasha Tampubolon.[31]

The FBI, moreover, was not the sole U.S. intelligence agency to reinstate the domestic-surveillance practices of the cold war era—though the extent of the CIA's, the NSA's, and the Department of Homeland Security's post-9/11 monitoring activities remains unknown, their secret actions for the most part having escaped public scrutiny. FBI, CIA, NSA, and Homeland Security officials have successfully preserved the secrecy of most of their claimed national-security records. Their success renders it impossible to ascertain the targets and scope of their investigations and, equally important, how the acquired information might have been used by either their officials or the White House. In one exception, in 2009, a classified report of an internal Justice Department investigation and congressional oversight was leaked to the *New York Times*. This investigation, the *Times* disclosed, had uncovered instances of "significant misconduct" by NSA analysts in intercepting the e-mail communications of American citizens having no links to suspected terrorists. This overcollection of e-mail communications, the authors of this internal report contended, had ostensibly been inadvertent, as NSA analysts had been unable to distinguish between foreign and domestic messages, in effect repeating the practice of the originally established program. In another case, senior NSA officials (it was subsequently learned) had blocked a proposed plan of NSA analysts to wiretap a member of Congress, traveling in the Middle East as part of a congressional delegation, owing to his contact with a suspected terrorist. In yet another known case, NSA analysts in the spring of 2005 intercepted Congresswoman Jane Harman's telephone conversation with an Israeli intelligence agent.[32] Released Homeland Security records, moreover, documented that the department's intelligence officials had improperly collected information about U.S. citizens and organizations engaged in lawful dissent (including pro- and antiabortion groups). Last, recently released Immigration Bureau records document that Muslim alien residents had been purposely targeted by Immigration Bureau agents in the fall of 2004. Although the actions of the Immigration agents were not known to the broader public at the time, their questioning was known to the Islamic community, with a resultant chilling effect. An already intimidated Muslim American would hesitate to challenge, during that year's presidential campaign, the Bush administration's potentially controversial policies involving the Iraq War and counterterrorism.[33]

The Bush administration's authorization of the NSA's surveillance operations further highlight the antidemocratic consequences of secret decision making. Thus, even though Congress had agreed to amend the 1978 Foreign Intelligence Surveillance Act, as part of the massive USA PATRIOT Act (specifically relating to the court-review and emergency standards), President Bush did not then request that Congress rescind the 1978 Foreign Intelligence Surveillance Act's prior court-review requirements enacted to "provide legislative authorization for all electronic surveillance conducted within the United States for foreign intelligence purposes." President Bush at the time knew that NSA Director Michael Hayden had informed CIA Director George Tenet (who had inquired at the behest of the White House) that the NSA could do "nothing more within existing [legal] authorities" to uncover terrorist activities. Asked then what the NSA could do "with more authority," Hayden outlined what became the Terrorist Surveillance Program, which President Bush secretly authorized on October 4, 2001 (three weeks before Congress approved the USA PATRIOT Act).

Under this secret program, NSA agents intercepted and recorded the communications (telephone, e-mail, and fax) "into and out" of the United States of unspecified individuals about whom there would be "a reasonable basis to conclude that one party to the communication is a member of al-Qa'ida, affiliated with al-Qa'ida, or a member of an organization affiliated with al-Qa'ida."[34] NSA operatives did not target specific subjects. Instead, through a process of "data mining," based on speculative criteria (communications, for example, expressing interest in flight schools or frequently sent to specific foreign regions, e.g., Pakistan), they sought to identify possible terrorists or terrorist sympathizers. In addition, because private telecommunication companies (AT&T, Verizon, Bell South) transmitted the bulk of electronic communications through fiber-optic cable, rendering them invulnerable to the NSA's sweeping of the airwaves, NSA officials solicited these companies' assistance to obtain access to these transmissions. In at least one known instance in 2005, Justice Department officials, to preclude discovery of this illegal program, withheld from a federal court during the trial of Muslim scholar Ali al-Timimi records confirming that the NSA had intercepted his telephone conversations.

The continued classification of relevant records pertaining to this program preclude a definitive understanding of the range of targets of such communication intercepts and any political (or other abusive) uses of the intercepted information. Isolated and inadvertent disclosures nonetheless suggest that a massive number of messages had been indiscriminately intercepted. Writer

James Bamford, for example, learned through one source that NSA staff supervisors had reviewed five thousand to seven thousand Middle Eastern communications daily. More revealing, and the by-product of the NSA's sharing the fruits of this interception program with the FBI, *New York Times* reporters discovered during interviews with unidentified FBI officials following the public exposure of this program in 2005 that the NSA's "steady stream" of information had led to "dead ends or innocent Americans" and had often amounted to "pointless intrusions on Americans' privacy." A July 2009 report[35] that the inspectors general of the Justice and Defense Departments, the NSA, the CIA, and the Office of National Intelligence issued confirmed this critical assessment. In their report, the inspectors general disclosed that most of the intelligence-agency officials whom they had interviewed "had difficulty citing specific instances" or "precise contributions" stemming from the intercepted communications in the uncovering of terrorist threats. Indeed, they concluded that the interception program, although "useful" as "one tool among many" and offering "value in some counterterrorism investigations," "generally played a limited role in the FBI's overall counterterrorism efforts."[36]

When secretly authorizing this NSA program, President Bush had assumed that his decision not to comply with the act's court-approval requirement would remain secret—an assumption that proved to be unwarranted. At least two participants in the execution of this program (Russell Tice, an NSA analyst, and Thomas Tamm, a career lawyer in the Justice Department's Office of Intelligence Policy and Review), troubled by the unwillingness of their more senior colleagues to challenge this illegal program, disclosed its existence to the *New York Times* in 2004.

The *Times*, however, delayed publishing this discovery until December 2005. Then, in a dramatic front-page expose, it reported that President Bush had secretly authorized this NSA interception program. Seeking to quell the resultant furor over his flaunting of the 1978 Foreign Intelligence Surveillance Act, President Bush brazenly defended the program as a "vital tool in our war against terrorists" and as narrowly targeting "people with known links to Al Qaeda and related terrorist organizations." His action, he further argued, was constitutional under the president's commander-in-chief powers and a 2001 congressional resolution authorizing military operations against those responsible for the 9/11 terrorist attack. Great care had been taken, he continued, to minimize any abuses during the program's operation, with NSA officials reviewing its operation every forty-five days to update targets and to assess their continuing intelligence value. The president, however, rebuffed congressional requests for access to the records of his authorization, the internal reviews, and the intercepted messages themselves.

Within a year, President Bush had to abandon his stonewalling strategy. His account of the program's inception and operation was undercut by disclosures that key congressional leaders had not been fully briefed and that in 2004 senior Justice Department officials (Attorney General Ashcroft, Deputy Attorney General James Comey, and the head of the Office of Legal Counsel, Jack Goldsmith) and FBI Director Mueller had questioned the program's legality. Their threats to resign had forced Bush that month to modify his authorization order. Two court suits also forced the president to shift his original stance.

The first of these, which the American Civil Liberties Union brought, challenged the constitutionality of the president's authorization. This suit eventually failed. A federal appeals court ruled (a ruling that the Supreme Court upheld) that the plaintiffs had failed to establish standing that their rights had been violated—a classic catch-22 situation, since the president's "state-secrets" claim denied to any potential plaintiff access to records that could establish that his or her communications had been intercepted. A more serious challenge, however, involved an Electronic Frontier Foundation class-action suit against AT&T for violating the privacy rights of its customers.

The plaintiffs in this latter case could meet the standing test owing to the mistaken 2004 disclosure to defense attorneys of a logbook that documented the interception of the phone calls of lawyers for an Oregon charity and their clients in Saudi Arabia. The foundation's case was further strengthened by the testimony of AT&T technician Mark Klein (who, in addition, produced AT&T documents that he had acquired as an employee) that AT&T officials had allowed the NSA to set up a special office in the company's switching center in San Francisco. This suit could not be stymied by the Bush administration's "states-secrets" argument, as it raised the issue "whether a telecommunications firm has the right to break the law."[37]

The Electronic Frontier case, and the possible future filing of other court cases against the cooperating telecommunication companies, in effect forced the Bush administration to abandon its claim of inherent presidential powers. Administration officials agreed to endorse amending the 1978 Foreign Intelligence Surveillance Act's court-approval requirement and to grant after-the-fact immunity to the participating telecommunication companies.

In the fall of 2007, Congress bowed to White House pressure that failing to act would benefit terrorists and enacted legislation authorizing, but only for a six-month period, NSA monitoring of international and domestic communications without a court warrant if NSA analysts "reasonably believed [the target] to be located outside the United States." The amendment to the 1978 act, moreover, restricted the so-called FISA court's review and approval responsibility to ensuring only that such interceptions complied with procedures that the president adopted.

At first, members of Congress resisted making these changes permanent. After difficult negotiations, congressional leaders reached a compromise with the White House in June 2008. The NSA would be permitted to intercept the communications (e-mail and telephone) of foreign individuals without having to obtain a court warrant or identify specific targets. In contrast, individualized court orders would be required to intercept the communications of U.S. citizens, although in "exigent" (emergency) situations, such interceptions would be permitted for seven days without an advance court order. In a key concession to the White House, Congress approved a section providing for the prompt dismissal of any lawsuit against a cooperating telecommunications company if a district court judge ruled that a presidential directive had authorized the interception.[38] The White House's principal concession to Congress involved acceptance of the stipulation that the revised 1978 act constituted the "exclusive" authority for counterterrorism and counterespionage interceptions and that the revisions would expire in 2012 unless Congress renewed them.[39]

The revised statute seemingly imposed stricter conditions governing the interception of strictly domestic communications. An internal Justice Department review of NSA operations conducted in the aftermath of this legislation's enactment, however, confirmed that the proposed distinction between domestic and international interceptions had not been honored. Leaked to the *New York Times,* this review confirmed that Justice Department investigators had discovered that NSA analysts had significantly "overcollected" domestic e-mail and telephone communications without prior court review and approval. American citizens had allegedly been inadvertently targeted owing to the difficulty NSA analysts encountered in distinguishing between domestic and international communications. Purportedly, after this discovery, Justice Department officials instituted procedures to "bring the program into compliance" with the law's court-approval requirements.[40]

Why, then, did Congress in the years 2001–2008 once again defer to the White House and the intelligence agencies? This deference appears unreasonable in light of the known abuses of power of White House, FBI, and NSA officials; the Bush administration's refusal to allow congressional access to all relevant records; and the known history of widespread White House, FBI, and NSA abuses of power during the World War II and cold war eras. This deference is even more troubling given how the actions and inactions of members of Congress in the 2001–2008 period differed from their responses (and also those of White House and FBI officials) in the 1940s and 1950s. Between 1941 and 1967, Congress consistently refused to enact administration-proposed bills to legalize wiretapping (even though at this time the United States confronted a far more serious threat than that posed by Al Qaeda, given the vastly greater political, military, and economic capabilities of the Soviet Union). Furthermore, during this earlier era, FBI officials, sensitive to Congress's wariness about FBI surveillance powers, had devised special Do Not File and June

Mail procedures to foreclose the possible discovery of their privately admitted authorization of illegal investigative techniques, while in 1948, 1950, and 1951 the Truman administration had decided against seeking explicit legislation that would legalize either a preventive detention program or the interception of international telegraph messages. The Truman administration's crafty strategy in the latter case offers a stark contrast between Congress's responses of the cold war era and its responses in the post-9/11 era. In both eras, presidents debated whether to seek legislation that explicitly granted immunity from prosecution to private corporations that had illegally assisted the intelligence agencies.

During World War II, the international telegraph companies (ITT World Communications, Western Union International, RCA Global) had forwarded to military intelligence telegraph messages (of the Soviet Union and the Axis powers) transmitted through their terminals in the United States. This assistance at the time was legal under wartime censorship legislation. Following the end of World War II, military intelligence officials pressured the companies to continue this arrangement, despite the expiration of the wartime authorization. Continued assistance through a program code-named Operation SHAMROCK, military officials had then assured company executives, would be legal, and they cited as authority a determination of the attorney general. In 1947, however, company executives reassessed their earlier decision, at which time they informed Secretary of Defense James Forrestal of their intention to cease cooperating. The courts had not yet (and might not) endorse the attorney general's interpretation of the legality of such assistance, they advised Forrestal; in addition, their union employees (with whom they had contentious relationships) might publicly expose such assistance.

The executives were persuaded to continue cooperating, having received two explicit assurances: first, that Attorney General Tom Clark, with President Harry Truman's concurrence, pledged not to prosecute them; and, second, that the administration would draft and secure enactment of a bill legalizing this assistance. Appropriate legislation was drafted and introduced in 1948. Nonetheless, while the bill to amend the 1934 Communications Act was under review by the Senate Judiciary Committee, administration officials asked the committee's chairman not to report it to the floor for a vote, fearing that this proposal might precipitate a divisive debate during the current presidential-election campaign. This legislative initiative, however, was not renewed following Truman's electoral victory in 1948. Instead, in 1949, Secretary of Defense Louis Johnson (Forrestal's successor) reaffirmed the nonprosecution pledge. Then, in 1951, without hearings having been held, issuance of a detailed report on the proposal, or even floor debate, Congress approved an obscure section, 21A, as part of an omnibus, noncontroversial bill to amend the federal code, H.R. 3899. This section criminalized the disclosure to any "unauthorized" person (that is, not authorized by the president) of information relating to codes and code breaking (the SHAMROCK program's original objective was to obtain coded Soviet telegraphic messages for deciphering purposes).[41]

Section 21A in effect addressed the remaining concern of company executives that their employees might disclose their participation in an illegal program. Should any employee publicly disclose the operation of this program after the enactment of Section 21A, he or she would be vulnerable to criminal prosecution.[42] Significantly, apart from the leadership of the House and Senate Judiciary Committees (and presumably the House Speaker and Senate majority leader), no member of Congress was aware that, by approving H.R. 3899, they had in effect immunized the executives of the international telegraph companies from criminal prosecution.

The Truman administration's cynical strategy to avoid a public debate over exempting NSA surveillance from the 1934 Communication Act's ban differed from Congress's responses of 2005–2008 regarding its passivity upon first learning of the Bush administration's purposeful violation of the Foreign Intelligence Surveillance Act or eventual agreement to immunize the telecommunication companies from any lawsuit brought by their customers over their violation of privacy rights. As such, Congress's differing responses of 2005–2008 from those of 1948–1951 highlight how an obsession over security led it to cede wide latitude to the White House and the intelligence agencies, purportedly to safeguard the nation from potential threats.

Why were members of Congress unwilling to challenge a direct presidential violation of FISA? Why did they not instead insist on accountability rather than defer once again to broad presidential "national-security" claims?

The answer to these questions is best captured in the changed language adopted during the cold war era to define how the nation should respond to international developments: "national security" rather than "national defense."

The original "national-defense" phrase reflected what had been a long-held conception of what constituted a responsible security policy—incorporated in President George Washington's 1796 farewell address warning against "entangling alliances" and in Congress's enactment of the so-called Neutrality Acts of 1935–1937. This phrase reflected the view that the United States could, on its own, determine its international role and that the principal threat to the nation's security derived from unnecessary involvement in international conflicts. Under this view, although the government should be prepared to repulse an actual invasion, the public and political leaders need not otherwise be concerned about the actions of foreign powers. The Neutrality Acts reaffirmed this sense of self-sufficiency (self-imposed restrictions on the nation's commercial and financial transactions) and an underlying concern to limit unilateral presidential initiatives (the provisions restricting a president's discretion to permit bank loans and the sale of arms). Consistent with this sense of self-sufficiency and suspicion of executive power, many Americans (conservatives as well as liberals) viewed with great skepticism an expanded FBI surveillance role. Indeed, Walter Trohan, the Washington bureau chief of the arch-conservative (and anti–New Deal) *Chicago Tribune*, published in that newspaper's Sunday magazine of June 21, 1936, a scathing biographical sketch of FBI Director Hoover depicting the FBI director as a New Deal bureaucrat and demagogue bent on expanding the FBI's power and in the process undermining limited government. Moreover, during the late 1930s and early 1940s, President Roosevelt's conservative isolationist critics claimed (correctly, as it turns out) that the FBI was monitoring their efforts to mobilize public opposition to the president's interventionist foreign-policy initiatives.

In contrast, the "national-security" phrase, which governed U.S. internal and international security policy after 1945, reflected a far different conception of the nation's interests that two 1947 decisions succinctly capture: Congress's enactment of the National Security Act and President Truman's executive order establishing a Federal Employee Loyalty Program.

The National Security Act's provisions creating the nation's first permanent espionage agency, the CIA, reflected a new view that a successful foreign policy required advance knowledge of the plans and capabilities of foreign powers. Presidents would need to be fully informed about actual and potential threats and also, through another agency created by the 1947 act, the National Security Council, correlate the nation's diplomatic, military, and economic resources. The act contributed to the evolution of a more centralized executive branch while placing a premium on the need for secrecy. The creation of the Federal Employee Loyalty Program was similarly based on the need to anticipate, in this case espionage that disloyal federal employees committed. Its purpose was to foreclose this possibility by denying employment to suspect individuals based not on their conduct but on their political beliefs and associations.

The year 1947 marked a significant watershed but not an abrupt break, as American conservatives remained committed to limited government and the rule of law. Accordingly, during the late 1940s and early 1950s, many conservatives opposed the Truman Doctrine, the Marshall Plan, and the NATO treaty as provocative; demanded changes in the proposed National Security Act to ensure that the CIA could not become a "gestapo"; (captured in the criticisms of Congressman Nixon, Senator McCarthy, HUAC, and the Senate Internal Security Subcommittee) depicted executive agreements and executive secrecy as responsible for Soviet expansion (attributing the "sell-out" and "betrayal" of Eastern Europe and China to President Roosevelt's secret executive agreements at the 1945 Yalta Conference); and accused Presidents Roosevelt and Truman of harboring "Communists in Government" (who were then able to influence crucial foreign-policy decisions and steal the secret of the atomic bomb).

Conservatives soon abandoned this antipathy toward presidential power and secrecy—captured in the enactment of the 1968 Omnibus Crime Control and Safe Streets Act (legalizing wiretapping and bugging) and opposing the challenges of the special Senate committee investigating the Watergate Affair to President Nixon's "national-security" and "executive-privilege" claims.

This obsession over possible security threats did not dissipate with the end of the cold war following the collapse of the Soviet Union and Communist governments in Eastern Europe and the Balkans in 1989–1991. A new perceived security threat—that of terrorism—once again underpinned demands for expanded surveillance initiatives. In the process, the seamy side of cold war surveillance and secrecy policy has been ignored—that ambitious, if sincerely motivated, presidents and intelligence agency officials, if granted broad discretion to monitor suspected terrorists, would once again abuse that power and promote a culture of lawlessness.

Notes

Introduction

1. Extant FBI case files document this earlier shift in approach and priorities. In response to a lawsuit challenging the National Archives's approval of FBI field office and headquarters record-disposition plans, in 1980, Judge Harold Greene ordered the National Archives and the FBI to develop a plan to ensure the preservation of FBI files of historical value. To address the housekeeping problem that the FBI's massive record holdings posed, the National Archives developed a plan to preserve a representative sample of FBI records. Under this plan, the number of preserved case files in the Espionage category created from the 1920s through 1980 totaled 239,282. In contrast, the preserved case files in the Domestic Security category totaled 1,790,191 for the period 1939–1980, and in the Internal Security category they totaled 1,271,195 for the years 1938–1980.

2. The name of the unit reflects the spelling adopted by the FBI in 1999. In 2001, the U.S. government adopted the spelling "Osama."

Chapter 1

1. U.S. Senate, Select Committee to Study Governmental Operations with Respect to Intelligence Activities, *Hearings on Intelligence Activities*, vol. 6, *Federal Bureau of Investigation*, 94th Cong., 1st sess., 1975, 558, 559; Raymond Batvinis, *The Origins of FBI Counterintelligence* (Lawrence: University Press of Kansas, 2007), 46–47.

2. Confidential Memos, Hoover, August 24 and 25, 1936, Franklin D. Roosevelt folder, Official and Confidential File of FBI Director J. Edgar Hoover (henceforth Hoover O&C).

3. Strictly Confidential Memo, Hoover to Tamm, September 10, 1936, Franklin D. Roosevelt folder, Hoover O&C; Senate Select Committee on Intelligence Activities, *Hearings on FBI*, 562–563.

4. Batvinis, *Origins of FBI Counterintelligence*, 3–28; Francis MacDonnell, *Insidious Foes: The Axis Fifth Column and the American Home Front* (New York: Oxford University Press, 1995), 49–61.

5. Senate Select Committee on Intelligence Activities, *Hearings on FBI*, 563–567; and *Final Report, Supplementary Detailed Staff Reports on Intelligence Activities and the Rights of Americans*, Book III, 94th Cong., 2d sess., 1976, 397–399.

6. Athan Theoharis, *The FBI and American Democracy: A Brief, Critical History* (Lawrence: University Press of Kansas, 2004), 173.

7. Memo, Belmont to Ladd, July 31, 1950, FBI 66-9330-204.

8. Memo, Hoover to Tamm and Clegg, November 18, 1940, FBI 66-9330-2.

9. Memo, FBI Director to Attorney General, November 18, 1940, FBI 66-9330-1.

10. Memo, FBI Director to Tamm and Ladd, November 18, 1940, FBI 66-9330-2. Confidential National Defense Informants were not "sources of information" but paid informers whose surveillance activities were targeted and controlled by a supervising FBI agent.

11. Memo, FBI Director to Tolson, Tamm, and Clegg, November 19, 1940, FBI 66-9330-3; Personal and Confidential Letter, FBI Director to All SACs, December 4, 1940, FBI 66-9330-7; Memo, Tamm to FBI Director, December 19, 1940, FBI 66-9330-9x; Memo, Brown to Tamm, January 6, 1941, FBI 66-9330-11.

12. Bureau Bulletin, No. 27, First Series 1942, April 15, 1942, FBI 66-9330-99.

13. Memo, Foxworth to FBI Director, September 3, 1941, FBI 66-9330-69.

14. Senate Select Committee on Intelligence Activities, *Hearings on FBI*, 409–411.

15. Senate Select Committee on Intelligence Activities, *Supplementary Detailed Staff Reports*, 414.

16. Senate Select Committee on Intelligence Activities, *Intelligence Activities and the Rights of Americans*, Book II, 94th Cong., 2d sess., 1975, 35; and *Supplementary Detailed Staff Reports*, 418–419. FBI officials, however, objected to the proposal to prosecute American citizens and instead urged department officials to consider "utilizing naturalization proceedings" or undertake a study to "control suspected citizens."

17. Memo, Hoover to Watson, October 25, 1940, and accompanying report, Present Status of Espionage and Counterespionage Operations of the Federal Bureau of Investigation, October 24, 1940; Memo, Roosevelt to Watson, October 31, 1940; Letter, Watson to Hoover, October 31, 1940; all in OF 10-B, Franklin Roosevelt Presidential Library; John Christgau, *"Enemies": Alien Internment* (Ames: Iowa State University Press, 1985), vii–viii, 33, 37, 50–85; Roger Daniels, *Without Trial: Japanese Americans in World War II* (New York: Hill and Wang, 1993), 24, 26, 31–33; Robert Goldstein, *American Blacklist: The Attorney General's List of Subversive Organizations* (Lawrence: University Press of Kansas, 2008), 25–27.

18. Recent disclosures of those whom the FBI had listed bear out Biddle's critical assessment—for example, those listed included radical attorney Carol Weiss King, United Automobile Workers union leaders Walter and Victor Reuther, radical Congressman Vito Marcantonio (listed because of his sharp criticisms of President Roosevelt's foreign-policy decisions), and then-UPI reporter Harrison Salisbury (listed allegedly because he was a "code expert" and "German spy"). Salisbury had been listed based solely on the uncorroborated allegations of his neighbor, whom military intelligence subsequently

concluded (when conducting its own investigation of this FBI listing) was unreliable and a "known prevaricator."

19. Senate Select Committee on Intelligence Activities, *Hearings on FBI*, 412–413.

20. Ibid., 414–415.

21. Theoharis, *FBI and American Democracy*, 174.

22. Memo, Callen to Rosen, February 6, 1945, FBI 66-9330-151; Bureau Bulletin, No. 16, Series 1945, February 21, 1945, FBI 66-9330-NR (Not Recorded).

23. Memo, FBI Executives Conference to FBI Director, February 13, 1945, FBI 66-9330-148.

24. Bureau Bulletin, No. 66, Series 1945, November 26, 1945, FBI 66-9330-NR; Memo, FBI Executives Conference to FBI Director, November 1, 1945, FBI 66-9330-171.

25. Memo, FBI Executives Conference to FBI Director, July 17, 1950, FBI 66-9330-205; Memo, Belmont to Ladd, July 31, 1950, FBI 66-9330-204.

26. Memo, FBI Executives Conference to FBI Director, July 17, 1950, FBI 66-9330-205.

27. Memo, FBI Executives Conference to FBI Director, July 17, 1950, FBI 66-9330-205; Memo, Belmont to Ladd, July 31, 1950, FBI 66-9330-204; Bureau Bulletin, No. 43, Series 1950, August 14, 1950, FBI 66-9330-NR; Letters, FBI Director to All SACs, January 27, 1951, FBI 66-9330-NR, and March 25, 1953, FBI 66-9330-NR; Memo, Ladd to Hoover, July 14, 1953, FBI 66-9330-328.

28. Memo, Stein to FBI Director, July 27, 1954, FBI 66-9330-354; Memo, Belmont to Boardman, August 3, 1954, FBI 66-9330-357; SAC Letter No. 54–42, August 17, 1954, FBI 66-9330-NR; Proposed Change to Manual of Instructions, August 10, 1954, FBI 66-9330-NR.

29. Memos, Baumgardner to Sullivan, September 17, 1964, FBI 66-9330-417, and February 16, 1965, FBI 66-9330-409.

30. Memos, Baumgardner to Sullivan, March 7, 1966, FBI 66-9330-417, and March 10, 1966, FBI 66-9330-416; Airtel, FBI Director to SAC Albany, March 11, 1966, FBI 9330-417.

31. Letter, FBI Director to All SACs, December 4, 1940, FBI 66-9330-9.

32. Memo, Baumgardner to Sullivan, December 22, 1965, FBI 66-9330-415.

33. Senate Select Committee on Intelligence Activities, *Supplementary Detailed Staff Reports*, 429–430.

34. Ibid., 430.

35. Senate Select Committee on Intelligence Activities, *Supplementary Detailed Staff Reports*, 436–438. Privately, FBI officials opposed providing the Justice Department examples of "Espionage Suspects and Government employees in Communist Underground," with Ladd pointing out that "the Bureau does not have evidence, whether admissible or otherwise, reflecting actual membership in the Communist Party." Ibid., 436–437.

36. Ibid., 438; Richard Freeland, *The Truman Doctrine and the Origins of McCarthyism: Foreign Policy, Domestic Politics, and Internal Security, 1946–1948* (New York: Alfred Knopf, 1972), 210–219, 293–298, 337–338.

37. Senate Select Committee on Intelligence Activities, *Supplementary Detailed Staff Reports*, 439; and *Hearings on FBI*, 416–420, 424–425.

38. Policies of the Government of the United States of America relating to the National Security, vol. 1, 1947–1948; NSC 17 A Report to the National Security Council,

June 28, 1948; NSC 17/3 A Report to the National Security Council, November 16, 1948; Memos, Coyne to Executive Secretary, National Security Council, November 7, 1949, March 15, 1951, November 30, 1951, October 31, 1952, and November 24, 1952; all in PSF, NSC, Harry Truman Presidential Library. Letter, Hoover to Souers, and accompanying report, August 7, 1950, PSF, FBI, Harry Truman Presidential Library.

39. Senate Select Committee on Intelligence Activities, *Hearings on FBI*, 416–420, 424–425.

40. When vetoing the Internal Security Act, President Truman had claimed that it "would actually weaken our internal security and would seriously hamper the Federal Bureau of Investigation and other security agencies." The detention standards of Title II, the president then contended, would "probably prove ineffective" and were of doubtful constitutionality "unless the writ of habeas corpus was suspended." When his veto was decisively overriden, White House aides thereupon contacted sympathetic members of Congress (notably the powerful chairman of the House Appropriations Committee, Clarence Cannon) and helped draft legislation to amend Title II to authorize suspending the writ of habeas corpus and permit the attorney general to "arrest and detain persons as to whom there are reasonable grounds to believe that they might engage in espionage, sabotage, or other activity inimical to the public's safety." Congress never even considered this legislative initiative. Then, in January 1951, President Truman adopted a different strategy of appointing a presidential Commission of Internal Security and Individual Rights, chaired by Admiral Chester Nimitz. The commission was directed to examine current internal security laws and procedures and to offer recommendations on the "need to change such laws, practices and procedures." The Nimitz Commission, however, never became operational; the Senate Judiciary Committee subsequently refused to report a proposed bill to exempt its members and staff from "conflict of interest rules" (which rules would have barred any appointee or staff from receiving any federal contract for two years after their appointment).

41. Ibid., 421; Senate Select Committee on Intelligence Activities, *Supplementary Detailed Staff Reports*, 442; and *Intelligence Activities and the Rights of Americans*, 54–55.

42. Ibid.

43. Senate Select Committee on Intelligence Activities, *Hearings on FBI*, 421; and *Supplementary Detailed Staff Reports*, 442. Although forwarding to the department the names of those individuals listed in the Security Index, FBI officials did not forward the names of certain espionage subjects "for security reasons," arguing that apprehension of the latter "would destroy chances of penetration and control of an operating Soviet espionage parallel or would destroy known chances of penetration and control of a 'sleeper' parallel." FBI officials, however, did not apprise Justice Department officials of this decision. Ibid., 442–443.

44. Senate Select Committee on Intelligence Activities, *Hearings on FBI*, 419–420, 422, 424–425; and *Supplementary Detailed Staff Reports*, 443.

45. Senate Select Committee on Intelligence Activities, *Supplementary Detailed Staff Reports*, 443–444.

46. Ibid.; and *Hearings on FBI*, 422–423.

47. Ibid., 423.

48. Ibid., 416–417, 420, 423–426; and *Supplementary Detailed Staff Reports*, 445.

49. Senate Select Committee on Intelligence Activities, *Hearings on FBI*, 427; and *Supplementary Detailed Staff Reports*, 445.

50. Ibid., 445.

51. Again, on his own, FBI Director Hoover sought alternative means to exploit this program in 1951 by authorizing a code-named Responsibilities Program, whereby FBI officials leaked to state governors the names of state employees (primarily college and university professors) listed in the Security Index. Hoover's objective was to effect the dismissal from state agencies of all those listed in the Security Index.

52. Ibid., 513–518.

53. Ibid., 542–544; Senate Select Committee on Intelligence Activities, *Hearings on FBI*, 655–658.

54. Senate Select Committee on Intelligence Activities, *Supplementary Detailed Staff Reports*, 552.

Chapter 2

1. 47 U.S.C. 605 (1934).

2. In 1924, Attorney General Harlan Fiske Stone had banned FBI wiretapping, an order affirmed by his successor, John Sargent, in 1928. Sargent's successor, William Mitchell, lifted the ban in 1931, a decision triggered by the transfer of the Prohibition Bureau from the Treasury to the Justice Department. Prohibition agents had been authorized to employ taps, and Mitchell decided to adopt uniform rules for both bureaus under his jurisdiction.

3. *Nardone v. U.S.*, 302 U.S. 379 (1937); the Roberts quote is from 382–384.

4. Memo, Tamm to Hoover, December 22, 1937, Wiretapping Use folder, Official and Confidential File of FBI Director J. Edgar Hoover (henceforth Hoover O&C); Memo, Holtzoff to Attorney General, January 25, 1938, Wiretapping folder, Homer Cummings Papers, University of Virginia Special Collections Library; Neal Katyal and Richard Caplan, "The Surprisingly Stronger Case for the Legality of the NSA Surveillance Program: The FDR Precedent," *Stanford Law Review* (Feb. 2008): 1042–1043.

5. *Nardone v. U.S.*, 308 U.S. 338 (1939).

6. Memo, Tamm to Hoover, January 4, 1940; Memo, Hoover to Solicitor General, March 13, 1940; Department of Justice press release, March 18, 1940; all in Wiretapping Use folder, Hoover O&C.

7. Raymond Batvinis, *The Origins of FBI Counterintelligence* (Lawrence: University Press of Kansas, 2007), 120, 133; Katyal and Caplan, "The FDR Precedent," 1049–1050.

8. Confidential Memo, Roosevelt to Jackson, May 21, 1940, Wiretapping Use folder, Hoover O&C.

9. Strictly Confidential Memo, Hoover to Tolson, Tamm, and Clegg, May 28, 1940, Wiretapping Use folder, Hoover O&C; Memo, Tolson to Hoover, May 21, 1941, FBI 62-116758.

10. Confidential "Personal Use for LBN [Louis B. Nichols] Only Cards from DML [D. Milton Ladd] 2/1/54" plus nine other note cards in Nichols's handwriting, Wiretapping folder, Official and Confidential File of FBI Assistant Director Louis Nichols (henceforth Nichols O&C).

11. U.S. House, Subcommittee on Government Information and Individual Rights, *Hearings on Inquiry into the Destruction of Former FBI Director Hoover's File and FBI Recordkeeping*, 94th Cong., 1st sess., 1975, 154–155.

12. U.S. House, Committee on the Judiciary, *Hearings on Wire Tapping for National Defense* and *Report No. 2574*, 76th Cong., 3d sess., 1940; Senate Select Committee on

Intelligence Activities, *Supplementary Detailed Staff Reports on Intelligence Activities and the Rights of Americans*, Book III, 94th Cong., 2d sess., 1976, 279–280; *U.S. Congressional Record*, vol. 86, 76th Cong., 3d sess., 1940–1941, 9950.

13. U.S. Senate, Subcommittee of the Committee on Interstate Commerce, *Hearings pursuant to S. Res. 224*, 76th Cong., 3d sess., 1940; and *Senate Report No. 1304*, 76th Cong., 3d sess., 1940.

14. U.S. Senate, *Report No. 1304*, 76th Cong., 3d sess., 1940.

15. U.S. House, *Report No. 2048*, 77th Cong., 2d sess., 1942.

16. Letter, Clark to Truman, July 17, 1946, Stephen Spingarn Papers, Harry Truman Presidential Library; Ovid Demaris, *The Director: An Oral Biography of J. Edgar Hoover* (New York: Harper's Magazine, 1975), 123.

17. *New York Times*, January 15, 1949, and April 1, 1949.

18. Athan Theoharis, *Spying on Americans: Political Surveillance from Hoover to the Huston Plan* (Philadelphia: Temple University Press, 1978), 100–104.

19. Alexander Charns, *Cloak and Gavel: FBI Wiretaps, Bugs, Informers, and the Supreme Court* (Urbana: University of Illinois Press, 1992), 32–33.

20. Personal and Confidential Memo, Hoover to McGrath, October 6, 1951; and Personal and Confidential Memo, McGrath to Hoover, February 26, 1952; both in Microphone Surveillance folder, Hoover O&C. Emphasis original.

21. Memo, Hoover to the Director's Files, June 9, 1952, Microphone Surveillance folder, Hoover O&C.

22. Charns, *Cloak and Gavel*, 33–34; Cabinet Meeting, December 15, 1953, Papers of the President, 1953–1961 (Ann Whitman file), Cabinet Series, Eisenhower Presidential Library.

23. *New York Times*, November 18, 1953; April 3, 1954; April 21, 1954; April 24, 1954; February 25, 1955; March 24, 1955; May 15, 1958; December 16, 1959. U.S. House, *Report No. 1461*, 83d Cong., 2d sess., 1954; U.S. House, Subcommittee No. 3 of the Committee on the Judiciary, *Hearings on Wiretapping for National Security*, 83d Cong., 1st sess., 1953; U.S. House, Subcommittee No. 5 of the Committee on the Judiciary, *Hearings on Wiretapping*, 84th Cong., 1st sess., 1955.

24. *New York Times*, April 21, 1954. In 1930, in contrast, FBI Director Hoover had emphatically denied that wiretapping was permitted, adding that "we have a rule in the Bureau that any employee engaged in wiretapping will be dismissed." U.S. House, Committee on Expenditures in the Executive Departments, *Hearings on Wiretapping in Law Enforcement*, 71st Cong., 3d sess., 1930, 26.

25. U.S. House, *Hearings on Wiretapping for National Security*; U.S. House, *Hearings on Wiretapping*.

26. U.S. House, *Hearings on Wiretapping for National Security*. Other bills under consideration by the Subcommittee offered similar definitions, with some simply referring to but never defining "national security."

27. U.S. Senate, Subcommittee on Constitutional Rights of the Committee on the Judiciary, *Hearings Pursuant to S. Res. 62 on Wiretapping, Eavesdropping, and the Bill of Rights*, Part 3, 86th Cong., 1st sess., 1959, 1014, 1021, 1022. Congressman Celler's bill defined "national security" as "one or more of the crimes punished under Chapter 7 (dealing with espionage) . . . , Chapter 105 (dealing with sabotage), or Chapter 115 (dealing with treason, sedition, and subversive activities) of this title, or Section 10 of the Atomic Energy Act of 1946 . . . , as amended, or a conspiracy to commit any such crimes."

28. Ibid., 1027.

29. U.S. Senate, *Senate Report No. 307*, 82d Cong., 1st sess., 1951; U.S. Senate, Select Committee on Improper Activities in the Labor or Management Field, *Hearings*, 85th Cong., 1st and 2d sess., 1957–1958, and 86th Cong., 1st sess., 1959; U.S. Senate, Committee on the Judiciary, *Hearings on S. 2813 and S. 1495*, 87th Cong., 2d sess., 1962, 2, 3.

30. U.S. Senate, *Hearings Pursuant to S. Res. 62 on Wiretapping, Eavesdropping, and the Bill of Rights*, 1481–1482; U.S. Senate, Subcommittee on Constitutional Rights of the Committee on the Judiciary, *Hearings on S. 1086 on Wiretapping and Eavesdropping Legislation*, 87th Cong., 1st sess., 1961, 363.

31. *New York Times*, January 30, 1968. Justice Department sources had admitted to the *Times* that as a result of the Supreme Court's ruling in *Kolod v. U.S.*, 390 U.S. 136 (1968), about twice as many such instances would be revealed. In *Kolod*, the Court rejected the Justice Department's position that Justice Department officials would first decide whether eavesdropping was arguably relevant to any of the evidence for prosecution. The Court held that this determination must be made by the district court after full disclosure by the government.

32. In *Irvine*, the Court struck down as unconstitutional the action of local police when installing a bug during a gambling investigation, finding particularly offensive the installation of the bug in a bedroom.

33. Memos, Nichols to Tolson, March 29, 1954, and April 14 and 27, 1954; Memo, Boardman to Hoover, March 31, 1954; Confidential Memo, Brownell to Hoover, May 20, 1954; all in Fred Black folder, Hoover O&C. Policy Brief, Microphones, July 11, 1966, FBI 66-5815-1283.

34. A New York state trooper in northern New York State, in the course of monitoring limousines with out-of-state license plates, had uncovered a meeting of organized-crime leaders of Italian descent from around the country at the estate of crime boss Joseph Barbara.

35. June Memo, Belmont to Tolson, July 2, 1959; June Memo, FBI Executives Conference to Tolson, July 20, 1959; both in Fred Black folder, Hoover O&C.

36. Senior FBI officials were alarmed by this stricter policy. Indeed, in May 1966, FBI Assistant Director James Gale protested over what he contended was the propensity of senior Justice Department officials of "advising the courts whenever they have knowledge" of FBI bugs "whether or not this coverage had any bearing on the case under consideration." Gale further privately revealed that of the 738 bugs that the FBI had installed between 1960 and 1966, Justice Department officials were aware of only 158. Memo, Gale to DeLoach, May 27, 1966, Fred Black folder, Hoover O&C.

37. Senate Select Committee on Intelligence Activities, *Supplementary Detailed Staff Reports*, 285–286, 298, 305–306.

38. Ibid., 301.

39. U.S. Senate, Subcommittee on Administrative Practice and Procedure of the Committee on the Judiciary, *Hearings on S. 928*, Part 1, 90th Cong., 1st sess., 1967, 3.

40. Ibid., 51, 56.

41. Athan Theoharis, "Misleading the Presidents: Thirty Years of Wiretapping," *The Nation*, June 14, 1971, 747.

42. Ibid.

43. These assurances proved to be unwarranted. Immediately after assuming office in 1969, the Nixon administration authorized FBI wiretapping of radical activists and organizations. In one such case, involving the radical Weather Underground, the

Supreme Court in *U.S. v. U.S. District Court* in June 1972 struck down the administration's claim that the president had the absolute right to authorize warrantless wiretaps during a "domestic-security" investigation.

44. Theoharis, "Misleading the Presidents," 747–751.

Chapter 3

1. This is not a comprehensive list of the subjects of FBI wiretapping and bugging operations but is merely suggestive of their scope and targets.

2. Do Not File Memo, Spear to Foxworth, May 17, 1941; Do Not File Memo, Tamm to Foxworth, June 6, 1941; Do Not File Memo, July 25, 1941; all in FBI 62-116758; Memo, Ladd to Hoover, February 7, 1945, FBI 62-2755-287.

3. White House aides were particularly concerned about Corcoran's contacts in the Justice Department, with White House aide Edward McKim lamenting that Corcoran, for all practical purposes, "has been Attorney General."

4. For background on Grunewald, see obituary and press clippings in FBI 62-9444. The extensive reports based on the two taps and FBI surveillance are included in two folders maintained in Hoover's Official and Confidential File: Henry Grunewald folder and "H" (Henry Grunewald) Summaries, FBI Report, Washington field office, September 7–13, 1943, FBI 87-2755-85; Memo, Belmont to Boardman, June 27, 1955, FBI 62-9444-NR. Douglas Charles, *J. Edgar Hoover and the Anti-Interventionists: FBI Political Surveillance and the Rise of the Domestic Security State, 1939–1945* (Columbus: Ohio State University Press, 2007), 51–52.

5. Edwin P. Hoyt, *The Vanderbilts and Their Fortunes* (Garden City, NY: Doubleday, 1962), 315–317, 332–339, 350–353, 356–358, 364–369, 379–380, 391–397. Personal and Confidential Letters, Hoover to Hopkins, November 25, 1941, August 31, 1942, September 14 and 21, 1942, and November 12, 1942, Harry Hopkins folder, Official and Confidential File of FBI Director J. Edgar Hoover (henceforth Hoover O&C). Log "Y," June 7, 1942, 8:50AM, FBI 62-116758; Summary Memo Re "Y," FBI 62-116758.

6. Blind Memo, March 11, 1942, FBI 100-94623-4; Memo, Hoover to Biddle, March 11, 1942, FBI 100-94623-4; Do Not File Memo, Ladd to Hoover, September 17, 1942, FBI 62-117658.

7. Wiretapping folder, Official and Confidential File of FBI Assistant Director Louis Nichols (henceforth Nichols O&C); "Y" (Lillian Moorehead) and "X" (John O'Brien) wiretap summaries, FBI 62-1167568. See, for example, Do Not File Memo, Ladd to Hoover, September 17, 1942; Blind and undated Memo re: "Y"; Memo, Ladd to Tamm, June 5, 1942; Memos, Ladd to Hoover, January 12 and 17, 1942; Do Not File Memo, Ladd to Tamm, March 11, 1942; all in FBI 62-116758.

8. FBI Report, New York field office, June 7, 1941; Letter, Hoover to [name withheld], December 2, 1940; Memo, McKee to Hoover, December 12, 1941; Letter, Hoover to McKee, December 24, 1941; and undated routing slip, Hoover to Tamm and Ladd; all in Mrs. Paul Fejos, née Inga Arvad, folder, Hoover O&C.

9. Letter, McKee to Hoover, January 22, 1942; FBI Reports, Washington field office, January 6 and 22, 1942; Memo, Ladd to Hoover, January 17, 1942; Memo, Hoover to Biddle, January 21, 1942; Personal and Confidential Letter, Hoover to McKee, January 30, 1942; Memo, Mumford to Ladd, January 21, 1942; Memo, Kramer to Ladd, January 28, 1942; all in Fejos-Arvad folder, Hoover O&C.

10. Memo, Carson to Ladd, January 1, 1942; Memo, Ladd to Kramer, January 29,

1942; Personal and Confidential Letter, Hoover to McKee, January 30, 1942; Letter, Hoover to McKee, February 11, 1942; all in Fejos-Arvad folder, Hoover O&C.

11. Memo, Burton to Ladd, February 3, 1942; Personal and Confidential Letters, McKee to Hoover, February 5, 10 (two), and 24, 1942; Wiretap Summaries, January 31, February 3, 5, 10, 17, 19, and 20, and March 5 and 13, 1942; Personal and Confidential Letters, Ruggles to Hoover, February 9, 11, and 23, 1942; FBI Report, Savannah Field Office, February 9, 1942; FBI Reports, Washington Field Office, February 12, March 4, and April 8, 1942; Memos, Ladd to Tamm, February 6 and 10, and March 2, 1942; Memo, Fitch to Ladd, February 11, 1942; Memo, Tamm to Hoover, February 3, 1942; Memo, Ladd to Hoover, February 6, 1942; all in Fejos-Arvad folder, Hoover O&C.

12. Memo, Ladd to Hoover, May 23, 1942; Personal and Confidential Letters, Hoover to SAC Washington, April 11 and May 6, 1942; Confidential Memo, White House to Hoover, May 4, 1942; all in Fejos-Arvad folder, Hoover O&C.

13. Memo, Jones to DeLoach, July 13, 1960, Senator John F. Kennedy folder, Hoover O&C; Memo, Bassett to Callahan, February 13, 1975, President John F. Kennedy folder, Hoover O&C.

14. Truman's request had been triggered by Hoover's unsolicited submission on April 23, 1945, of a report detailing some of the political activities of disgruntled Roosevelt loyalists. Truman responded to this report by thanking the FBI director and requesting "future communications along this line whenever in your [Hoover's] opinion they are necessary."

15. Summary Memo Re: Philip Jaffe, March 3, 1953, Philip Jaffe folder, Part II; Memo, Ladd to Hoover, June 5, 1950, Philip Jaffe folder, Part IV; both in Nichols O&C. White House Security Survey (1945) folder, Hoover O&C.

16. Athan Theoharis and John Stuart Cox, *The Boss: J. Edgar Hoover and the Great American Inquisition* (Philadelphia: Temple University Press, 1988), 239–241, 244–246.

17. Letter, Vaughan to Hoover, April 23, 1945, OF 10-B, Truman Presidential Library.

18. Truman had dispatched Hopkins to meet with Stalin to discuss critical foreign-policy issues and, as important, to allay the Soviet premier's suspicions that Truman had abandoned Roosevelt's foreign-policy commitments. Hopkins's meetings with Stalin lasted from May 26 through June 6, 1945.

19. Strictly Personal and Confidential Memo, Gurnea to Hoover, June 2, 1945; Memo, Ladd to Hoover, June 5, 1950; and Memo, Nichols to Tolson, June 13, 1950; all in Philip Jaffe folder, Part IV, Nichols O&C. Memo, Ladd to Hoover, May 23, 1945, and attached transcripts of Prichard's intercepted conversations with Frankfurter and Pearson of May 8, 13, 16, and 17, 1945, Technical Summaries Sent to the White House folder, Hoover O&C.

20. In a subsequent massive report to the White House summarizing the results of the FBI investigation of the Hopkins leak, the FBI director attributed this failure to the widespread dissemination of classified records throughout the federal bureaucracy. He counseled Truman that "until there is a tightening up of the handling and dissemination of highly confidential government documents, such leaks of information will continue." Letter, Hoover to Vardaman, August 17, 1945, and accompanying Report, July 31, 1945, White House Security Survey folder, Hoover O&C.

21. Technical Summaries Sent to the White House folder, Hoover O&C.

22. Memos, Hoover to Tolson, Nichols, and Ladd, May 30 and 31 (two), 1950, and Summary Memo Re: Philip Jaffe, March 3, 1953, Philip Jaffe folder, Part II; Memo, Nich-

ols to Hoover, May 27, 1950, Philip Jaffe folder, Part I; Blind Memo, May 29, 1950, Philip Jaffe folder, Part IV; all in Nichols O&C. Correlation Summary Re: Thomas Corcoran, January 26, 1956, FBI 62-63007-36.

23. Memo, Nichols to Hoover, November 8, 1953; Memo, Ladd to Hoover, June 5, 1950; both in Philip Jaffe folder, Part IV, Nichols O&C. Theoharis and Cox, *The Boss*, 271–273.

24. *New York Times*, May 4, 5, 6, 9, 11, 23, and 25, 1943; and June 2, 1943.

25. Memo, [agent's name withheld] to Conroy, January 18, 1944, Director folder, Nichols O&C.

26. Memo, [agent's name withheld] to Conroy, January 18, 1944; Highly Confidential Memos, [agent's name withheld] to Conroy, January 18 (three), 1944; Strictly Confidential Letter, Conroy to Hoover, January 19, 1944; all in Director folder, Nichols O&C.

27. Strictly Confidential Letter, Conroy to Hoover, January 19, 1944, Director folder, Nichols O&C.

28. Routing slip, Hoover to Tolson et al., undated but ca. January 20, 1944, Director folder, Nichols O&C. Letters of reprimand were then included in the personnel files of all the FBI agents handling this investigation (either for not reporting or not acting upon this information immediately), which contained the further warning that "No repetition will be tolerated." Personal and Confidential Letter, Conroy to Hoover, January 21, 1944; Memos, Conroy to [three agents' names withheld], January 19, 1944; Memo, Nichols for Personnel Files of Conroy and [three agents' names withheld], February 5, 1944; all in Director folder, Nichols O&C.

29. Note card in Nichols's handwriting undated but ca. January 20, 1944, Director folder, Nichols O&C. Do Not File Memos, Nichols to Tolson, January 24 (two), 1944; signed statement of John Monroe, January 24, 1944; all in John Monroe folder, Hoover O&C.

30. *New York Times*, September 19, 1945; October 12, 1945; March 21 and 30, 1946; and April 19, 1946.

31. Significantly, the Monroe wiretap transcripts were maintained separately from other FBI wiretap records in Hoover's secret office file—confirming the FBI director's personal interest in and awareness of their contents.

32. John Monroe Technical Summaries folder, Hoover O&C.

33. Do Not File Memo, Tamm to Hoover, November 5, 1945, Wiretapping folder, Nichols O&C. FBI officials, moreover, continued to barrage the White House before and after November 1945 with reports of alleged Communist influence in the meat-packing, telephone, maritime, railroad, and retail industries. See, for example, Personal and Confidential Letters, Hoover to Vaughan, October 31, 1945; November 15, 1945; January 25 and 29, 1946; May 15, 1946; June 5 and 10, 1946; December 13, 1946, PSF FBI, Truman Presidential Library.

34. Athan Theoharis, *Spying on Americans: Political Surveillance from Hoover to the Huston Plan* (Philadelphia: Temple University Press, 1978), 170.

35. *New York Times*, June 22, 2007; June 27, 2007; and July 1, 2007. Tim Wiener, *Legacy of Ashes: The History of the CIA* (New York: Doubleday, 2007), 193–194, 593; Timothy Naftali, ed., *The Presidential Recordings John F. Kennedy: The Great Crises*, vol. 1 (New York: Norton, 2001), 188–201, 443–444, 593–594, 597–599; Robert Dallek, *An Unfinished Life: John F. Kennedy 1917–1963* (Boston: Little Brown, 2003), 374–375, 529; Scott Monjes, *The Central Intelligence Agency: A Documentary History* (Westport, CT: Greenwood, 2008), 77–78, 177.

36. Senate Select Committee on Intelligence Activities, *Supplementary Detailed Staff Reports on Intelligence Activities and the Rights of Americans*, Book III, 94th Cong., 2d sess., 1976, 313, 328–330, 346; and *Intelligence Activities and the Rights of Americans*, 9, 64, 64n259, 64n262, 65, 65n263, 201, 227, 233–234.

37. Theoharis, *Spying on Americans*, 191–194.

38. The NSA had the capability to sweep the airwaves to intercept all electronic communications and then, based on specified words or names, to single out communications containing those terms or names.

39. Normally, defense attorneys would have confined their discovery motions to the FBI. They would not have suspected that the NSA might have monitored their clients and, had they sought an NSA response, would have been rebuffed by the court.

40. Athan Theoharis, "Illegal Surveillance: Will Congress Stop the Snooping?" *Nation*, February 2, 1974, 140–141.

41. Senate Select Committee on Intelligence Activities, *Supplementary Detailed Staff Reports*, 739–740, 739n18, 756–761; and *Hearings on the National Security Agency and Fourth Amendment Rights*, vol. 5, 94th Cong., 1st sess., 1975, 15–16, 158–163.

Chapter 4

1. The FBI was originally named the Bureau of Investigation and acquired the name of Federal Bureau of Investigation only in 1935.

2. Hoover's Personal and Confidential File was destroyed by his administrative assistant, Helen Gandy, in the months after his death—pursuant to his explicit order. The extant Official and Confidential File contains 164 folders (filed and organized alphabetically) recording the FBI's collection and retention of derogatory personal information on prominent Americans (Presidents John Kennedy and Lyndon Johnson, First Lady Eleanor Roosevelt, Democratic presidential nominee and Illinois Governor Adlai Stevenson, syndicated columnist Joseph Alsop, and various members of Congress) and recounting the conduct and authorization of illegal investigative techniques (wiretaps, bugs, break-ins).

3. U.S. House, Subcommittee of the Committee on Government Operations, *Hearings on Inquiry into the Destruction of Former FBI Director J. Edgar Hoover's Files and FBI Recordkeeping*, 94th Cong., 1st sess., 1975, 139, 154–155.

4. Athan Theoharis and John Stuart Cox, *The Boss: J. Edgar Hoover and the Great American Inquisition* (Philadelphia: Temple University Press, 1988), 92–93.

5. See SAC Letters file, FBI 66-3286; Athan Theoharis, ed., *From the Secret Files of J. Edgar Hoover* (Chicago: Ivan R. Dee, 1991), 3–4.

6. The Teapot Dome affair was a major scandal that led to the indictment of President Warren Harding's Secretary of the Interior Albert Fall and the resignation of Attorney General Harry Daugherty. The scandal involved Fall's fraudulent disposition of valuable oil reserves in Teapot Dome, Wyoming, and Elk Hills, California, and Daugherty's refusal to investigate the matter.

7. Do Not File Memo, Sullivan to DeLoach, July 19, 1966, "Black Bag Jobs" folder, Official and Confidential File of FBI Director J. Edgar Hoover (henceforth Hoover O&C). During congressional testimony in 1975, FBI Assistant Director Charles Brennan concurred with Senator Richard Schweiker's characterization of the Do Not File procedure as "the perfect coverup" and "really total deception" in permitting FBI officials to deny that the FBI central records system contained any record of illegal conduct. Such denials, Schweiker observed, "would be technically" truthful "because of the way the

wording is constructed." Senate Select Committee on Intelligence Activities, *Hearings on Intelligence Activities*, vol. 2, *Huston Plan*, 94th Cong., 1st sess., 1975, 130–131.

8. House Subcommittee on Government Operations, *Hearings on Hoover's Files and FBI Recordkeeping*, 141–145, 156–170.

9. Memo, Hoover to Tolson and eleven other FBI assistant directors, March 19, 1953, FBI 66-2095-100.

10. The transferred records had been created in the 1950s and mid-1960s.

11. On Gandy's testimony, see House Subcommittee on Government Operations, *Hearings on Hoover's Files and FBI Recordkeeping*, 36–64, 139–140, 203–205. The preservation of the Official and Confidential File and Gandy's transfer of records in 1971 from the Personal File are recorded in Senate Select Committee on Intelligence Activities, *Hearings on Federal Bureau of Investigation*, vol. 6, 94th Cong., 1st sess., 1975, 351–356.

12. It is unclear when the Tolson Personal File was first created. Hoover authorized the creation of the Nichols Official and Confidential File in October 1941. At the time, the FBI director admonished senior FBI officials to exercise "discretion" when forwarding records for inclusion in the Nichols file to avoid "congest[ing]" this file with "material which rightly belongs in the general Administrative files of the Bureau." The Dwight Eisenhower folder in this file succinctly captures how senior FBI officials exploited the FBI's resources to advance their own bureaucratic and political agenda. On the one hand, this file records how senior FBI officials surreptitiously collaborated with Eisenhower administration officials to impugn the loyalty and character of liberal Democrats (Eleanor Roosevelt, Harry Truman) and to promote McCarthyite politics. Conversely, this file records the efforts of FBI officials to corroborate spurious allegations of Eisenhower's involvement in illicit sexual activities: an allegation that he had continued an affair with Kay Summersby, the British officer who served as his driver during World War II, and another allegation that he was involved in an affair with the wife of Herbert Hyde, an attorney employed in the General Services Administration. House Subcommittee on Government Operations, *Hearings on Destruction of Hoover's Files*, 154–155; Dwight Eisenhower folder, Official and Confidential File of FBI Assistant Director Louis Nichols (henceforth Nichols O&C).

13. On the Tolson File and its unexpected existence, see Memo, McDermott to Jenkins, June 11, 1975, FBI 66-17404-94; on DeLoach's Confidential File and its apparent destruction, see Athan Theoharis, "The National Archives and FBI Records," *Government Publications Review* 10 (1983): 253–254.

14. On Nichols, see Anthony Summers, *Official and Confidential: The Secret Life of J. Edgar Hoover* (New York: Pocket Star, 1993), 200–201; on Felt, see W. Mark Felt, *The FBI Pyramid from the Inside* (New York: Putnam's, 1979), 144.

15. The Coplon case is more extensively reviewed in Theoharis and Cox, *The Boss*, 256–261.

16. Strictly Confidential Bureau Bulletin, No. 34, Series 1949, July 8, 1949, FBI 66-03-992; Confidential Bureau Bulletin, No. 16, Series 1951, April 20, 1951, FBI 66-03-1119.

17. SAC Letter, No. 69, Series 1949, June 29, 1949, FBI 66-1372-1; Memo, Tolson to Hoover, December 7, 1949, FBI 66-8160-1579; No Number SAC Letter, December 22, 1949, FBI 66-1372; Memo, Hoover to Ladd, Clegg, Fletcher, Nichols, and Rosen, December 28, 1949, FBI 66-1372-2; Memo, Branigan to Belmont, May 28, 1954, FBI 66-1372-11; Memo, SAC New York to Hoover, August 3, 1954, FBI 62-10026A; Memo, Wannall to Sullivan, January 17, 1969, FBI 66-1372-49x. Memo, Nichols to Tolson, January 12, 1950; Memo, Fletcher to Ladd, January 11, 1950; both in Judith Coplon folder, Nichols O&C.

18. Memo, Proposed Change in Manual for Field Stenographers, October 12, 1955, FBI 66-1934-7393.

19. Kenneth O'Reilly, *Hoover and the Un-Americans: The FBI, HUAC, and the Red Menace* (Philadelphia: Temple University Press, 1983), 128, 338n60. In a later interview with Anthony Summers, McCaughey elaborated on Mundt's covert relationship with Hoover and the FBI director's willing helpfulness. Summers, *Official and Confidential*, 190–191.

20. Memo, Cartwright to Nichols, November 4, 1944, FBI 62-3286-156; Memo, FBI Executives' Conference to Hoover, November 17, 1944, FBI 62-3286-157; Memo, Waikart to Nichols, August [unclear] 1948, FBI 66-3286-339; Memo, Nichols to Hoover, October 12, 1950, FBI 66-16304-71.

21. The Black case is more fully discussed in Theoharis and Cox, *The Boss*, 368–393. Relevant documents, moreover, are reprinted in Theoharis, *From the Secret Files of J. Edgar Hoover*, 153–176, 267–275.

22. Memo, SAC Washington to FBI Director, March 6, 1970, FBI 66-3286-53; Memo, FBI Director to Washington SAC, March 11, 1970, FBI 66-3286-53. When processing my FOIA request for the FBI's Record Destruction File, FBI personnel withheld in their entirety four other records relating to the Washington SAC's recommendation: see NR (Not Recorded) records dated March 9, 17, and 24, 1970, and May 4, 1970.

23. These records never had any evidentiary value. They would, however, have contradicted Chambers's self-serving explanation as to why he had not disclosed Hiss's espionage activities earlier: a humanitarian desire not to cause Hiss any more harm than "necessary to revealing Communist activities." During his December 1948 grand-jury testimony, Chambers had also named Wadleigh as another State Department employee who had given him classified State Department documents in 1937–1938. Wadleigh during his grand-jury appearance admitted to having done so but subsequently described his unsettling meeting with Chambers following his return to Washington in January 1939 from an assignment in Turkey. Chambers had telephoned him, demanding a meeting. Fully expecting that Chambers would have been accompanied by FBI agents (having learned of Chambers's defection), Wadleigh agreed to this meeting, at which Chambers demanded a loan, describing his dire economic situation. Interpreting this request as an attempt at blackmail, Wadleigh paid what he considered a bribe. His loan apparently paid off. Although Chambers did name Wadleigh (and others) during his meeting with Assistant Secretary of State Adolf Berle in September 1939, he omitted Wadleigh's name in his interviews with the FBI in 1942 and 1945 and in his August 1948 HUAC testimony.

24. Deposition and Affidavit, FBI agent Martin Wood in *Salant v. U.S. Department of Justice*, CA 7-893, March 30, 1978; Answers to Interrogatories, E. Ross Buckley in *Salant v. U.S. Department of Justice*, CA 77-893, March 2, 1978, 7–10. Memo, Baltimore SAC to FBI Director, December 18, 1950, FBI 74-6-4707. Bulky Material File re: Whittaker Chambers, Baltimore, Maryland, September 13, 1949, FBI 65-1642-1-B.

25. Athan Theoharis, "Bureaucrats Above the Law: Double-Entry Intelligence Files," *Nation*, October 22, 1977, 304, and "The National Archives and FBI Records," 251–255; *The Chronicle of Higher Education*, January 21, 1980, 1, 4; Susan Steinwall, "The FBI Files Case: Implications for Archivists" (seminar paper, University of Wisconsin-Madison Library Science 976, copy in author's possession); John Rosenberg, "The FBI's Field Office Files," *Nation*, March 3, 1979, 231–232, and "The FBI Shreds Its Files: Catch in the Information Act," *Nation*, February 4, 1978, 108–111; National Archives and

Records Administration and Federal Bureau of Investigation, *Appraisal of the Records of the Federal Bureau of Investigation: A Report to the Honorable Harold H. Greene, United States District Court for the District of Columbia* (Washington, D.C., November 9, 1981); Gerald Haines and David Langbert, *Unlocking the Files of the FBI: A Guide to Its Records and Classification System* (Wilmington: Scholarly Resources, 1993).

26. Seth Rosenfeld, "FBI's 'Sex Deviate' Files Come to Light," *San Francisco Examiner*, January 13, 1991. The National Archives review and approval of this record-destruction proposal is Memo, Wolfinger re: Disposition Job No. NO1-65-78-5, December 27, 1977, and request for Record Disposition Authority, James Awe, January 15, 1978. The reference to the Sex Deviate program is in Memo, FBI Executives Conference to FBI Director, October 14, 1953, FBI 62-93875-NR. The Sex Deviate index card on Stevenson is Sex Deviate Index Card Stevenson, Adlai Ewing, Adlai Stevenson folder, Hoover O&C.

27. The 1966 memorandum describing the Do Not File procedure recorded that this practice began in 1942 and, at the bottom of the memorandum, Hoover had penned his order terminating this practice.

28. Senate Select Committee on Intelligence Activities, *Hearings on the Huston Plan*, vol. 2, 94th Cong., 1st sess., 1975, 277–280.

29. Justice Department and FBI officials subsequently conceded that the phrases "innovative" or "special" techniques were euphemisms for break-ins.

30. Athan Theoharis, "FBI Surveillance: Past and Present," *Cornell Law Review* 69, no. 4 (1984): 884–888.

31. FBI agents safeguarded the identity of their sources by employing assigned "symbol numbers." A symbol number consists of the acronym of the reporting field office and a consequently assigned number (e.g., CHI [Chicago] 267). When the source was a "sensitive source" (i.e., an illegal investigative technique), the symbol number would also include an asterisk (e.g., CHI 267*). FBI officials at FBI headquarters found it essential to maintain an index of sensitive sources, as such a finding would readily confirm whether a reported source was an individual, who could be surfaced as a witness during a trial, or an illegal investigative technique, which could not be introduced as evidence unless otherwise verified.

32. Report, Webster to Civiletti, February 19, 1980, 22.

33. Athan Theoharis, "The Importance of F.O.I.A.: New Light on Old Black-Bag Jobs," *Nation*, July 11–18, 1981, 46–47.

34. In 1975, FBI officials had misled not only the Church Committee about past FBI break-ins but also Justice Department officials, the court, and Congress. For one, in 1975, they withheld from Justice Department attorneys, and thus the court, information responsive to a 1973 SWP discovery motion for all records of FBI break-ins targeting the SWP. Justice Department attorneys first learned in 1976 of the extant records that documented that FBI agents had broken into SWP offices 204 times between 1958 and 1966 and immediately amended their denial. The SWP eventually prevailed in its suit seeking damages, receiving a settlement of $264,000 for violation of their constitutional rights. In a second instance, in 1974, FBI officials withheld from investigators of the General Accounting Office (GAO) information relating to FBI break-ins involving Weather Underground activists. At the time, the GAO was conducting an investigation of FBI "domestic-security" investigations at the request of the House Subcommittee on Civil and Constitutional Rights.

35. Because released FBI files are heavily redacted—with FBI officials redacting all the names of individuals in the Surreptitious Entries file on personal privacy grounds—and in addition because all FBI files on radical and left-liberal activists and

organizations have not been released, this list of the targets of FBI break-ins is woefully incomplete.

36. The Contreras and Mossadegh record destruction was reported in *New York Times*, May 29, 1997, and November 14, 2003. The Clarridge "privacy channels" and "shadow file" is recorded in *Report of the Independent Counsel for the Iran/Contra Matter*, vol. 1, *Investigations and Prosecutions* (Washington, DC: Reports of the Independent Counsel, 1993), 255–259. Helms's record destruction is from Commission on CIA Activities within the United States, *Report to the President* (Washington, DC: Government Printing Office, 1975), 203–204, and Thomas Powers, *The Man Who Kept the Secrets: Richard Helms and the CIA* (New York: Knopf, 1979), 157, 158. Angleton's secret office file is from Tom Mangold, *Cold Warrior: James Jesus Angleton: The CIA's Master Spy Hunter* (New York: Simon and Schuster, 1991), 328–329. CIA drug-testing programs and records destruction is from Senate Select Committee on Intelligence Activities, *Hearings on Intelligence Activities*, vol. 1, *Unauthorized Storage of Toxic Agents*, 94th Cong., 1st sess., 1975, 6, 11, 21–23, 245, and *Final Report, Foreign and Military Intelligence*, Book I, 94th Cong., 2d sess., 1976, 390, 394, 402–406, 404n76, 408, 408n90; and U.S. Senate, Select Committee on Intelligence and Committee on Human Resources, Subcommittee on Health and Scientific Research, *Joint Hearings on Project MKULTRA, the CIA's Program of Research in Behavioral Modification*, 95th Cong., 1st sess., 1977, 2–5, 8–10, 14, 15, 21–23, 25, 38, 45–55, 65n2, 65, 66, 70, 71, 74, 82–88, 84n75, 84n76, 84n77, 88n90, 103–107, 134, 137. Blake's testimony is from U.S. Senate, Committee on the Judiciary, Subcommittee on Administrative Practice and Procedure, *Hearings on Oversight of the Freedom of Information Act*, 95th Cong., 1st sess., 1977, 68, 73–85, 93, 525–532. McCone's order, Director of Central Intelligence Directive No. 117, February 21, 1967, Center for National Security Studies Library, Washington, D.C. The special handling orders are from U.S. House, Committee on Government Operations, Subcommittee on Government Information and Individual Rights, *Hearings on Freedom of Information Act: Central Intelligence Agency Exemptions*, 96th Cong., 2d sess., 1980, 28–30, 62, 67; see also the testimony of Deputy CIA Director Bobby Inman in U.S. Senate, Select Committee on Intelligence, *Hearings on Intelligence Reform Act of 1981*, 97th Cong., 1st sess., 1981, 13–14.

37. Senate Select Committee on Intelligence Activities, *Hearings on National Security Agency and Fourth Amendment Rights*, vol. 5, 94th Cong., 1st sess., 1975, 7–24, 31–33, 145–163; and *Supplementary Detailed Staff Reports on Intelligence Activities and the Rights of Americans*, Book III, 94th Cong., 2d sess., 1976, 736–764, 781–782.

38. For Lay's admission, see Senate Select Committee on Intelligence Activities, *Interim Report, Alleged Assassination Plots Involving Foreign Leaders*, 94th Cong., 1st sess., 1975, 55–60, 56n2. The "do not log" procedure and record destruction are from *New York Times*, November 28, 1986; February 23, 1987; February 24, 1987; June 9, 1987; June 10, 1987; July 10, 1987. One of North's reconstructed "Do Not Log" messages is reprinted in *Report of the Congressional Committees Investigating the Iran-Contra Affair*, 100th Cong., 1st sess., 1987, app. A, vol. 2, 1321, 1322.

Chapter 5

1. Strictly Confidential Letter, Hoover to Watson, October 25, 1940, and accompanying report "Present Status of Espionage and Counter Espionage Operations of the Federal Bureau of Investigation"; Personal and Confidential Letter, Hoover to Watson, May 22, 1941; both in OF 10-B, Franklin Roosevelt Presidential Library.

2. Letters, Hoover to Watson, November 16, 1939, September 30, 1943, October 27, 1943, and March 21, 1944; Personal and Confidential Letters, Hoover to Hopkins, October 24, 1942, May 7, 1943, August 7, 1944, and December 24, 1944; General Intelligence Survey in the United States, September 1944 and January 1945; all in OF 10-B, Roosevelt Presidential Library. Letter, Morgenthau to Hoover, April 16, 1940; Letter, Hoover to Morgenthau, April 14, 1940; both in Morgenthau Diaries, vol. 294, 231–232, Roosevelt Presidential Library.

3. Nelson was a prominent Communist Party leader at the time residing in Oakland, California.

4. Personal and Confidential Letter, Hoover to Hopkins, May 7, 1943, OF 10-B, Roosevelt Presidential Library. Robert Benson and Michael Warner, eds., *Venona: Soviet Espionage and the American Response 1939–1957* (Washington, DC: National Security Agency/Central Intelligence Agency, 1996), 51–54, 105–112. Kai Bird and Martin Sherwin, *American Prometheus: The Triumph and Tragedy of J. Robert Oppenheimer* (New York: Knopf, 2005), 188–190. Report, San Francisco, April 22, 1947, FBI 100-203581-5421; Letter, Hoover to SAC New York, May 15, 1943, FBI 100-203581-5. FBI 100-190625 (CINRAD file), vol. 1, serials 6–18; vol. 52, 26, 206, 207; vol. 53, 226–230; Letters, FBI Director to SAC San Francisco, April 17, 1943, FBI 100-190625-21 and FBI 100-190625-24; Letter, SAC San Francisco to FBI Director, April 10, 1943, FBI 100-190625-30; Memo, Ladd to Hoover, April 28, 1943, FBI 100-109625-33.

5. Letters, Hoover to SAC New York, April 9, 1943, FBI 100-203581-7, and May 15, 1943, FBI 100-203581-5; Teletypes, Hoover to San Francisco, undated but May 1943, FBI 100-203581-47; Memo, Ladd to Welch, April 24, 1943, FBI 100-203581-64; Letter, Hoover to Conroy, May 24, 1943, FBI 100-203581-102; Personal and Confidential Letters, Hoover to SAC San Francisco, June 22, 1943, FBI 100-203581-270, and April 7, 1943, FBI 100-203581-5; Personal and Confidential Letter, Pieper to Hoover, June 18, 1943, FBI 100-203581-407; Letter, Pieper to Hoover, April 7, 1943, FBI 100-203581-689; Memos, Ladd to FBI Director, January 21, 1947, FBI 100-203581-2668, and July 15, 1947, FBI 100-203581-2733; Letter, FBI Director to SAC Philadelphia, April 9, 1943, FBI 100-203581-11; Letter, FBI Director to SAC Chicago, April 8, 1943, FBI 100-203581-13.

6. Bird and Sherwin, *American Prometheus*, 176, 184–193, 231–235. Letter, Pieper to FBI Director, April 7, 1943, FBI 100-203581-x; Letter, Hoover to Pieper, April 24, 1943, FBI 100-203581-x17; Letters, Hoover to Strong, April 22, 1943, FBI 100-203581-x25, and June 22, 1943, FBI 100-203581-87; Letter, Hoover to SAC New York, May 15, 1943, FBI 100-203581-5; Memo, Ladd to Welch, April 24, 1943, FBI 100-203581-64; Personal and Confidential Letters, Hoover to Strong, June 22, 1943, FBI 100-203581-176, June 25, 1943, FBI 100-203581-267, September 18, 1943, FBI 100-203581-487, and September 28, 1943, FBI 100-203581-547; Confidential Letter, Hoover to Lansdale, September 8, 1943, FBI 100-203581-587; Report, San Francisco, April 22, 1943, FBI 100-203581-542; Narrative, New York, January 30, 1945, FBI 100-203581-3914.

7. Eventually code-named the Venona Project, this operation involved the interception of Soviet messages sent by Soviet consular and embassy officials in New York and Washington to their handlers in Moscow.

8. Military intelligence analysts, working closely with the FBI, were never able to identify the Soviet spy whose assigned code name disguising his identity was PERS. McNutt's identity was first uncovered in 2005 as the result of the privileged access to KGB records granted to former Soviet intelligence agent Alexander Vassiliev.

9. Benson and Warner, *Venona*, xii–xiii, xv, xix, xxv–xxvi, 201–202, 255–256, 299–300, 327–328, 335, 341–342, 363–364, 365, 381, 387–389, 425–426, 441–442; *New*

York Times, November 12, 2007; Steven Usdin, "Tracking Julius Rosenberg's Known Associates," *Studies in Intelligence* 49, no. 3 (2005): 13–19; John Haynes, Harvey Klehr, and Alexander Vassiliev, *Spies: The Rise and Fall of the KGB in America* (New Haven, CT: Yale University Press, 2009), 35–39, 340–343.

10. The FBI never discovered McNutt's espionage activities, as agents were never able to identify him as the code-named PERS.

11. Athan Theoharis, *Chasing Spies: How the FBI Failed in Counterintelligence but Promoted the Politics of McCarthyism in the Cold War Years* (Chicago: Ivan Dee, 2002), 45–47, 82.

12. Benson and Warner, *Venona*, xxvi, 363–364, 441–442; Joseph Albright and Marcia Kunstel, *Bombshell: The Secret Story of America's Unknown Atomic Spy Conspiracy* (New York: Times Books, 1997), 6–7, 66–70, 108–114, 119–128, 136, 152–153, 215–218, 226–233; Theoharis, *Chasing Spies*, 31–32, 81–84. See also the FBI files on the Sax investigation, FBI 65-59122, and, specifically, Memo, Ladd to FBI Director, April 25, 1950, FBI 65-59122-15; Report, New York, May 10, 1950, FBI 65-59122-37; Report, Albuquerque, May 4, 1950, FBI 65-59122-38; the memo terminating the investigation is Memo, [name deleted] to Branigan, May 8, 1953, FBI 65-59122-403.

13. Report, San Francisco, December 15, 1944, FBI 100-203561-3702.

14. Memo for File, COMRAP, February 6, 1948, reprinted in Benson and Warner, *Venona*, 105–115.

15. Theoharis, *Chasing Spies*, 47–49, 66.

16. Report, San Francisco, December 15, 1944, FBI 100-203581-3702.

17. Unsolicited defectors had also been the key to two earlier seemingly successful FBI counterintelligence operations—the so-called Sebold and Dasch cases. While visiting relatives in Germany in February 1939, William Sebold was pressured by agents of the German espionage service, Abwehr, to spy on behalf of Germany. Fearing that refusing to cooperate could endanger his relatives, Sebold agreed but on returning to the United States contacted the FBI. Sebold thereafter became a key participant in a sting operation under which, with FBI assistance, a radio transmitter station was set up in Centerpoint, Long Island, to relay to Germany information that Abwehr's American recruits provided. The operation lasted one year and resulted in the apprehension of thirty-three Abwehr recruits. In contrast, George Dasch was a member of one of two four-man sabotage squadrons that German submarines transported, with one landing in Amagansett, Long Island, and the other in Jacksonville, Florida. Coast Guard officer John Cullen unexpectedly discovered the Amagansett squad, of which Dasch was a member, on landing. Claiming to be fishermen, the four bribed Cullen. Returning with his colleagues the next day, Cullen found the uniforms and equipment that the squad members had buried in the sand. In the interim, Dasch had gotten cold feet that they would be discovered and contacted the FBI, at which time he apprised agents of the plans and identified code names and U.S. contacts of the other members of the Amagansett and Jacksonville sabotage teams.

18. Allen Weinstein and Alexander Vassiliev, *The Haunted Wood: Soviet Espionage in America—The Stalin Era* (New York: Random House, 1999), 103–107; FBI Report, Underground Soviet Espionage Organization (NKVD) in Agencies of the United States Government, October 21, 1946, 1, 28, 30, 33–34, 37, 46–47, 49, 70, 74, 75, 77, 96, 138, 142, 146, 150, 190, 216–217, 229, 231–232, 249–250, 258, 260, 262, 279, 282, Harry Truman Presidential Library; Gary May, *Un-American Activities: The Trials of William Remington* (New York: Oxford University Press, 1994), 88–89; Memo, SAC Washington to FBI Director, March 6, 1970, FBI 66-3286-53; John Haynes and Harvey Klehr,

Venona: Decoding Soviet Espionage in America (New Haven, CT: Yale University Press, 1999), 163.

19. Ironically, Lore himself had been involved in Soviet espionage activities at the same time as Chambers during the mid-1930s. His principal known action involved recruiting State Department employee David Salmon (who headed the department's Communications and Records Division) to provide copies of the department's communications with its overseas ambassadors. Soviet agents, however, eventually discovered that Lore had scammed them by pocketing monthly stipends of two claimed other recruits when his sole source was Salmon. In 1937, they severed relations with Lore. Haynes, Klehr, and Vassiliev, *Spies*, 156–158, 197–200.

20. Memo, Foxworth, August 18, 1941, reprinted in Edith Tiger, ed., *In Re Alger Hiss*, vol. 2 (New York: Hill and Wang, 1980), 208–209; Allen Weinstein, *Perjury: The Hiss-Chambers Case* (New York: Knopf, 1978), 340.

21. Weinstein, *Perjury*, 340–341.

22. Perlo headed the second espionage ring (Silvermaster the first) providing classified government reports to Bentley. Report, New York, November 30, 1945, FBI 65-56402-220; Memo, Hoover to Tolson, Tamm, Ladd, and Carson, October 11, 1945, FBI 62-116606-1; Memo, [name redacted] agent to [name redacted] agent, December 10, 1948, serial #198, FBI file on Alger Hiss. Memo, Ladd to FBI Director, November 13, 1953, FBI 101-2668-52.

23. Weinstein, *Perjury*, 357–358; Tiger, *In Re Alger Hiss*, 249–253, 257–275, 282–288; Memo, Tamm to FBI Director, October 8, 1945; Memo, Hoover to Tolson, Tamm, Ladd, and Carson, March 19, 1946; Memo, Hoover to Tolson, Tamm, Ladd, and Clegg, March 19, 1946; Memo, Hoover to Tolson, Tamm, and Ladd, March 20, 1946; Memo, Hoover to Tolson, Tamm, and Ladd, March 21, 1946; all FBI 62-116606-1; Conversation, Hoover with Byrnes and Attorney General, March 21, 1946, FBI 101-2668-52.

24. Memo, Conroy to FBI Director, March 28, 1946, reprinted in Edith Tiger, *In Re Alger Hiss*, Vol. 1 (New York: Hill and Wang, 1979), 253–257.

25. New York to Moscow, No. 594, May 1, 1944; No. 600, May 2, 1944; No. 613–614, May 3, 1944; No. 654, May 9, 1944; No. 724, May 19, 1944; No. 740, May 24, 1944; No. 799, June 3, 1944; No. 907, June 26, 1944; No. 951, July 4, 1944; No. 1143–1144, August 10, 1944; No. 1145, August 11, 1944; and No. 87, January 19, 1945. Kravchenko was being followed, although by FBI and not NKVD agents (the NKVD was the immediate predecessor to the KGB).

26. Zubilin's official status at the time was second secretary of the Soviet embassy in Washington. He was, in fact, and this was known to the FBI, the head of NKVD operations in the United States.

27. Memo, FBI Director to SAC New York, October 21, 1958, FBI 10035817-NR. Memos, Ladd to FBI Director, April 4, 1944, FBI 100-275683-52; April 3, 1944, FBI 100-275683-53; April 7, 1944, FBI 100-275683-63; and April 11, 1944, FBI 100-275683-168. Memos, Buckley to Ladd, April 4, 1944, FBI 100-275683-57, and April 5, 1944, FBI 100-275683-66. Letter, unidentified to Berle, April 10, 1944, FBI 100-275683-[unclear]. Memo, Ladd to Tamm, May 11, 1944, FBI 100-275683-331; Memo, Barton to Ladd, May 26, 1944, FBI 100-275683-231. Memo, Hoover to Tamm, Ladd, and Tolson, January 5, 1945, FBI 100-275683-327. Memo, Tamm to Ladd, December 22, 1944, FBI 100-275683-331. Memo, Tamm, December 26, 1944, Kravchenko, Victor folder, Official and Confidential File of FBI Director J. Edgar Hoover (henceforth Hoover O&C).

28. Memo, Branigan to Sullivan, February 9, 1966, Kravchenko, Victor folder, Hoover O&C. Memo, Hoover to Attorney General, March 30, 1944, Francis Biddle

Papers, FBI, Roosevelt Presidential Library (henceforth Biddle Papers, FDR). Memos, Hoover to Attorney General, March 14, 1944, FBI 100-275683-2; and February 15, 1944, FBI 100-275683-3. Teletypes, Conroy to FBI Director, April 4, 1944, FBI 100-275683-54; April 28, 1944, FBI 10-275683-178; May 6, 1944, FBI 100-275683-186; May 10, 1944, FBI 100-275683-188; May 11, 1944, FBI 100-275683-195; May 16, 1944, FBI 100-275683-197; May 18, 1944, FBI 100-275683-200; June 6, 1944, FBI 100-275683-221; and July 28, 1944, FBI 100-275683-250. Memo, Buckley to Ladd, April 10, 1944, FBI 100-275683-69. Memo, Ladd to Tamm, April 6, 1944, FBI 100-275683-97. Memo, Conroy to FBI Director, April 6, 1944, FBI 100-275683-98. Memos, Ladd to FBI Director, April 15, 1944, FBI 100-275683-123; and April 11, 1944, FBI 100-275683-168.

29. Memos, Hoover to Attorney General, February 15, 1944, FBI 100-275683-3; March 23, 1944, FBI 100-275683-5; March 24, 1944, FBI 100-275683-6; and August 26, 1944, FBI 100-275683-268. Memos, Ladd to FBI Director, March 24, 1944, FBI 100-275683-7; April 15, 1944, FBI 100-275683-123; and April 18, 1944, FBI 100-275683-157. Teletypes, Conroy to FBI Director, [date unclear but circa April 1944], FBI 100-275683-35; April 3, 1944, FBI 100-275683-36; May 10, 1944, FBI 100-275683-188; June 6, 1944, FBI 100-275683-221; June 24, 1944, FBI 100-275683-228; June 26, 1944, FBI 100-275683-229; July 28, 1944, FBI 100-275683-250; July 29, 1944, FBI 100-275683-256; and August 14, 1944, FBI 100-275683-270. Letter, Hoover to SAC Washington, March 10, 1944, FBI 100-275683-42. Memo, FBI Supervisor to Ladd, April 2, 1944, FBI 100-275683-44. Memos, Buckley to Ladd, April 10, 1944, FBI 100-275683-69; August 18, 1944, FBI 100-275683-265; and August 24, 1944, FBI 100-275683-273. Memo, Conroy to FBI Director, April 6, 1944, FBI 100-275683-987. Memo, Hoover to SAC New York, June 12, 1944, FBI 100-275683-245. Memo, [name redacted] to Ladd, August 3, 1944, FBI 100-275683-259. Report, [Syracuse agent's name redacted], October 24, 1944, FBI 100-275683-299. Teletype, Hoover to SAC Syracuse, January 11, 1945, FBI 100-275683-307. Memo, Strickland to Ladd, December 20, 1944, FBI 100-275683-325. Memo, Mumford to Ladd, July 11, 1946, FBI 100-275683-362.

30. Memos, Biddle, April 1, 1944; and Hoover to Attorney General, March 30, 1944; both Biddle Papers, FDR. Memo, Branigan to Sullivan, February 9, 1966, Kravchenko, Victor folder, Hoover O&C. Memo, Hoover to Tamm and Ladd, February 18, 1944, FBI 100-275683-1. Memos, Hoover to Tolson, Tamm, and Ladd, April 1, 1944, FBI 100-275683-18; and March 29, 1944, FBI 100-275683-111x.

31. Memo, Hoover to Attorney General, March 30, 1944, Biddle Papers, FDR. Memo, Hoover to Tolson, Tamm, and Ladd, March 29, 1944, FBI 100-275683-111x.

32. Memos, Hoover to Attorney General, March 30, 1944; and Biddle, April 1, 1944; both Biddle Papers, FDR. Memos, Hoover to Tolson, Tamm, and Ladd, April 1, 1944, FBI 100-275683-18; and March 29, 1944, FBI 100-275683-111x.

33. Memo, Biddle, April 1, 1944, Biddle Papers, FDR. Memo, Hoover to Tolson, Tamm, and Ladd, April 1, 1944, FBI 100-275683-18.

34. Memo, Branigan to Sullivan, February 9, 1966, Kravchenko, Victor folder, Hoover O&C. Memo, Ladd to FBI Director, April 4, 1944, FBI 100-275683-52.

35. FBI reports of April 1944 are so heavily redacted that it is impossible to ascertain which of them had been based on the FBI agents' interviews with Kravchenko. A redacted Teletype, Conroy to FBI Director, April 18, 1944, FBI 100-275683-90 suggests that Kravchenko might have identified three SGPC officials (Serov, Rudenko, Kladov) as NKVD agents. The unredacted Memo, Hoover to Attorney General, March 30, 1944, Biddle Papers, FDR; and Memo, Branigan to Sullivan, February 9, 1966, Kravchenko, Victor folder, Hoover O&C described in general terms Kravchenko's proffered information.

36. Memos, Hoover to Attorney General, March 14, 1944, FBI 100-275683-2; March 23, 1944, FBI 100-275683-6; and August 26, 1944, FBI 100-275683-268. Letters, Hoover to SAC New York, March 14, 1944, FBI 100-275683-11; and July 22, 1944, FBI 100-275683-245. Memo, Hoover to Tolson, Tamm, and Ladd, April 1, 1944, FBI 100-275683-18. Memos, Ladd to FBI Director, March 20, 1944, FBI 100-275683-43; March 14, 1944, FBI 100-275683-44; March 21, 1944, FBI 100-275683-48; March 3, 1944, FBI 100-275683-206; and November 9, 1944, FBI 100-275683-310. Letter, Hoover to SAC Washington, March 14, 1944, FBI 100-275683-42. Memo, Ladd to Buckley, April 3, 1944, FBI 100-275683-176. Memo, SAC Philadelphia to FBI Director, May 4, 1944, FBI 100-275683-184. Teletypes, Hoover to SAC New York, June 12, 1944, FBI 100-275683-224; September 18, 1944, FBI 100-275683-299; and November 11, 1944, FBI 100-275683-311. Teletypes, Conroy to FBI Director, June 24, 1944, FBI 100-275683-228; and June 26, 1944, FBI 100-275683-229. Memo, [name redacted] to Ladd, August 3, 1944, FBI 100-275683-259. Memo, Buckley to Ladd, August 24, 1944, FBI 100-275683-267. Teletype, Hoover to SAC Syracuse, January 11, 1945, FBI 100-275683-307. Memo, Nichols to Tolson, April 5, 1946, FBI 100-275683-354.

37. Kravchenko, in fact, became a consultant to the House Committee on Un-American Activities and an avid proponent of McCarthyite politics. The John Birch Society actively promoted his book, *I Chose Freedom*, as a featured title at its bookstores.

Chapter 6

1. Letter, Hoover to SAC Los Angeles, November 21, 1942, FBI 100-138754-3. Report, [agent's name withheld], February 18, 1943, FBI 100-138754-4.

2. Letter, Hoover to SAC Los Angeles, June 21, 1943, FBI 100-138754-5; Teletypes, Hoover to SAC Los Angeles, July 3, 1943, FBI 100-138754-7, and July 9, 1943, FBI 100-138754-10. The suspect films either portrayed the Soviet Union sympathetically or were decidedly anti-Fascist.

3. The seven were *Mission to Moscow, Action in the North Atlantic, Hangmen Also Die, Keeper of the Flame, Edge of Darkness, Our Russian Front*, and *This Land Is Mine*.

4. These nine were *North Star, For Whom the Bell Tolls, Through Embassy Eyes, Russian People, Song of Russia, Boy from Stalingrad, Girl from Leningrad, Seventh Cross*, and *Secret Service in Darkest Africa*.

5. Report, [agent's name withheld], July 10, 1943, FBI 100-138754-9; Letter, Hood to FBI Director, July 8, 1943, and accompanying Memo re: *Mission to Moscow*, July 2, 1943, FBI 100-138754-13; Letter, Hood to FBI Director, May 27, 1943, and accompanying Memo re: *Mission to Moscow*, May 14, 1943, FBI 100-138754-14.

6. Letter, Hood to FBI Director, August 9, 1943, and accompanying Memo, FBI 100-138754-19; undated and unserialized Memo, Hoover to Tamm and Ladd; Report, [agent's name withheld], February 16, 1944, FBI 100-138754-32.

7. Report, [agent's name withheld], August 25, 1943, FBI 100-138754-21.

8. Report, [agent's name withheld], October 11, 1943, FBI 100-138754-22.

9. Letter, Hoover to SAC Los Angeles, April 20, 1944, FBI 100-138754-27; Letter, Hood to FBI Director, June 28, 1947, FBI 100-138754-173; Memo, Coyne to Ladd, July 9, 1947, FBI 100-138754-[unclear]; Memo, Ladd to FBI Director, October 2, 1947, FBI 100-138754-251x1.

10. Report, [agent's name withheld], April 20, 1944, FBI 100-138754-26; Letter, Hoover to SAC Los Angeles, May 8, 1944, FBI 100-138754-29. First prepared in June

1944, this list was updated monthly and listed Communist employees with the films with which they were affiliated. See Letter, Hood to FBI Director, June 3, 1944, FBI 100-138754-35.

11. Personal and Confidential Memo, Hoover to Attorney General, October 31, 1944, and accompanying undated report re: Communist Infiltration of the Motion Picture Industry, FBI 100-138754-59.

12. Membership in the Communist Party violated no law, and the Hollywood film industry was not covered under the Federal Employee Loyalty Program that President Truman instituted in March 1947.

13. Memos, Nichols to Tolson, July 2, 1945, FBI 100-138754-96, and July 3, 1945, FBI 100-138754-97; Memo, Ladd to Tamm, July 3, 1945, FBI 100-138754-98; Memo, Hoover to Tolson and Ladd, July 4, 1945, FBI 100-138754-99.

14. Memo, Hoover to Attorney General, March 13, 1947, FBI 61-7582-1455.

15. Memo, Tolson to Hoover, May 12, 1947, FBI 61-7582-1462.

16. Letter, Hood to FBI Director, May 12, 1947, FBI 61-7582-1465; Teletype, Los Angeles to FBI Director, May 13, 1947, FBI 61-7582-1463; Memo, Nichols to Tolson, May 13, 1947, FBI 61-7582-1465.

17. The additional two included the spouses of two of the nine whom Thomas requested: Bertolt Brecht, Edward Dmytryk, Hanns Eisler, Paul Henreid, Lisa Henreid, Regina Kaus, Fritz Kortner, Johanna Kortner, Peter Lorre, Adrian Scott, and Salka Viertel.

18. Memo, Coyne to Ladd, July 11, 1947, FBI 100-138754-185; Teletype, Hoover to SAC Los Angeles, May 13, 1947, FBI 61-7582-1464; Teletype, Hood to FBI Director, May 13, 1947, FBI 61-7582-1466; Letter, Hood to FBI Director, May 14, 1947, and accompanying undated Memo re: Communist Activities in Hollywood, FBI 61-7582-1468.

19. Memo, Hoover to Tolson, Tamm, Ladd, and Nichols, June 24, 1947, FBI 100-138754-165.

20. Memo, Coyne to Ladd, July 11, 1947, FBI 100-138754-185; Memo, FBI Director to SAC New York, July 25, 1947, FBI 100-138754-[unclear]; Memos, FBI Director to SAC Los Angeles, July 2, 1947, FBI 100-138754-[unclear], and July 11, 1947, FBI 100-138754-176; Letters, Hood to FBI Director, June 28, 1947, FBI 100-138754-137; July 15, 1947, FBI 100-138754-[unclear]; July 25, 1947, FBI 100-138754-x175; and August 5, 1947, and accompanying Report, [agent's name withheld], August 4, 1947, FBI 100-138754-188; Letter, Scheidt to FBI Director, July 25, 1947, FBI 100-138754-174; Teletypes, Hoover to SAC Los Angeles, June 24, 1947, FBI 100-138754-166, and August 21, 1947, FBI 100-138754-192.

21. A special FBI records procedure, blind memoranda were prepared on plain white nonletterhead stationery without identifying the sender or recipient, thereby disguising the FBI as the source of the assistance to a favored recipient.

22. Memos, Nichols to Tolson, August 21, 1947, FBI 100-138754-219; August 27, 1947, FBI 100-138754-219; August 29, 1947, FBI 100-138754-221; September 2, 1947, FBI 100-138754-[unclear]; and September 10, 1947, FBI 100-138754-224; Memo, Coyne to Ladd, undated and unserialized, captioned "Request of House Committee on Un-American Activities for a Check of Bureau Files on 40 Individuals Identified with the Motion Picture Industry," FBI 100-138754.

23. Memo, Tolson to FBI Director, September 11, 1947, FBI 100-138754-218; Memo, Ladd to FBI Director, September 3, 1947, FBI 100-138754-122; Memo, Tamm to FBI Director, September 12, 1947, FBI 100-138754-225; Memo, Coyne to Ladd, September 17, 1947, FBI 100-138754-251x. The 100-138754 file does not contain copies of the

prepared memoranda. One of the forty was included, however, in the FBI's file on Larry Parks; see Victor Navasky, *Naming Names* (New York: Viking, 1980), 317n.

24. The testimony of the ten witnesses—Edward Dmytryk, Adrian Scott, John Lawson, Dalton Trumbo, Alvah Bessie, Herbert Biberman, Lester Cole, Ring Lardner, Jr., Albert Maltz, and Sam Ornitz—during HUAC's October 1947 hearing led to their being cited for contempt of Congress owing to their refusal to answer questions about their Communist Party membership and associations.

25. Letters, Hood to FBI Director, September 13, 1947, FBI 100-138754-230, and September 17, 1947, FBI 100-138754-[unclear].

26. Richard Freeland, *The Truman Doctrine and the Origins of McCarthyism: Foreign Policy, Domestic Politics, and Internal Security, 1946–1948* (New York: Knopf, 1972), 240. Memo, Nichols to Tolson, October 28, 1947, FBI 100-138754-286; Memo, Coyne to Ladd, October 28, 1947, FBI 10-138754-305; Report, [agent's name withheld], November 8, 1947, FBI 100-138754-308.

27. On the Crum wiretap, see Memo, Ladd to FBI Director, October 8, 1947, FBI 100-138754-248; Memo, SAC San Francisco to FBI Director, November 13, 1947, FBI 100-138754-[unclear]. On the Popper wiretap and transcripts of the intercepted conversations, see, for example, Memo, Coyne to Ladd, November 10, 1947, FBI 100-138754-309; Memos, Hottel to FBI Director, October 18, 1947, FBI 100-138754-338; November 15, 1947, FBI 100-138754-318; December 8, 1947, and accompanying Wiretap Summary, FBI 100-138754-364; December 29, 1947, FBI 100-138754-373; January 14, 1948, and accompanying Wiretap Summary, FBI 100-138754-386.

28. Memos, FBI Director to Attorney General, November 26, 1947 (two), FBI 100-138754-322 and FBI 100-138754-323; December 30, 1947, FBI 100-138754-372; April 2, 1948 (two), FBI 100-138754-423 and FBI 100-138754-438; April 8, 1948, FBI 100-138754-441; April 10, 1948 (two), FBI 100-138754-437 and FBI 100-138754-450; April 26, 1948, FBI 100-138754-451. Memos, FBI Director to Quinn, March 23, 1948, FBI 100-138754-419; April 23, 1948, FBI 100-138754-452; May 7, 1948 (two), FBI 100-138754-458.

29. Memo, Quinn to FBI Director, April 12, 1948, FBI 100-138754-446.

30. Indeed, dating from the 1920s, the FBI compiled and maintained files on the nation's most prominent authors (including Ernest Hemingway, Archibald MacLeish, Kay Boyle, Lillian Hellman, Dashiell Hammett, Sherwood Anderson, Pearl Buck, Truman Capote, Allen Ginsburg, Arthur Miller, E. B. White, Richard Wright, John Steinbeck, and Upton Sinclair) as well as the nation's most eminent sociologists (Talcott Parsons, W.E.B. DuBois, Ernest Burgess, Helen Lynd, Pitirim Sorokim, C. Wright Mills, Edwin Sutherland, and the American Sociological Association). Mike Keen, *Stalking the Sociological Imagination: J. Edgar Hoover's Surveillance of American Sociology* (Westport, CT: Greenwood Press, 1999). Natalie Robins, *Alien Ink: The FBI's War on Freedom of Expression* (New York: William Morrow, 1992). Herbert Mitgang, *Dangerous Dossiers: Exposing the Secret War against America's Greatest Authors* (New York: Donald Fine, 1988).

31. Senate Select Committee on Intelligence Activities, *Supplementary Detailed Staff Reports on Intelligence Activities and the Rights of Americans*, Book III, 94th Cong., 2d sess., 1976, 447.

32. FBI agents also monitored and, in this case, wiretapped another critic, the radical journalist I. F. Stone.

33. Informal Memo, Nichols, September 6, 1950; Letter, Ernst to Nichols, September 22, 1950; both in Morris Ernst folder, Official and Confidential File of FBI Assistant

Director Louis Nichols (henceforth Nichols O&C). Memo, fml (Francis Lurz) to Nichols, undated, FBI 66-04-1181.

34. Personal Attention Strictly Confidential SAC Letter No. 65, Series 1950, September 6, 1950, FBI 66-04-1189; Memo, Nichols to Hoover, September 2, 1950, FBI 61-7582-1693; Kenneth O'Reilly, *Hoover and the Un-Americans: The FBI, HUAC, and the Red Menace* (Philadelphia: Temple University Press, 1983), 140–141. Sanford Ungar, *FBI* (Boston: Little Brown, 1975), 376; Frank Donner, *The Age of Surveillance* (New York: Knopf, 1980), 111.

35. Memo, Nichols to Tolson, February 27, 1953, FBI 62-88217-943. Memo, Hoover to McGranery, August 25, 1952, FBI 62-88217-NR.

36. Memo, Nichols to Tolson, June 19, 1956, FBI 94-4-386951; Memos, Nichols to Tolson, June 21 and 26, 1956, *The FBI Story* folder, Official and Confidential File of FBI Director J. Edgar Hoover (henceforth Hoover O&C); Memos, Nichols for the File, November 28, 1956, FBI 66-04-1725x and FBI 66-04-1782x. Memo, Nichols to Tolson, May 10, 1955, FBI 77-68662-1x; Memo, Callan to Rosen, September 15, 1955, FBI 77-68662-26; Memos, Hoover to Tolson and Nichols, March 16, 1956, FBI 77-68662-26, and July 2, 1956, FBI 77-68662-NR. Ungar, *FBI*, 373–374.

37. Letter, Hoover to Overstreet, December 7, 1956, FBI 100-114575-70; Memos, Sullivan to Belmont, September 19, 1958, FBI 100-1114575-88; October 1, 1958, FBI 100-1114575-90; November 25, 1958, 100-1114575-92.

38. Letter, [name redacted] to Hoover, November 16, 1940, Fejos/Arvad folder, Hoover O&C.

39. Letter, Hoover to [name redacted], December 2, 1940, and Report, FBI agent M. M. Cummings, June 7, 1941; both in Fejos/Arvad folder, Hoover O&C.

40. Memo, Nichols to Tolson, November 14, 1941, Fejos/Arvad folder, Hoover O&C. Wenner-Gren had become a subject of FBI interest in 1940 owing to his financial and commercial interests and relations with German officials. FBI officials subsequently closed the resulting "espionage" investigation of Wenner-Gren having uncovered no evidence confirming these suspicions. Following the Japanese attack on Pearl Harbor, however, Wenner-Gren was placed on the State Department's Proclaimed List, and his activities in Latin and South America were closely monitored throughout the war years (although, once again, no evidence was uncovered of his involvement in espionage or sabotage). Letter, Morgenthau to Hoover, August 9, 1940; Personal and Confidential Letter, Hoover to Morgenthau, August 3, 1940; and Blind Memo re: Axel Wenner-Gren, August 2, 1940; all in Morgenthau Diaries, vol. 291, 38–48, Franklin Roosevelt Presidential Library. Personal and Confidential Letter, Gaston to Hoover, August 17, 1940; Personal and Confidential Letter, Hoover to Morgenthau, August 16, 1940, and accompanying Blind Memo, August 15, 1940; both in Morgenthau Diaries, vol. 294, 257–259, Roosevelt Presidential Library. Memo, Klaus to Morgenthau, October 17, 1940, Morgenthau Diaries, vol. 323, 72, Roosevelt Presidential Library. Memo, Coe to Morgenthau, February 23, 1945, and accompanying Memo re: Axel Wenner-Gren, Morgenthau Diaries, vol. 822, 47–54, Roosevelt Presidential Library.

41. Memo, McKee to Hoover, December 12, 1941, Fejos/Arvad folder, Hoover O&C.

42. Telephone Message to Hoover, December 17, 1941; and Memo, Hoover to Tolson, Tamm, and Ladd, December 17, 1941; both in Fejos/Arvad folder, Hoover O&C.

43. Routing Slip, Hoover to Tamm and Ladd, undated [but December 24, 1941]; and Letter, Hoover to McKee, December 24, 1941; both in Fejos/Arvad folder, Hoover O&C.

44. Memo, FBI Director to Attorney General, January 21, 1942; and Secret Serial Removal Charge Out National Security Electronic Surveillance File, February 2, 1942; both in Fejos/Arvad folder, Hoover O&C.

45. Memo, [name withheld] to Hoover, February 2, 1942; and follow-up reports identifying the names of Arvad's interviewees and resulting columns described in Reports, Welch, February 21 and May 5, 1942; all in Fejos/Arvad folder, Hoover O&C.

46. Memos, Tamm to Hoover, March 2 and 6, 1942; ARV Summary [Arvad wiretap summary], March 7, 1942; Memo, Ladd to Tamm, March 9, 1942; all in Fejos/Arvad folder, Hoover O&C.

47. Personal and Confidential Letter, Hoover to Watson, April 27, 1942, and accompanying Blind Memo re: Iquitos and Axel Wenner-Gren Expeditions, OF 10-B, Roosevelt Presidential Library. Blind Memo, April 23, 1942, PSF Justice Department-Francis Biddle, Roosevelt Presidential Library.

48. Confidential Memo, Roosevelt to Hoover, May 4, 1942, OF 10-B, Roosevelt Presidential Library.

49. Personal and Confidential Letter, Hoover to McKee, May 6, 1942; Memos, Ladd to Hoover, May 23 and June 16, 1942; all in Fejos/Arvad folder, Hoover O&C.

50. The latter was due to the fact that the various memoranda recording this investigation were originally maintained in FBI Assistant Director Louis Nichols's secret office file until July 1960, when this file was transferred to Hoover's office.

51. Memo, Biddle on Conference with the President, April 22, 1942, Francis Biddle Papers, Franklin Roosevelt, Roosevelt Presidential Library (henceforth Biddle Papers, FDR).

52. Blind Summary Memo, March 19, 1940, *New York Daily News* folder, Nichols O&C.

53. Personal and Confidential Letter, Hoover to Morgenthau, July 2, 1940; and Letter, Morgenthau to Hoover, July 10, 1940; both in Morgenthau Diaries, vol. 281, 268–270, Roosevelt Presidential Library. Personal and Confidential Letter, Hoover to Watson, July 30, 1941, and accompanying Memo re: Generoso Pope, July 30, 1941, OF 10-B, Roosevelt Presidential Library.

54. The offending column described the "debacle" as the "largest naval defeat in the nation's history," saying that many of the destroyed ships "were close together, one tied to each other side by side," and that the destroyed planes "were lined up in neat rows, wing to wing."

55. FBI officials, in fact, closely monitored Pearson's columns, convinced that the syndicated columnist was untrustworthy with Hoover, at one time describing him as a "coyote." On at least one occasion, in June 1953, FBI agents intercepted (that is, they opened and photocopied) his correspondence. See, for example, Memo, Hoover to Tolson, DeLoach, and Gale, November 25, 1968, Personal File of FBI Associate Director Clyde Tolson File; Letter, Pearson to Downes, June 9, 1953, Drew Pearson folder, Hoover O&C.

56. Telegram, Andersen to Early, December 12, 1941; Memo, Early to Hoover, December 12, 1941; Personal and Confidential Letter, Hoover to Early, December 12, 1941; Telegrams, Early to Thomason (*Chicago Daily News*), Sorrells *Pine Bluff [AK] Commercial*, and Andersen, December 12, 1941; all in PSF FBI, Roosevelt Presidential Library.

57. Memo, Rowe to Hoover, January 20, 1944; and Personal and Confidential Letter, Hoover to Tully, January 25, 1944; both in OF 10-B, Roosevelt Presidential Library.

58. Paul Clancy, "The Bureau and the Bureaus," *Quill*, February 1976, 18. Memo, Hoover to Tolson, Sullivan, Bishop, Brennan, and Rosen, November 25, 1970, Tolson File.

59. Letters, Dulles to Hoover, April 1, 1957, and accompanying Memo undated [but February 23, 1957]; April 5 and 16, 1957; Letters, Hoover to Dulles, April 9 and 19, 1957; Memo, Roach to Belmont, April 26, 1957, and accompanying "A" and "B" enclosures; Memo, Scatterday to Belmont, October 28, 1958; Memo, Hoover to Tolson, Boardman, and Belmont, April 17, 1957; Memos, Hoover to Tolson, Boardman, Belmont, and Nichols, April 17 and May 10, 1957; Memo, FBI Director to Attorney General, May 2, 1957; all in Joseph Alsop folder, Hoover O&C.

60. *Washington Post*, April 13, 1995. David Barrett, *The CIA and Congress: The Untold Story from Truman to Kennedy* (Lawrence: University Press of Kansas, 2005), 236, 300, 323, 356, 361, 364, 368.

61. Memo, Hoover for Personal File, April 14, 1959, Alsop folder, Hoover O&C.

62. Memo, Hoover for Personal File, April 14 and 23, 1959, Alsop folder, Hoover O&C. Barrett, *CIA and Congress*, 368–369.

63. Athan Theoharis, *Spying on Americans: Political Surveillance from Hoover to the Huston Plan* (Philadelphia: Temple University Press, 1978), 175–179. Senate Select Committee on Intelligence Activities, *Supplementary Detailed Staff Reports*, 681–682, 687–707, 711–721.

64. Not only were FBI agents required to monitor local press coverage of the FBI; Hoover maintained two lists about reporters and their attitudes based on their writing: a Special Correspondents list (those deemed favorable and who should be assisted) and a Not to Contact list (those considered unfriendly and to be shunned). The actions of *Reader's Digest* editor Fulton Oursler and *American Mercury* publisher Lawrence Spivak offer a case in point. Eager to stanch the controversy precipitated by the revelations of FBI wiretapping during Judith Coplon's trial and to contain any damage "in view of the Lowenthal book," FBI officials arranged to have the *Reader's Digest* publish an article by Morris Ernst (a prominent ACLU attorney and Hoover ally) defending the FBI. Oursler, however, found Ernst's submission inconsistent with the *Digest's* style. Accordingly, FBI Assistant Director Louis Nichols, working with Oursler, incorporated a series of anecdotes and enlivened the writing. In contrast, upon learning in 1948 that Spivak purportedly had commissioned *New York Times* reporter Anthony Leviero to write a "smear article" about Hoover impugning his managerial style and hinting at his homosexuality, FBI officials confronted Spivak. The *American Mercury* publisher denied having commissioned a "smear article" or that he would ever publish an article critical of Hoover or the FBI. And, when advised that the FBI director accepted his denial, Spivak ironically deemed this incident "a wonderful demonstration of a free country, that had this occurred in any other country he would have been shot." Apprised of the FBI's interest and actions in approaching Spivak, Leviero decided not to write the article. See Morris Ernst and American Mercury folders, Nichols O&C.

65. Cover Memo, Watson, undated and appended to Personal and Confidential Letter, Hoover to Watson, February 28, 1941, OF 10-B, Roosevelt Presidential Library.

66. Memo, Biddle, December 6, 1941, Biddle Papers, Franklin Roosevelt, FDR. Douglas Charles, *J. Edgar Hoover and the Anti-Interventionists* (Columbus: Ohio State University Press, 2007), 119–126.

67. Memo, Hoover to Attorney General, February 7, 1942, Pearl Harbor folder, Nichols O&C. The week before Hoover had protested to Biddle about John O'Donnell's

New York Daily News article criticizing the FBI's failure to have monitored Japanese activities prior to the Pearl Harbor attack. Memo, Hoover to Attorney General, January 26, 1942, Pearl Harbor folder, Nichols O&C. Charles, *Hoover and the Anti-Interventionists*, 132–133, 136.

68. Personal Letter, Mitchell to Biddle, August 25, 1942, and reply, August 31, 1942; Personal and Confidential Letters, Hoover to Watson, June 20, 1942, and accompanying Blind Memorandum re: Stanley Johnson; and November 17, 1942, and accompanying Blind Memorandum re: Stanley Johnson; Memo, Early to Surles, October 30, 1942; Memo, Grogan to Early, November 6, 1942; Memo, Early to McCrea, October 26, 1942; Memo, Train to McCrea, October 28, 1942; Memo, McCrea to Early, October 29, 1942; Memo, Early to Hoover, November 10, 1942; Memo, Winegar to Tully, December 12, 1942; all in OF 10-B, Roosevelt Presidential Library.

69. FBI agents had apparently obtained a copy of this telegram from one of their sympathetic sources employed by the transmitting Postal Telegram company.

70. Personal and Confidential Letter, Hoover to Watson, February 23, 1942, OF 10-B, Roosevelt Presidential Library.

71. Memo, Roosevelt to Hoover, January 21, 1942, PSF Justice J. E. Hoover, Roosevelt Presidential Library. Memo, Roosevelt to Attorney General, May 11, 1942, OF 10-B, Roosevelt Presidential Library. Memo, Roosevelt to Hoover, March 25, 1943; Personal and Confidential Letter, Hoover to McIntyre, March 31, 1943; Personal and Confidential Letter, Hoover to Watson, September 28, 1943; and Memo, LD to Watson, September 29, 1943; all in OF 5286, Roosevelt Presidential Library.

72. Confidential Memo, Early to President, March 20, 1942, PSF Justice Department; and Memo, Roosevelt to Attorney General, April 3, 1942, OF 1994; both in Roosevelt Presidential Library.

73. Memos re: content analysis of *Chicago Tribune, New York Daily News*, and *New York Journal American*, May 19, 1942, Biddle Papers, Propaganda Domestic, FDR.

74. Memos, Tamm to Hoover, July 2 and 10, 1940, Herbert Hoover folder, Nichols O&C.

75. The referenced memorandum is no longer extant. FBI Director Hoover had instituted the blue-memorandum procedure in 1940 to ensure that the specially sensitive communications of senior FBI officials were not serialized or indexed in the FBI's central records system and thus could be safely destroyed after appropriate action had been taken.

76. Do Not File Memo, Ladd to FBI Director, February 4, 1942, and accompanying photostats of Mrs. Roosevelt's correspondence with AYC leaders, American Youth Congress folder, Nichols O&C.

77. All these allegations were false. The counterintelligence unit had not bugged Lash's meetings with Mrs. Roosevelt, but only with Trude Pratt; the unit's members were not sent to the South Pacific, and, indeed, its head, Paul Boyer, was given a sensitive assignment at the military's code-breaking unit at Arlington Hall. Bissell, in fact, was promoted to lieutenant general, while Lash was not sent overseas "within ten hours" but weeks later was assigned to a safe weather station unit in the South Pacific.

78. Do Not File Memo, Burton to Ladd, December 31, 1943, and accompanying MID reports, Joseph Lash folder, Hoover O&C. Burton's memo and related records are also reprinted in Joseph Lash, *Love, Eleanor: Eleanor Roosevelt and Her Friends* (Garden City, NY: Doubleday, 1982), 463–488, 492–493.

79. This denial was technically truthful, as the surveillance records were not included in the FBI's central records system but rather in the FBI director's secret office file.

80. Informal Memo, Nichols to FBI Director, January 18, 1951, Joseph Lash folder, Hoover O&C.

81. Memo, Nichols to FBI Director, January 8, 1953, Dwight Eisenhower folder, Nichols O&C.

82. Informal Memo, Nichols to FBI Director, February 2, 1954, Joseph Lash folder, Hoover O&C; Senate Select Committee on Intelligence Activities, *Intelligence Activities and the Rights of Americans*, Book II, 94th Cong., 2d sess., 1976, 52.

83. Cartha DeLoach, *Hoover's FBI: The Inside Story by Hoover's Trusted Lieutenant* (Washington, DC: Regnery, 1995), 43–44.

84. Informal Memo, Scheidt to FBI Director, April 17, 1952; Informal Memo, Ladd to FBI Director, June 24, 1952; Informal Memo, Jones to Nichols, July 24, 1952; Letter, Love to Hoover, November 12, 1952; Memo, Springfield SAC to Hoover, February 9, 1953; Memo, Belmont to Ladd, March 3, 1953; Memos, Belmont to Ladd, January 6 and March 3, 1953; Memo, Springfield SAC to Hoover, February 9, 1953; Memo, Cleveland to Evans, October 3, 1964; all in Adlai Stevenson folder, Hoover O&C.

85. Technically truthful, as the report on Stevenson's alleged homosexuality was not included in the FBI's central records system.

86. Informal Memo, Ladd to FBI Director, August 15, 1952, Adlai Stevenson folder, Hoover O&C.

87. This denial was again technically truthful in that FBI agents had not directly investigated Stevenson but had simply collected information about his personal conduct and political activities.

88. Memo, Belmont to Ladd, January 19, 1953, Adlai Stevenson folder, Hoover O&C.

89. Personal and Confidential Memo, Nichols to FBI Director, August 29, 1952, Adlai Stevenson folder, Hoover O&C.

90. Memo, Nichols to Tolson, November 1, 1956, Adlai Stevenson folder, Hoover O&C.

91. *New York Times*, April 19, 1950; April 25, 1950; April 26, 1950; May 1, 1950; May 20, 1950.

92. *New York Times*, May 21, 1950; May 22, 1950; May 25, 1950; June 8, 1950; June 15, 1950; December 16, 1950.

93. Athan Theoharis, ed., *From the Secret Files of J. Edgar Hoover* (Chicago: Ivan Dee, 1991), 346–356.

94. Summary Memo re: Senator Henry Cabot Lodge, Jr., Jones to Nichols, November 14, 1946; and Memo, Rosen to Ladd, December 17, 1952; both in Henry Cabot Lodge folder, Hoover O&C.

95. *New York Times*, April 28, 1951.

96. Memo, FBI Executives Conference to FBI Director, October 14, 1953, FBI 62-93875-NR. Memo, Boardman to FBI Director, October 28, 1954, FBI 62-93875-2503. Memo, [agent's name withheld] to Rosen, October 22, 1954, FBI 62-93875-NR.

Chapter 7

1. And, similarly, that the CIA and the NSA, despite their international intelligence responsibilities, had at times instituted formal programs targeting American citizens engaged in political dissent.

2. Good luck (in this case the ineptness of Soviet agents) also enabled military-intelligence analysts to decode these Soviet consular messages. Military analysts had discov-

ered in 1946 that, when transmitting their messages to Moscow, Soviet agents had reused one-time pads, an action that enabled the analysts to decode these messages. The Soviet agents, who had employed code words to disguise the names of their American recruits, in one case had cited the actual names of Hall and Sax and in another (Coplon, Greenglass, Rosenberg) had provided extensive background information, thereby enabling military-intelligence agents (with FBI assistance) to identify the code-named spies.

3. This misplaced focus on prominent political activists also informed the FBI's counterterrorist investigations of the pre-9/11 era, captured in the seemingly prescient recommendation of the FBI's Phoenix-based agent, Kenneth Williams. In July 2001, two months prior to the 9/11 attack, Williams recommended that the FBI launch a nationwide investigation of Middle Eastern alien residents attending flight schools. His recommendation, however, was rebuffed. Williams's concern centered on the activities of Zakaria Soubra, a British citizen of Middle Eastern descent who had helped organize and had attended demonstrations opposing U.S. policy in the Middle East and who, when interviewed by the FBI, displayed a photo in his apartment of Osama Bin Laden and maintained that U.S. forces in the Middle East were "legitimate targets of Islam." The FBI's post-9/11 investigation of Soubra uncovered no evidence that Soubra had collaborated with or had any knowledge of the 9/11 attack. More significantly, Williams had missed another Middle Eastern alien resident who had attended flight school in the Phoenix area over the past five and a half years, Hani Hanjour. Hanjour was one of the nineteen 9/11 terrorists and piloted the plane that crashed into the Pentagon. The Soubra-Hanjour case confirms that although all terrorists are militants, not all militants are terrorists, requiring the need to distinguish between advocacy and intent. This distinction was lost on the so-called Kean Commission and the Joint House and Senate Intelligence Committee investigators who cited Williams's recommendation as an example of the FBI's passive counterterrorist approach of the pre-9/11 era. The belief that a more aggressive approach that connected the dots would avert planned terrorist operations also underlay the media's, Congress's, and the White House's contention that the aborted Christmas Day 2009 terrorist incident was a preventable intelligence failure. They cited the lack of coordination and the failure to act on what was at best murky and nonspecific intelligence that, in hindsight, seemed to indicate a planned terrorist operation.

4. Senate Select Committee on Intelligence Activities, *Supplementary Detailed Staff Reports on Intelligence Activities and the Rights of Americans*, Book III, 94th Cong., 2d sess., 1976, 567, 571, 574, 631, 695, 740, 743, 746–747, 749–750; *Hearings on Mail Opening*, vol. 4, 94th Cong., 1st sess., 1975, 31; Senate Select Committee on Intelligence Activities, *Hearings on National Security Agency and Fourth Amendment Rights*, vol. 5, 94th Cong., 1st sess., 1975, 12, 21. *New York Times*, June 22, 2007; June 27, 2007. James Bamford, *The Puzzle Palace* (New York: Houghton Mifflin, 1982), 319.

5. Senate Select Committee on Intelligence Activities, *Intelligence Activities and the Rights of Americans*, Book II, 94th Cong., 2d sess., 1976, 289–341; see 289, 293, 294, 297.

6. Loch Johnson, *A Season of Inquiry: The Senate Intelligence Investigation* (Lexington: University Press of Kentucky, 1985), 227–249.

7. S. 2525, February 9, 1978; U.S. Senate, Select Committee on Intelligence, *Report No. 95-17, Annual Report of the Senate*, 95th Cong., 1st sess., 1977. S. 1612, *Federal Bureau of Investigation Charter Act of 1979*, July 31, 1979; U.S. Senate, Subcommittee on Administrative Practice and Procedure of the Committee on the Judiciary, *Hearings on FBI Statutory Charter, Parts 1 and 2*, 95th Cong., 2d sess., 1978.

8. U.S. Senate, *Report No. 95-701 Foreign Intelligence Surveillance Act of 1978*, 95th

Cong., 2d sess., March 14, 1978; Neal Katyal and Richard Caplan, "The Surprisingly Stronger Case for the Legality of the NSA Surveillance Program: The FDR Precedent," *Stanford Law Review* (Feb. 2008): 1029–1032.

9. *Attorney General's Guidelines for FBI Domestic Security Investigations*, reprinted in John Elliff, *The Reform of FBI Intelligence Operations* (Princeton, NJ: Princeton University Press, 1979), 196–202.

10. Ibid., 133.

11. Ibid., 145.

12. Memo, SAC Pittsburgh to Webster, March 14, 1979, FBI 100-6839-239, citing an April 1978 FBI Airtel. The SAC reported that his office's investigation of the RCP had concluded that "the RCP encouraged its members at one time to acquire weapons and engage in firearms training, but discontinued this practice."

13. *New York Times*, June 25, 1982.

14. Press Release, Department of Justice, March 7, 1983; Attorney General's Guidelines on Domestic Security/Terrorism Investigations, 32 *Criminal Law Reports*, 3087–3092. The Smith guidelines required that "preliminary inquiries" involving "sensitive criminal matters" (i.e., "any alleged criminal conduct involving corrupt action by a public official or political candidate, the activities of a foreign government, the activities of a religious organization or a primarily political organization or the related activities of any individual prominent in such an organization, or activities of the news media") "be notified" to the U.S. attorney or "appropriate Department of Justice official" "as soon as practicable after the opening of the inquiry, and the fact of the notification shall be recorded in writing." In contrast, the Smith guidelines' standards for authorizing and reviewing "racketeering enterprise" investigations were more stringent: The FBI director or designated FBI assistant director may "authorize" such investigations "upon a written recommendation setting forth the facts and circumstances reasonably indicating the existence of a racketeering enterprise whose activities involve violence, extortion, narcotics, or systematic public corruption." Any racketeering investigation "not involved in these activities" could be authorized "only by the Director upon his written determination, concurred in by the Attorney General, that such investigation is warranted by exceptional circumstances." See p. 3088–3089 and 3091.

15. U.S. Senate, Select Committee on Intelligence, and U.S. House, Permanent Select Committee on Intelligence, *Report on Joint Inquiry into Intelligence Community Activities before and after the Terrorist Attacks of September 11, 2001*, S. Report No. 107-351, 107th Cong., 2d sess., 2003, 20–22; *The 9/11 Commission Report: Final Report of the National Commission on Terrorist Attacks upon the United States* (New York: Norton, 2004), 74, 76–78, 261–262.

16. *New York Times*, May 30, 2002; May 31, 2002. *Attorney General Guidelines on General Crime, Racketeering Enterprise and Terrorist Enterprise Investigations*, May 30, 2002, available at www.doj.gov/olp/index/#agguide (accessed April 2002).

17. This provision concerning the retention and dissemination of incidentally obtained information invited the resumption of the FBI's earlier abusive practices, exemplified by the FBI's indirect monitoring of the personal and political activities of John Kennedy; Eleanor Roosevelt; Martin Luther King, Jr.; Adlai Stevenson; Harrison Salisbury; the Washington press corps; and the so-called Hollywood Ten and the COINTELPRO, Sex Deviate, and Responsibilities programs. In effect, this provision would permit the recurrence of such abusive practices as FBI agents' collaboration with (1) Immigration Bureau officials in the planning and execution of the infamous Palmer raids of January 1920, (2) local and state police Red Squads during the cold war era, and

(3) the NSA when naming those U.S. citizens whose international communications were to be intercepted under the code-named Operation MINARET program.

18. In fact, as Inspector General Glenn Fine disclosed in 2010, FBI officials retained information relating to political activities even when there was no discovery of a crime or act of terrorism. *New York Times*, September 21, 2010.

19. *New York Times*, September 13, 2008; September 17, 2008; October 4, 2008. *Milwaukee Journal Sentinel*, September 12, 2008; October 29, 2009. *The Attorney General's Guidelines for Domestic FBI Operations*, September 29, 2008, 5–13, 16–22, 31, 34, 40, available at www.usdoj.gov/opa/pr/2008/October/08-Opa-890 (accessed October 2009).

20. Independent of this intradepartmental review, individuals detained under these rulings brought suit against Attorney General John Ashcroft and Justice Department attorney John Yoo, seeking compensatory damages for the illegal violation of their rights. Whereas government officials could traditionally have been immune from such suits involving their official conduct, in three separate cases federal judges in unprecedented rulings refused to dismiss these lawsuits. To date, no final ruling has been reached on these Justice Department officials' liability. *New York Times*, September 5, 2009; *Milwaukee Journal Sentinel*, September 29, 2009.

21. Indeed, one commentator characterized the legal analysis as "insane," another as "very weak, embarrassingly weak, just short of reckless," and a third had demanded that the authors of the leaked memorandum should "face professional sanctions."

22. *New York Times*, April 17, 2009; April 21, 2009; April 22, 2009; April 23, 2009; May 6, 2009; July 11, 2009; July 13, 2009; February 20, 2010; February 27, 2010. *Unclassified Report of the President's Surveillance Program*, Report # 2009-0013-0709, July 10, 2009, 11–13, 16, 19, 27, available at www.usdoj.gov/oig/report/0709 (accessed July 2009). Office of Professional Responsibility, Final Report Investigation *into the Office of Legal Counsel's Memoranda Concerning Issues Relating to the Central Intelligence Agency's Use of 'Enhanced Interrogation Techniques' on Suspected Terrorists*, July 29, 2009, available at http://judiciary.house.gov/hearings/pdf/OPRFinal Report 090729. pdf (accessed August 2009). Memo, Margolis to Attorney General and Deputy Attorney General, January 5, 2010, available at http://judiciary.house.gov/hearings/pdf/DAG Margolis Memo 100105.pdf (accessed March 2010).

23. *New York Times*, July 10, 2009; July 13, 2009; July 14, 2009; July 18, 2009; August 20, 2009.

24. *New York Times*, February 4, 2003; February 23, 2003; September 25, 2005; August 19, 2009. *Milwaukee Journal Sentinel*, December 3, 2001; June 17, 2002; February 22, 2003; March 3, 2003; December 8, 2003. AP wire story, November 6, 2006, available at http://news.yahoo.com/s/ap/2006 (accessed November 2006).

25. *New York Times*, September 17, 2001; September 18, 2001; September 20, 2001; September 21, 2001; September 28, 2001; October 1, 2001; October 2, 2001; October 4, 2001; October 12, 2001; October 13, 2001; October 18, 2001; October 25, 2001; October 26, 2001; October 27, 2001. U.S. Department of Justice, Office of the Inspector General, *A Review of the Federal Bureau of Investigation Uses of National Security Letters*, March 2007, available at http://usdoj.gov/oig/report/0703 (accessed March 2007).

26. *New York Times*, November 17, 2002; November 23, 2002; July 18, 2005; December 20, 2005; October 13, 2006; October 31, 2008; September 21, 2010. *Milwaukee Journal Sentinel*, March 25, 2003; March 16, 2006; September 21, 2010. Defending Dissent Foundation Letter, November 2008, 4.

27. Despite the release in 2009 of the 2004 report of the CIA inspector general on

CIA detention and interrogation practices, CIA officials refused to make public hundreds of pages of CIA documents relating to these practices. *New York Times*, September 2, 2009.

28. Furthermore, although military personnel at Guantanamo's Camp Delta prison facility routinely videotaped all training exercises of initial reaction force (IRF) squads, the videotape of a (subsequently) publicized beating of Army Specialist Sean Baker by one of the IRF squads was "somehow lost." Joseph Margulies, *Guantanamo and the Abuse of Presidential Power* (New York: Simon and Schuster, 2006), 172–173.

29. *New York Times*, February 13, 2005; February 16, 2005; March 19, 2005; November 9, 2005; April 12, 2007; April 13, 2007; June 19, 2007; October 7, 2007; November 13, 2007; December 7, 2007; December 8, 2007; December 9, 2007; December 10, 2007; December 11, 2007; December 12, 2007; December 13, 2007; December 15, 2007; December 18, 2007; December 21, 2007; December 22, 2007; December 30, 2007; January 3, 2008; January 4, 2008; January 17, 2008; January 18, 2008; January 19, 2008; January 25, 2008; February 7, 2008; February 20, 2008; March 1, 2008; April 18, 2008; April 27, 2008; June 17, 2008; November 11, 2008; March 3, 2009; March 7, 2009; July 3, 2009; February 23, 2010. Office of Professional Responsibility, *Final Report*, July 29, 2009, 5n3, 14.

30. In January 2010, the Justice Department's Office of Legal Policy authorized this informal, discretionary practice, issuing a directive stipulating that "under certain circumstances" (the language describing these circumstances having been redacted on release of this directive), FBI agents could "ask for and obtain these records on a voluntary basis from the providers without legal process or a qualifying emergency."

31. *New York Times*, March 10, 2007; March 21, 2007; August 9, 2008; January 21, 2010. *Washington Post*, March 18, 2007. *Milwaukee Journal Sentinel*, January 23, 2010. U.S. Department of Justice, Office of the Inspector General, *A Review of the Federal Bureau of Investigation Use of National Security Letters*, March 2007, available at www .usdoj.gov/oig/report/0703 (accessed March 2010).

32. The Israeli agent, and not Congresswoman Harman, was the target of this authorized wiretap. This interception recorded the agent's request that Harman intercede with the Justice Department to forestall indictments of two American pro-Israeli lobbyists. Ironically, Harman's action was apparently not pursued, and Attorney General Alberto Gonzales blocked a CIA request to brief the congressional leadership about her action (normal practice whenever a member of Congress was a subject of a national-security investigation) out of concern that this could publicly compromise the NSA surveillance program (not publicized until December 2005) and further because of Harman's helpful intercession in October–November 2004 when urging the *New York Times* not to publicize its discovery that year of this secret NSA surveillance program.

33. As the *New York Times* reported on December 18, 2009, FBI agents' heavy-handed surveillance and interrogation practices not only sowed fear among Muslim Americans but also served to discourage their cooperation with FBI intelligence investigations.

34. Once implemented, the NSA intercepted the communications of numerous individuals who had no links with foreign terrorist movements or governments. These included journalists, foreign-aid workers, and military personnel stationed abroad (primarily in the Middle East). The intercepted communications were automatically recorded, some of which involved the intimate communications between spouses, with NSA analysts, in some cases, circulating to their peers transcripts recording the "phone sex" of the intercepted parties. *New York Times*, October 10, 2008; October 11, 2008.

Milwaukee Journal Sentinel, October 10, 2008. James Bamford, *The Shadow Factory: The Ultra-Secret NSA from 9/11 to the Eavesdropping on Americans* (New York: Doubleday, 2008), 1, 3, 129–134.

35. The 2008 legislation legalizing the Terrorist Surveillance Program's interception activities contained a provision requiring the inspectors general of the participating agencies to conduct a "comprehensive review" and to report the results to the House and Senate Intelligence and Judiciary Committees. The resultant report was based on reviews of relevant records and interviews of more than two hundred individuals having some involvement with the program; however, White House Chief of Staff Andrew Card, Justice Department attorney Yoo, Attorney General Ashcroft, and aide to Vice President Cheney David Addington declined to be interviewed. *Unclassified Report*, 2–4.

36. *Unclassified Report*, 5–6, 32–33, 38. *New York Times*, December 16, 2005; December 18, 2005; December 21, 2005; December 22, 2005; December 24, 2005; January 17, 2006; February 11, 2006; May 13, 2006; May 14, 2006; May 17, 2006; May 18, 2006; July 1, 2006; August 24, 2007; October 20, 2007; October 26, 2007; November 7, 2007; December 16, 2007; March 30, 2008; December 8, 2008; April 16, 2009; April 21, 2009; July 11, 2009. *Washington Post*, January 1, 2006. James Bamford, *A Pretext for War: 9/11, Iraq, and the Abuse of America's Intelligence Agencies* (New York: Doubleday, 2004), 105–108, 112–114; and Bamford, *Shadow Factory*, 107–123, 128–134, 162–163, 176–196, 212–233, 266–267, 341–345. Eric Lichtblau, *Bush's War: The Remaking of American Justice* (New York: Pantheon, 2008), 137–159.

37. In March 2010, Judge Vaughn Walker ruled that the plaintiffs had been "subjected to unlawful surveillance" and were entitled to damages. Judge Walker rejected the government's claimed authority under President Bush's order and found that NSA surveillance had violated the prior court-review requirement of the 1978 Foreign Intelligence Surveillance Act. His ruling accordingly raised the further question whether the Barack Obama administration would appeal and, if not, would prosecute Bush administration officials for having violated the law. *New York Times*, March 31, 2010; April 2, 2010.

38. Following Congress's approval of this immunity section, Federal Judge Walker dismissed the Electronic Freedom Foundation's suit against the telecommunications companies in June 2009. Foundation attorneys planned to appeal this ruling and expressed their pleasure over this ruling, that Judge Walker had retained the plaintiff's claims against not the company but the government over this program as well as the suit brought by the Oregon-based charity that had been targeted under this program. *New York Times*, June 4, 2009.

39. Lichtblau, *Bush's War*, 139, 167–170, 173–185, 187–201. Bamford, *Shadow Factory*, 188–196, 278–292, 302–308. Harold Bruff, *Bad Advice: Bush's Lawyers in the War on Terror* (Lawrence: University Press of Kansas, 2009), 159–160, 179. *New York Times*, December 16, 2005; December 18, 2005; December 20, 2005; December 21, 2005; December 22, 2005; December 23, 2005; December 24, 2005; January 2, 2006; January 4, 2006; January 7, 2006; January 17, 2006; January 19, 2006; January 20, 2006; February 1, 2006; February 5, 2006; February 7, 2006; February 22, 2006; March 8, 2006; April 7, 2006; April 13, 2006; April 29, 2006; May 12, 2006; May 13, 2006; May 16, 2006; May 17, 2006; May 18, 2006; June 4, 2006; June 13, 2006; June 24, 2006; July 9, 2006; July 21, 2006; April 14, 2007; May 2, 2007; May 16, 2007; May 17, 2007; June 28, 2007; July 25, 2007; July 27, 2007; July 29, 2007; August 1, 2007; August 4, 2007; August 6, 2007; August 11, 2007; August 17, 2007; August 19, 2007; August 21, 2007; August 24, 2007; September 9, 2007; October 3, 2007; October 9, 2007; October 3, 2007; October 9, 2007; October 11,

2007; October 16, 2007; October 18, 2007; October 19, 2008; October 20, 2007; October 26, 2007; November 7, 2007; November 16, 2007; December 16, 2007; December 18, 2007; January 23, 2008; January 25, 2008; February 9, 2008; February 13, 2008; February 14, 2008; February 23, 2008; February 27, 2008; March 1, 2008; March 11, 2008; March 15, 2008; April 28, 2008; June 10, 2008; June 20, 2008; June 21, 2008; July 2, 2008; July 10, 2008. *Milwaukee Journal Sentinel,* June 26, 2008; June 27, 2008; June 28, 2008; July 11, 2008; December 15, 2008.

40. *New York Times,* April 16, 2009; April 17, 2009; June 17, 2009. *Milwaukee Journal Sentinel,* April 17, 2009.

41. Bamford, *Puzzle Palace,* 302–315; Bamford, *Body of Secrets: Anatomy of the Ultra-Secret National Security Agency from the Cold War to the Dawn of a New Century* (New York: Doubleday, 2001), 434–440; and Bamford, *Shadow Factory,* 165–168. Senate Select Committee on Intelligence Activities, *Hearings on National Security Agency,* 57–60; and *Supplementary Detailed Staff Reports,* 740–741, 765–776. U.S. House, Subcommittee of the Committee on Government Operations, *Hearings on Nonverbal Communications by Federal Intelligence Agencies,* 94th Cong., 1st and 2d sess., 1975–1976, 209–210, 324. Memo, Snyder to Bureau of the Budget, June 8, 1948, John Snyder Papers, Bureau of the Budget, Harry Truman Presidential Library. *U.S. Congressional Record,* 82d Cong., 1st sess., 1951, vol. 97, Parts 4 and 10, 5390, 5533–5540, 13211, 13549, 13747–13748, 13783, 13784, 13786. U.S. House, Committee on the Judiciary, *Report No. 462, Amending Certain Titles of the U.S. Code, and for Other Purposes,* May 15, 1951, 7–8, 30–31. U.S. Senate, Committee on the Judiciary, *Report No. 1020, Amending Certain Titles of the United States Code, and for Other Purposes,* October 16, 1951, 3, 9, 32–33.

42. When the Church Committee voted in November 1975 to disclose Operation SHAMROCK, it did so over the objections of its conservative members and the Gerald Ford administration. The critics of this decision claimed that such disclosure would harm national security and questioned whether Congress had the authority to in effect declassify this secret program. The committee's majority rejected both contentions, claiming that Congress had the constitutional authority to oversee executive-branch operations, adding that disclosure was warranted in light of the program's illegality. Senate Select Committee, *Hearings on the National Security Agency,* 46–64. Furthermore, during March 1976 testimony before a Subcommittee of the House Committee on Government Operations, the chairman of the Federal Communications Commission (FCC) Richard Wiley claimed that this section of H.R. 3899 prevented the FCC from enforcing violations of the 1934 Communications Act by denying to the FCC the facts necessary to making "an intelligent investigation of any possible violation," as the FCC was not "authorized" by the president to receive such information. House Subcommittee, *Hearings on Interception of Nonverbal Communications,* 162–170, 180–182.

Index

Lowenthal, Max, xiii, 117–119, 191n64
Lowther, G. K., 123
Lukianov, Serghi, 92
Lynd, Helen, 188n30
Lyons, Eugene, 104
Lyons, Leonard, 46

MacLeish, Archibald, 188n30
Mailer, Norman, 117
mail opening, xii, 90, 98, 101, 104, 190n55
Malamuth, Charles, 46, 104
Malone, John, FBI break-in records maintained
    by, 86
Maltz, Albert, 188n24
Manly, Chesly, 128
Mann, Heinrich, 46
Mann, Thomas, 30, 46
Mann Act, 79, 86
Mansfield, Mike, 75, 82, 87
Marcantonio, Vito, listed in the Custodial
    Detention index, 168n18
March, Fredric, 76, 116
March on Washington Movement, 30, 46
Mardian, Robert, 63
Margolis, Benjamin, 46
Margolis, David, on the Office of Professional
    Responsibility report, 152–153
Marsh, Henry, 47
Marshall, George, 132
Marshall, Thurgood, 80
Marshall Plan, 164
McCarran, Patrick, 106
McCarran Act of 1950, 17, 18, 19, 22
McCarthy, Joseph R., 33, 55, 106, 137, 143, 164
McCarthyism, 106, 137–138
McCaughey, Robert, 78, 179n19
McClellan, John, on wiretapping legislation,
    40–43
McClellan Committee, 36
McCone, John: and Project Mockingbird, 61;
    and special records procedures, 88
McCormack, John, 101
McCormick, Robert, 128
McDermott, John, 75
McElroy, Neil, 126
McGranery, James, 136; Amerasia case, 55; and
    authorization of FBI bugging, 37; and the
    preventive detention policy, 19–21
McGrath, J. Howard, 68–69; and authorization
    of FBI bugging, 33–34, 37; and FBI wiretap-
    ping, 32–34; and the preventive detention
    policy, 17–18
McGuire, M. F., 10
McHugh, Ray, 106

McInerney, James, and the preventive deten-
    tion policy, 18
McKee, Sam K., 49–50, 122
McKim, Edward, 52, 54, 56, 174n3
McLane, James, 63
McManus, Jack, 116
McNutt, Russell, 94, 95, 107, 142, 182n8,
    183n10
Media, Pennsylvania, break-in, 141
Meredith, Burgess, 116
MHCHAOS, 142, 144
microphone surveillance. See bugging
MID. See Military Intelligence Division
Milestone, Lewis, 116
Military Intelligence Division (MID): bug-
    ging, 131; and Eleanor Roosevelt, 131–133;
    and FBI liaison, 5–6, 12, 92–93, 132–134,
    182n8; and Soviet espionage, 92–94; Venona
    Project, 95–96, 182n7, 193n2; wiretapping,
    131
Miller, Arthur, 188n30
Miller, Earl, 134
Miller, Edward, 84, 85
Miller, Jack, 37
Miller, James, 45
Miller, Merle, 119
Mills, C. Wright, 87, 188n30
Mironov, Vassili, 92
Mission to Moscow, 109
Mitchell, John, 69, 73; and preventive deten-
    tion policy, 22
Mitchell, Kate, 46, 53, 55, 87
Mitchell, William, 171n2
MKULTRA, 87
Monroe, John, xiii, 57–59
Moorehead, Lillian, 46–48
Moose, Richard, 63
Morgan, Edward, 99
Morgenthau, Henry, 26–27, 124, 132
Morris, Robert, 106
Morros, Boris, 45, 92, 107
Mossadegh, Mohammad, 87
Mueller, Robert, III, xi, 149
Muhammad Ali, 31, 46
Muhammad, Elijah, 31, 46
Mukasey, Michael: and FBI "domestic"
    operations guidelines, 149–151; and
    Office of Professional Responsibility report,
    152
Mukasey guidelines, 149–151, 195n17
Mundt, Karl, 78–79, 106
Murphy, George, 133–134
Muskie, Edmund, 63
Myer, Francis, 59

Athan G. Theoharis is Emeritus Professor of History at Marquette University and author of twenty books, including *The Boss: J. Edgar Hoover and the Great American Inquisition* (coauthored with John Stuart Cox) and *Chasing Spies: How the FBI Failed in Counterintelligence but Promoted the Politics of McCarthyism in the Cold War Years.*